Faith of Our Fathers

Edited by
Mary Sennholz

The Foundation for Economic Education, Inc.
Irvington-on-Hudson, New York

Faith of Our Fathers
Copyright © 1997 by The Foundation for Economic Education

The Foundation for Economic Education, Inc.
30 South Broadway
Irvington-on-Hudson, NY 10533

Publisher's Cataloging in Publication
(Prepared by Quality Books, Inc.)

Faith of our fathers / edited by Mary Sennholz.
    p. cm.
    Includes index.
    ISBN: 1-57246-063-6

    1. United States—History.   2. United States—Politics and
government.   3. United States—Civilization.   4. Conduct of life.
I. Sennholz, Mary, 1913–

E156.F35   1997   973
                                     QBI97-40315

Library of Congress Catalog Card Number: 97-60345

Front cover: Christ Church, as seen from South Street, Philadelphia.
Cover design by Beth R. Bowlby
Manufactured in the United States of America

Table of Contents

III. The Rights of Man

IV. The Crisis of Our Age

Introduction

Man does not seek society for its own sake, but that he may benefit from the company of his fellow man. He yearns for comfort, protection, and productivity, which safeguard his life and promote his happiness. He lives and thrives in society, and is incapable of living alone. Man gives order and structure to society by way of a constitution or agreement in convention, custom, and tradition, thereby touching upon the manner in which he lives.

A constitution comprises the fundamental principles of government of a country, either implicitly in its laws and customs, as in Great Britain, or in one or several fundamental documents, as in the United States. Written in 1787 and ratified in 1789, the Constitution of the United States was the first written constitution which became a model for many subsequent constitutional documents written since then.

Several of the essays collected in this anthology search for the opinions, doctrines, and values of the men who wrote the Constitution. They dwell on two particular precepts and self-evident truths that guided the Founding Fathers. There was the theory of the social contract as developed by John Locke in the seventeenth century. It became the basis of the idea that government must reflect the will of all the people and their natural rights, which in turn became the ideological justification for both the American and the French revolutions.

The Founding Fathers were united in the belief that preservation of certain natural rights was an essential part of the social contract, and that "consent of the governed" was fundamental to any exercise of political power. The Declaration of Independence enumerated the king's violations of the rights of the colonists. It presented not only a justification for the revolution but also a unique statement of general principles and an abstract theory of government. Based on the belief in natural rights, the opening paragraph asserts the fundamental American ideal of government: "We hold these truths to be self-evident, that all men are created equal, and that they are endowed by their Creator with certain unalienable Rights, that among them are Life, Liberty, and the pursuit of Happiness. That to secure these rights, Governments are instituted among Men, deriving their just powers from the consent of the governed."

God-given natural rights were the guiding light of the Founding Fathers. The stirring closing paragraph of the Declaration of Independence was not only the formal pronouncement of independence but also a powerful appeal to the Creator of all rights: "We, therefore, the Representatives of the United States of America, in General Congress, Assembled, appealing to the Supreme Judge of the world for the rectitude of our intentions, do, in the Name, and by authority of the good People of these Colonies, solemnly publish and declare, that these United Colonies are and of Right ought to be free and independent States." In the final sentence of defiance they appealed to the Almighty for His protection: "And for the support of this declaration, with a firm reliance on the protection of divine Providence, we mutually pledge to each other our Lives, our Fortunes and our Sacred Honor."

To the Founding Fathers, the God of nature and the God of Scripture was the same God. Surely, there were differences in the understanding of natural law and the interpretation of revealed law, but the differences did not raise a doubt on the common bond, the Judeo-Christian faith. It was the spiritual and moral foundation on which America was built. To the Founding Fathers the world was ordered well. They looked upon the future of their country with confidence and in the knowledge that, in the end, all things would work together in freedom. The Reverend Frederick Faber later could write:

> Faith of our fathers, God's great power
>   Shall win all nations unto thee
> And through the truth that comes from God
>   Mankind shall then be truly free.

Throughout the nineteenth century this optimism slowly gave way to alien philosophies that are highly critical of all ramifications of freedom and that were to become the guidepost for most Americans. Positivism, a philosophical doctrine that denies the validity of first principles, teaches that such principles are unfathomable and that the only knowledge is scientific knowledge. If there are no first principles, there can be no economic principles. In order to prevent confusion and chaos, man obviously needs direction, command, and instruction by authority. This is why many Americans, especially those who profess to be rational and scientific, keep the company of central planners calling on legislators, regulators, judges, and policemen to retrieve order out of chaos.

Other Americans unwittingly embrace the philosophy of materialism which explains all political, social, and economic phenomena as entirely dependent on matter, beyond which nothing needs to be explained. Modern communism is based on it, socialist doctrines are derived from it, and political interventionism builds on it. The sociological doctrine of class struggle, the economic doctrines of labor theory of value, of labor exploitation, business concentration, and monopolization are popular offshoots. Countless labor laws and regulations spring from it.

Several essays in this anthology point at the sway of positivistic and materialistic doctrines as the ideological causes of the crisis of our age. In his essay on "The Psychology of Cultism," Dr. Ben Barker describes some of the symptoms of the crisis: "There is no prayer in the schools and unionized, socialist teachers insidiously program our youth. Mindless violence and senseless trivia beam at us from our television, our newspapers are full of lies and scantily clad females posing for underwear ads. Heroin is the opiate of the ghetto, alcohol of the middle class community, and cocaine of the wealthy. Valium, which we supply, is abused by all social classes."

The moral precepts and the self-evident truths that guided our Founding Fathers may not be fashionable in our time, but they are as inescapable and inexorable as they have been throughout the ages. We are free to ignore and disobey them, but we cannot escape the rising price we must pay for defying them.

February 1997   MARY SENNHOLZ

I. THE SPIRIT OF '76

The Founding of the American Republic

Clarence B. Carson

Scribes are quite often merciless tyrants in dealing with characters out of the past, spearing them with an assortment of verbs and freezing them in predetermined categories with their adjectives, much as a butterfly collector does with his helpless insects. There is no surer way to shatter the integrity of an individual or to distort a historical epoch than by the indiscriminate use of categories. No man of wit is likely to believe that a category comprehends him, even when it is well chosen. But when categories drawn from other times and places are imposed upon men and events which are foreign to them, the result can only be to confuse the subject under discussion.

Some twentieth-century historians have done just this to American history of the late eighteenth century. They have called Americans of the time by names, some of which were unknown to them and others which they would have disavowed; they have categorized them as revolutionaries or reactionaries, democrats or aristocrats, nationalists or states' righters, liberals or conservatives, and other such categories. They have tried to thrust the events into revolutionary and "social" revolutionary categories, categories drawn from other revolutions and other circumstances. It is

Dr. Carson has written and taught extensively, specializing in American intellectual history. This article appeared in the September 1972 issue of *The Freeman*.

a journalistic habit into which many historians have fallen to attribute an absoluteness to the views and thrusts of men which violates both what they intend and do. Debates, even great historical debates, can be quite misleading. Men often advance positions with more certainty than they feel, appear to be unalterable in their determination, yet may shortly yield to the other side with good humor when they have lost. Some historians appear to have no difficulty whatever in discovering men's motives, but the fact is that we are not privy to their motives.

The subject to be treated below is the reforms and innovations made by Americans mostly in the decade after the declaring of independence. The above prelude was made necessary because the present writer both wishes to make known the fact that he is familiar with the crosscurrents of interpretation of these years by twentieth-century historians and to disavow many of the categories that have been used. After the Americans broke from England they did make some changes; they did sometimes differ among themselves as to what the direction of change should be; but there is no need to question their motives or any solid basis for saying for certain what they were. Above all, there is no need to push this one into that category and that one into this, with the category being excessively large for the matter at issue and much too confining for the man over any period of time. More rubbish has been written about the class positions and interests of the men of these times than any other in American history, so far as I can make out. The present writer has neither the space nor inclination to spend energy upon trying to refute what has not been well established, in any case.

The Main Thrust of Changes

What is established is that there were some changes made during these years. The main thrust of these changes is the freeing of the individual: freeing him from foreign domination, from various government compulsions, from class prescriptions, and for greater control of his own affairs. And, in conjunction with these, there was an effort to erect safeguards around him that would protect him in the exercise of his rights. The thrust to do these things was made along several different paths, and each of these is worth some attention.

A primary aim of the Americans was independence. They wanted to be independent of England, of course; that was what the war was fought about. Many Americans had come to believe that they could only have the requisite control of their affairs by separating from the mother country. This was achieved, of course, by terms of the Treaty of Paris. But Americans longed also to be independent of European entanglements. Time after time, during the colonial period, Americans had been drawn into wars that originated in Europe but spread to the New World. Americans wanted to be free of the dynastic quarrels, the imperial ambitions, and the trade wars which rended Europe and shook much of the rest of the world. To many Americans, Europe was the symbol and embodiment of corruption, decadence, and foreclosed opportunity. To be independent of Europe was, in the final analysis, to be free to follow courses which had not yet, at any rate, proven to be so laden with disaster.

Independence did not mean, nor should it be taken to

connote, the rejection of either the English or European heritage. Indeed, there was little irrational rejection of either heritage that comes to mind. Though Americans rejected European aristocracy they did not, for that reason, change names of places in this country derived from aristocrats.

Perhaps, the most extensive thrust of this period was to the freeing of the individual from government compulsion. Libertarian sentiment had been maturing for some considerable while in America; it was fostered both by legal trends and religious and other intellectual development. Once the break from England came, Americans used the occasion to cut away a body of restraints no longer in accord with their outlook.

Religious Liberty

Religious liberty was widely secured within a decade or so of the break from England. Much of it came by way of the disestablishment of churches. The establishment most readily dispensed with was that of the Church of England. While the Church of England was established throughout the South as well as in New York, it was not very popular; many of its clergy remained loyal to England, and adherents of it were outnumbered by dissenters in most states. Its disestablishment was made even easier because it was a national church; membership in it was tied to loyalty to the king of England. The Church of England was everywhere speedily disestablished. But these actions were not simply prompted by convenience, for there was increasing belief in religious liberty. Several states had no established churches: namely, New Jersey, Rhode Island, Pennsylvania, and Delaware. But they used the opportunity afforded by independence to remove or reduce restrictions. Some of the disabilities of Roman Catholics were cut away.

The established Congregational church was maintained for several decades longer in Massachusetts, Connecticut, and New Hampshire. There was, however, some liberalization in these states. The Massachusetts constitution of 1780 affirmed that every man had the right to worship in his own way, that no church should be subordinated to any other, and that tax moneys could be used to support ministers other than Congregationalists. However, church attendance was required still, and ministers were supported from taxes.[1] "New Hampshire followed in the steps of Massachusetts, but Connecticut held out much longer against what its citizens regarded as the forces of iniquity. They allowed dissenters to escape payment of taxes to the established church if they presented the clerk of the local church with a certificate of church attendance signed by an officer of the dissenter's own church."[2]

The constitutions of New Jersey, Georgia, North and South Carolina, Delaware, and Pennsylvania "explicitly provided that no man should be obliged to pay any church rate or attend any religious service save according to his own free and unhampered will."[3] But Virginia made the greatest effort to assure religious liberty. This might have been a reaction to the fact that Virginia had the longest establishment and one of the most rigorous. Thomas Jefferson, James Madison, and George Mason were leading advocates of religious liberty, but they did not succeed in getting their ideas into law until 1786. This was done by the Virginia Statute of Religious Freedom, which proclaimed religious liberty a natural right. An impressive preface states the case:

Whereas, Almighty God hath created the mind free; that all attempts to influence it by temporal punishments or burthens, or by civil incapacitations, tend only to beget habits of hypocrisy and meanness, and are a departure from the plan of the Holy author of our religion. . . .

The legally effective portion of the statute reads this way:

That no man shall be compelled to frequent or support any religious worship, place, or ministry whatsoever, nor shall be enforced, restrained, molested, or burthened in his body or goods, nor shall otherwise suffer on account of his religious opinions or beliefs; but that all men shall be free to profess, and by argument to maintain, their opinion in matters of religion, and that the same shall in no wise diminish, enlarge, or affect their civil capacities.[4]

This was the beginning of religious liberty in America.

Freeing the Slaves

The movement for freeing the slaves reached a peak in the 1780s which it would not soon attain again. Even before the break from England, the slave trade was acquiring a bad reputation in America, but such efforts as were made to restrict it were negated by the mother country. Fiske says, "The success of the American Revolution made it possible for the different states to take measures for the gradual abolition of slavery and the immediate abolition of the foreign slave-trade."[5] Nor was sentiment against slavery restricted to states in which there were few slaves. Some of the outstanding leaders from the South during this period, most of them slaveholders, spoke out against slavery. Henry Laurens, a leader in South Carolina, wrote in 1776: "You know my Dear Sir. I abhor slavery . . . —in former days there was no combatting the prejudices of Men supported by Interest, the day I hope is approaching when from principles of gratitude as well [as] justice every Man will strive to be foremost in shewing his readiness to comply with the Golden Rule. . . ."[6] Thomas Jefferson argued in his *Notes on the State of Virginia* that slavery had a bad influence on the manners and morals of the white people as well as its devastating effects on the Negroes. He longed for and hoped to see the day when all slaves would be emancipated. He warned his countrymen of the impending impact on them if this were not done: "And can the liberties of a nation be thought secure when we have removed their only firm basis, a conviction in the minds of the people that these liberties are the gift of God? That they are not to be violated but with his wrath? Indeed I tremble for my country," he said, "when I reflect that God is just; that his justice cannot sleep forever. . . ."[7]

Some states began to act almost as soon as the opportunity arose. In 1776, Delaware prohibited the importation of slaves and removed all restraints on their manumission. Virginia stopped slave imports in 1778; Maryland adopted a similar measure in 1783. Both states now allowed manumission at the behest of the owner. In 1780, Pennsylvania not only prohibited further importation of slaves but also provided that after that date all children born of slaves should be free. Similar enactments were made in the early 1780s in New Hampshire, Connecticut, and Rhode Island.

In Massachusetts, the supreme court decided that on the basis of the constitution of 1780 slavery was abolished in that province. Even North Carolina moved to discourage the slave trade in 1786 by taxing heavily such slaves as were imported after that time. In order to protect free Negroes, Virginia made it a crime punishable by death for anyone found guilty of selling a freed Negro into slavery.[8]

How far sentiment against slavery had gone may well be best indicated by the Northwest Ordinance (1787), an act of all the states, as it were, in Congress assembled. The act provided: "There shall be neither slavery nor involuntary servitude in the said territory, otherwise than in the punishment of crimes whereof the party shall have been duly convicted. . . ." This article was passed, according to one of its proponents, without opposition.[9]

Individual Liberties

The bills of rights drawn and adopted in the various states contained provisions intended to assure individual liberties. These bills of rights were usually drawn and adopted along with constitutions but were frequently separate documents. They were usually cast in the language of natural rights theory. For example, Article I of the Massachusetts Declaration of Rights states:

> All men are born free and equal, and have certain natural, essential, and unalienable rights; among which may be reckoned the right of enjoying and defending their lives and liberties; that of acquiring, possessing, and protecting property; in fine, that of seeking and obtaining their safety and happiness.[10]

Virginia was the first state to draw both a constitution and a bill of rights. Actually, Virginia's Bill of Rights was adopted June 12, 1776, while the would-be state was still a colony. It was the work primarily of George Mason, was circulated among the states, and became a model for such instruments.

The Virginia Bill of Rights guaranteed trial by jury in both criminal and civil cases, prohibited excessive bail and fines, declared general warrants to be oppressive, and acknowledged freedom of the press. The protections of a person accused of a crime were spelled out:

> That in all capital or criminal prosecutions a man hath a right to demand the cause and nature of his accusation, to be confronted with the accusers and witnesses, to call for evidence in his favour, and to a speedy trial by an impartial jury of his vicinage, without whose unanimous consent he cannot be found guilty; nor can he be compelled to give evidence against himself; that no man may be deprived of his liberty, except by the law of the land or the judgment of his peers.

The only specific protection of property, other than the provision for jury trial in civil cases, was the requirement that men "cannot be taxed or deprived of their property for publick uses, without their own consent, or that of their representatives so elected. . . ."[11]

The Massachusetts Declaration of Rights of 1780, the work mainly of John Adams, was considerably more thorough. In regard to property, it said: "No part of the property of any individual can, with justice, be taken from him, or applied to public uses, without his consent, or that of the representative body of the people. . . . And whenever the public exigencies require that the property of any individual should be appropriated to public uses, he shall receive a reasonable compensation therefor."[12] Other rights were alluded to than those mentioned in the Virginia Bill: freedom from unreasonable searches, the right to bear arms, the right of peaceful assembly, the prohibition of ex post facto laws, the prohibition of attainders by the legislature, as well as most of those covered in Virginia.

Northwest Ordinance

The Northwest Ordinance sums up, in Article II, what may well be considered a contemporary consensus of the protections of the rights of the people most needed:

> The inhabitants of the said territory shall always be entitled to the benefits of the writs of *habeas corpus*, and of the trial by jury; of a proportionate representation of the people in the legislature, and judicial proceedings according to the course of the common law. All persons shall be bailable, unless for capital offences, where the proof shall be evident or the presumption great. All fines shall be moderate; and no cruel or unusual punishment shall be inflicted. No man shall be deprived of his liberty or property, but by the judgment of his peers, or the law of the land; and should the public exigencies make it necessary, for the common preservation, to take any person's property, or to demand his particular services, full compensation shall be made for the same. And, in the just preservation of rights and property, it is understood and declared, that no law ought ever to

be made, or have force in the said territory, that shall, in any manner whatever, interfere or affect private contracts or engagements, *bona fide,* and without fraud, previously formed.[13]

Some recent writers have claimed that the Founders distinguished between "human rights" and property rights in favor of "human rights." It should be clear from the above that no such distinction can be discerned, nor has the present writer ever seen a quotation from the original that could reasonably be construed to show that the Founders made any such distinction.

Property was, however, freed from various feudal restraints during this period and made more fully the possession of the individual holding title to it. The most general encumbrance on property ownership was the quitrent—a periodical payment due to king or proprietor on land, a payment that originated in the late Middle Ages as money payments displaced personal servitude. Such claims were speedily extinguished following the break from England, and land thereafter was held in "fee simple." Such royal prerogatives as the right of the monarch to white pines on private land were, of course, nullified. States abolished entail, also, a move which enhanced the authority of the owner to dispose of his lands.

With the Declaration of Independence, the whole edifice of mercantilism as imposed from England was swept away. One historian describes the impact of this as follows: "As a result of the American Revolution, freedom of enterprise, that is, the equal opportunity of any individual to engage in any economic activity he chooses in order to amass wealth, and to hold onto his wealth or dispose of it as he pleases, became a living reality in America to a greater degree than before."[14]

Abolition of Classes

Another sort of innovation may be described as anti-class in its character. Fixed classes are supported and maintained by government where they exist. Americans of this period wanted to remove government support of classes and prevent the growth of special privileges by which classes are shaped. Some of the actions already described were, in part, anti-class measures. For example, the established Church of England was hierarchical and, in England particularly, a major support of class arrangements. Its disestablishment in America struck at the root of government support of class structures. Entailment was a means of perpetuating great estates, just as quitrents were devices for maintaining aristocracies. Other actions were taken that were even more pointedly aimed at removing government from its role as class perpetuator.

One of these was the abolition of primogeniture. Primogeniture was the rule that the estate of one who died without a will should go either whole or in larger part to the eldest son. States abolished this rule and adopted the practice of dividing the estate equally among the children when the father died intestate. The tendency of this was for great estates to be broken up from time to time.

Various sorts of provisions were made in state constitutions to prevent the growth of aristocratic privileges. For example, the Virginia Bill of Rights had this provision:

> That no man, or set of men, are entitled to exclusive or separate emoluments or privileges from the community, but in consideration of publick services; which, not being descendible, neither ought the offices of magistrate, legislator or judge to be hereditary.[15]

The Massachusetts Declaration held:

> No man, nor corporation, or association of men, have any other title to obtain advantages, or particular and exclusive privileges, distinct from those of the community, than what arises from the consideration of services rendered to the public; and this title being in nature neither hereditary, nor transmissible to children, or descendants, or relations by blood; the idea of a man born a magistrate, lawgiver, or judge, is absurd and unnatural.[16]

The animus against titles of nobility found expression sometimes. So strong was the animus against hereditary positions that the Society of Cincinnati, a voluntary association of officers who had served in the War for Independence, found it expedient to abandon the rule that membership could be inherited to allay the indignation against them. Frequent elections and restrictions on the amount of time one could serve in office were efforts to prevent the emergence of a ruling class, at least in part.

The kind of equality sought by prohibitions against governmentally fostered classes was equality before the law. So far as any other equality was concerned, American opinion of the time accepted differences in wealth and social station as inevitable and desirable results of differences in ability and effort. Undoubtedly, there were those in that day who would have liked to have some portions of the wealth and estates of others—who coveted what was not theirs—as there are in any day, but they were either inarticulate or ashamed to profess their views. Some historians have made much ado about the confiscation and sale of Loyalist estates during the war. This is treated as if it were a redistributionist scheme, and there is an attempt to give factual support to this notion by pointing out that large estates were sometimes broken up before they were offered for sale. This did sometimes happen, but it does not follow that it was done with any motive of equalizing holdings. Small parcels attract more bidders than large ones; hence, the price attained for large estates was likely to be increased by dividing them up. Moreover, large estates were sometimes formed or added to by buying several parcels.[17]

Limitations on Government

There were some general changes in governments during this period, changes in degree from what they had been under British rule. The main tendency was to make the state governments more dependent upon the popular will than they had been during the colonial period. The new state constitutions required that all state officers either be chosen by the electorate or appointed by those who had.

The main impetus behind making governments depend more closely on the electorate was a profound fear of government. This distrust of government was most clearly shown in the distrust of governors and courts, those parts of the government that had not been popularly chosen during the colonial period. The colonists feared the legislatures, too, or so the limitations on them would indicate, but out of their colonial experience, they feared them less than the other branches. In point of fact, Americans relied rather heavily on a narrow and provincial colonial experience in making their first constitutions. Probably, Massachusetts and New York should be excepted from these strictures.

The office of governor—or whatever the executive

might be called, for some states abandoned briefly that colonial title—was stripped of much of the power and most of the independence enjoyed by colonial chief executives. Colonial governors had usually possessed an absolute veto over legislation. The new executives were stripped of the veto power in all but two of the states—Massachusetts and New York—, and in these the power was somewhat weakened. In all the states but New York the legislatures or the constitutions governed the assembling and dispersal of the legislative branch. In eight of the states, the chief executive was elected by the legislature, and he was made, thereby, greatly dependent upon it. His tenure of office was usually quite brief. In nine states, it was only twelve months, and nowhere was it for a longer period than three years. To prevent the growth of personal power in the hands of the governor, most state constitutions limited the number of terms he could serve in a given period.[18]

Courts and Legislatures

The courts generally were made more dependent on legislatures than they had been formerly. The Pennsylvania constitution described the relationship this way: "The judges of the supreme court of judicature shall have fixed salaries, be commissioned for seven years only, though capable of reappointment at the end of that term, but removable for misbehavior at any time by the general assembly. . . ."[19] Even so, the principle of separation of powers generally prevailed as between the courts and the legislature more fully than between governors and legislatures.

The legislatures were subject to frequent elections, a device for making them closely dependent upon the electorate. In ten of the states the lower house was subject to annual elections; in two states their terms were only for six months. The members of the upper house usually had somewhat longer terms, but one state did not even have an upper house.[20] Even so, the powers of the legislatures were quite extensive. Thomas Jefferson complained that in Virginia:

> All the powers of government, legislative, executive, and judiciary, result to the legislative body. . . . An *elective despotism* was not the government we fought for, but one which should not only be founded on free principles, but in which the powers of government should be so divided and balanced among several bodies of magistracy, as that no one could transcend their legal limits, without being effectually checked and restrained by the others.[21]

What had been generally done was this: Americans in establishing their state governments had sought to check them by the electorate rather more than by an internal balance of powers. The people could, however, use their influence to abet arbitrary government as well as to check it.

There was also some extension of the franchise during this period. In addition, several legislatures were reapportioned to give inhabitants in the backcountry a more nearly proportionate voice in government. One of the trends, in this connection, was the movement of state capitals inland from the coast to make them more accessible to the backcountry.

Most of these were changes of degree rather than of kind. To call them revolutionary, as some twentieth-century historians have, is a distortion of what happened and a stretching of the meaning of revolution beyond reasonable confines. Insofar as they were changes from what had prevailed, they were culminations of trends long afoot. Americans had been tending toward religious liberty in practice long before they established it in fundamental law. They had been evading, so far as they could, quitrents, primogeniture, and entail. Their new governmental structures embodied much of what they had been contending with the British for. Bills of rights, bicameral legislatures, and weak executives, were built on the British model. The assault on special privilege did run contrary to recent British practice to some extent, but it was quite in accord with what Americans had been doing almost since they had reached the New World. If in their early enthusiasms in government building they did not attend to a broader experience than their colonial one, this did not make their acts revolutionary, only precipitate. They were clear enough that they wanted to protect the individual from government in the enjoyment of his rights; they did not at first realize how much more this took than felicitously phrased declarations. Weak governments do not make liberty and property secure; that is the office of powerful governments internally restrained. Many Americans were to learn this lesson, and that rather quickly. But just as their first experiments were not revolutionary in character, no more were their later alterations a counterrevolution.

---

1. See Merrill Jensen, *The New Nation* (New York: Vintage Books, 1950), p. 132.

2. *Ibid.*, p. 133.

3. John Fiske, *The Critical Period of American History* (Boston: Houghton Mifflin, 1916), p. 78.

4. Jack P. Greene, ed., *Colonies to Nation* (New York: McGraw-Hill, 1967), pp. 390–391.

5. Fiske, *op. cit.,* p. 71.

6. Greene, *op. cit.,* p. 397.

7. Ibid., p. 398.

8. See Fiske, *op. cit.,* pp. 74–75.

9. See Robert A. Rutland, *The Birth of the Bill of Rights* (New York: Collier, 1962), p. 109.

10. Henry S. Commager, ed., *Documents of American History,* I (New York: Appleton-Century-Crofts, 1962, 7th ed.), p. 107.

11. *Ibid.,* p. 104.

12. *Ibid.,* p. 108.

13. Greene, *op. cit.,* pp. 472–473.

14. Dumas Malone and Basil Rauch, *Empire for Liberty,* I (New York: Appleton-Century-Crofts, 1960), p. 196.

15. Commager, *op. cit.,* p. 103.

16. *Ibid.,* p. 108.

17. See Frederick B. Tolles, "A Re-evaluation of the Revolution as a Social Movement," George A. Billias, ed., *The American Revolution* (New York: Holt, Rinehart and Winston, 1970, 2nd ed.), pp. 66–67.

18. See Richard Hofstadter, *et al., The United States* (Englewood Cliffs, N.J.: Prentice Hall, 1967, 2nd ed.), p. 160.

19. Greene, *op. cit.,* p. 343.

20. Hofstadter, *op. cit.,* pp. 159–160.

21. Quoted in Nelson M. Blake, *A History of American Life and Thought* (New York: McGraw-Hill, 1963), p. 100.

Madison's Answer to Machiavelli

John Wesley Young

An abiding problem in political thought, one that has vexed the soul of many a philosopher and statesman, is the problem of how to establish and keep order in society. Without order, without accepted standards of civility and right conduct, a nation will lack peace, justice, and prosperity. Without order it will sink backward into barbarism and brute existence.

The problem of order is especially complex for peoples who live under representative governments. Dictators can brandish the bayonet and the bludgeon to restrain and humble their subjects, but on what can republics depend? How can a self-governing citizenry, the repositories of political sovereignty in a free society, rule themselves equitably and with dignity? How can they live together in liberty without soon abusing that liberty and butchering one another like savages?

The answer is that to balance the blessings of order and liberty, republics must depend upon the virtue of the people themselves. But how to plant in the breasts of the people those good old republican virtues—honesty, frugality, temperance, self-sacrifice, and vigilance against tyranny—without which they will descend into anarchy and ulti-

John Wesley Young, an educator, wrote this article for the July 1977 issue of *The Freeman*.

mate despotism, the victims of an enterprising Napoleon or Caesar?

There is one medium, important above all others, for transmitting virtue to republican populaces: religion. As Washington stated in his Farewell Address, "Of all the dispositions and habits which lead to political prosperity, religion and morality are indispensable supports." But that suggests yet another question: What should be the legal relation of religion to government in a republic? Broadly speaking, among republicans there are two schools of thought on the subject.

Two Points of View

One school, a comparatively recent development in political thought, contends that the best approach to religion in republics is simply to make government leave it alone. To entangle church with state, it is argued, will surely corrupt both. The church best serves society when it is free from interference by civil government.

The other school, a much older one, advocates using the authority of republican government to foster and maintain religion—that is, to "establish" it, either through outright legal recognition and subsidization, or through less comprehensive forms of assistance, such as Sabbath laws or religious tests for public office. Since virtue is necessary to the prosperity and progress of a republic, and religion is necessary to virtue, we ought—or so the reasoning goes—to use the power of government to promote religion among the citizens.

To many spokesmen for this school it does not seem to matter so much *which* religion or *which* form of Christianity is promoted as that the religion should help produce dutiful and patriotic men and women.

Consider the views of one of these spokesmen, Niccolò Machiavelli of Florence (1469–1527). Better known for having authored *The Prince,* a kind of handbook for intelligent tyrants, Machiavelli, in a puzzling and perverse way, was actually an ardent apologist for popular government. His study of ancient history convinced Machiavelli that, as he writes in his *Discourses on the First Ten Books of Titus Livius,* "the observance of divine institutions is the cause of the greatness of republics." Neglect such observance, Machiavelli warns, and a republic perishes. "For where the fear of God is wanting, there the country will come to ruin, unless it be sustained by the fear of the prince, which may temporarily supply the want of religion."[1] In that case, of course, a republic ceases to be a republic. Religion, then, is essential to republics because it gives them cohesion and durability. The best republicans are pious republicans.

So far, so fine. But interestingly enough, Machiavelli singles out for praise the legendary Sabine king, Numa Pompilius, who took the early Romans, "a very savage people" and taught them habits of obedience by using religion as a social cement. Indeed, Machiavelli attributes more historical importance to Numa than to Romulus, Rome's founder; for Numa's invention of religious forms made possible the rise of Rome to republican greatness.[2]

And just how did Numa use religion as a social cement? Machiavelli doesn't say in great detail, but we learn from Plutarch, an ancient Greek historian, that Numa filled the imaginations of Romans "with religious terrors, professing that strange apparitions had been seen, and dreadful voices heard; thus subduing and humbling their minds by a sense of supernatural fears."[3]

In other words, Numa exploited the superstitions of a primitive people. Machiavelli himself notes approvingly that, throughout the period of the Republic, religious sanctions were sometimes used with great effect to inspire, discipline and direct the Roman armies "on the eve of battle with that confidence which is the surest guaranty of victory."[4] For example, during the long siege of the city of Veii in the fourth century B.C., when the Roman troops grew weary and threatened to quit the campaign, their generals told them that some of the sacred oracles had forecast the fall of the city when Lake Albano, in central Italy, should overflow its banks, as in fact it had recently done. Actually the oracles had made no such forecast; but the Roman regulars did not know that. Their resolve to fight on revived and toughened, and finally they seized the city.[5]

Its Use to the State

Observe that Machiavelli's concern is not for the truth of the sacred "prophecy," which he well knows was a fraud, but rather for its effect on the army, its utility to the Roman state. It spurred the soldiers' spirits, brought about the defeat of an enemy, and hence helped to make the world safe for Roman republicanism. It worked; therefore it was good.

> And therefore everything that tends to favor religion (even though it were believed to be false) should be received and availed of to strengthen it. . . . Such was, in fact, the practice observed by sagacious men [in antiquity]; which has given rise to the belief in

the miracles that are celebrated in religions, however false they may be. For the sagacious rulers have given these miracles increased importance, no matter whence or how they originated; and their authority afterwards gave them credence with the people. Rome had many such miracles. . . .[6]

Machiavelli thinks that even in modern times men, however sophisticated, can be led to believe in sham miracles and supernatural manifestations. As proof he points to Florence, the cultured Italian city where, for a short time in the late fifteenth century, many normally staid and stolid people were mesmerized by the preaching of Savonarola, the fire-breathing Dominican reformer who claimed to have conversed with God.[7]

Now the trouble with this utilitarian approach to the problem of order, religion and republican virtue is just that—its utilitarianism. Besides its utter contempt for truthfulness, the spirit of it is decidedly unrepublican. For in picking out the Roman solution to the problem, Machiavelli has not picked out a peculiarly *republican* solution. Roman religion, in fact, was no different in its essential relation to the state from the religions of Egypt, the Mesopotamian kingdoms, the Seleucid Empire, or any other ancient autocracy. It, too, like the other religions, proceeded *downward* from the leaders to the masses. Often the leaders employed it as a propaganda tool, a device for duping the multitude.

Machiavelli does not dwell, for instance, on the exceptionally cynical use made of religion in the later Roman Republic, especially during the civil wars that climaxed with Julius Caesar's dictatorship. Religion became in great degree the instrument of oligarchs and demagogues. Many important Roman statesmen of the period—Servilius, Lep-

idus, Pompey, Cicero, and Caesar himself, among others—
were also priests of the state religion, and they manipulated
that religion in order to reinforce their grip on the government.[8] It is difficult to reconcile this sort of practice with the
power of free choice implicit in republicanism.

But in vain would anyone raise that objection to Machiavelli. For he *wants* utilitarian religion—not quite in the
form into which it degenerated in Rome, perhaps, but at
any rate an established religion, a religion that is only an
arm or extension of the state, a religion that teaches the
martial virtues. This explains Machiavelli's personal hostility to Christianity as he perceives it to be lived by men of
his age. Because of its other-worldliness, he feels, Christianity has made them too effeminate, too indifferent to
their country's liberty, too apt "to suffer than to achieve
great deeds."[9] He doesn't care a jot whether religion edifies
or uplifts individuals, so long as it buoys the state.

Religion as a Social Cement

Without doubt the Machiavellian position is an extreme
one. And yet it is true that after Machiavelli's death, and
well into the modern era, most republicans continued to
treat religion, the Christian religion included, as a social
cement more than a "sovereign balm" for the soul. They
may have lacked Machiavelli's cynicism, they may even
have been devout believers, but in the matter of religion's
relation to republican government they were still Machi-
avellians after a fashion.

Think of any famous republican political philosopher
prior to about 1780, and almost certainly he will have advocated in some sense the mixing of politics with formal religion. He may, like the Genevese Rousseau or the English-

man James Harrington, have favored toleration for most dissenting sects, but he could not have brought himself to call for complete severance of church from state.[10] He could not have visualized full religious liberty—an almost untried freedom until the eighteenth century—invigorating a republic. To abandon men wholly to their private judgment in religion, his instincts would have told him, would kindle social chaos and destroy the state, no matter how well-ordered and free its purely political institutions might be. Remove the official religious props and any popular government would crash down like the house of Dagon.

Not for more than two centuries after Machiavelli did any prominent republican sally forth to assault such ideas. Significantly, the definitive refutation of Machiavelli came, not from the continent of Europe, but from the New World, from the pen of James Madison, quite possibly the profoundest political thinker who ever lived.

Spiritual Crisis in 1780s

A bit of historical background is necessary. In the early 1780s the thirteen newly confederated republics of America were faced with a spiritual crisis no less grave than the political crisis which had forced them, in 1776, to cut their connection with the British Empire. As so often happens in the midst of war and in its aftermath, America suffered a sort of moral depression. This is an often-overlooked aspect of our Revolutionary history, but it was much commented-on by contemporaries.

Political and moral corruption were reportedly proliferating and threatening to unfit the people for republican freedom. Newspapers bemoaned the evaporation of virtue because of "the visible declension of religion, . . . the rapid progress of licentious manners, and open profanity."[11] Clergymen warned of impending divine judgment upon an impenitent people, but they were plainly not the only ones alarmed. "Justice & Virtue," wrote George Mason to Patrick Henry in May 1783, "are the vital Principles of republican Government; but among us, a Depravity of Manners & Morals prevails, to the Destruction of all Confidence between Man & Man."[12] Mason wondered if America's independence would prove a blessing or a curse.

What would the new republican governments do, in these circumstances, to retrieve the disappearing virtue of the people?

For a time they yielded, or seemed to yield, to the utilitarian temptation. To cite the most notable example, Article II of the Massachusetts State Constitution, drawn up in 1780, granted freedom of worship "in the manner and season most agreeable to the dictates of [the citizen's] own conscience"; but the very next article, declaring that "the happiness of a people, and the good order and preservation of civil government, essentially depend upon piety, religion and morality," empowered the state legislature to require local governments and "religious societies" to provide for "public worship of GOD, and for the support and maintenance of public protestant teachers of piety, religion and morality, in all cases where such provision shall not be made voluntarily."[13] In other words, the Massachusetts constitution-makers were harnessing religion—in this instance "protestant" religion—to the state.

Virginia Considers Tax Support of Teachers

Similarly, in 1784, a bill was introduced in the Virginia General Assembly calling for an annual tax assessment to support teachers of the Christian religion in "the general diffusion of Christian knowledge," knowledge which would help "preserve the peace of society."[14] With apparent impartiality the bill would have permitted each taxpayer to designate which Christian denomination his tax contribution would go to. Along with many Presbyterians and the recently disestablished Episcopal Church, honest republicans like Patrick Henry, George Washington, John Marshall, and Richard Henry Lee supported the measure.

Legislative opponents of the assessment, among them James Madison, managed to postpone for almost one year a final vote on the bill. Meanwhile they launched a campaign to work up opposition to it from the grassroots. The big gun in their arsenal of intellectual weapons was a pamphlet by Madison, "A Memorial and Remonstrance Against Religious Assessments."[15]

In the numerous collections of American historical documents, Madison's pamphlet does not appear nearly as often as Thomas Jefferson's more eloquent Statute for Religious Freedom, but Madison's is in truth the superior statement on religious rights. It should be read in its entirety, but for our purposes we may draw out of it that thread of thought which refutes the Machiavellian thesis. Without referring directly to the Florentine, Madison demolishes with impeccable logic the old Machiavellian argument that established religion is necessary to sound civil government.

To begin with, civil society, according to Madison, is not the highest good. Other things take precedence over it. A man's duty to his Creator, for example, is prior to any duty to society. Government, even with the force of majority opinion pressed behind it, must not encroach upon man's natural right to worship the Almighty as conscience obliges him. Obedience belongs first to God, the "Universal Sovereign." Civil obligations come second.

A Power to be Feared

Notice here that Madison has stood Machiavelli on his head. The Florentine republican makes the stability of popular government an end in itself, with individual rights tacitly subordinated to that end. But to the Virginian any truly popular government will respect popular rights, especially the right of free worship. This conviction of Madison necessarily determines his attitude to established religion. Because he would protect men's rights and their power of free choice, he must oppose the slightest suggestion of enforced conformity to a particular religious system, Christian or non-Christian, even if the state needs the underpinning of virtue that religion provides.

After all, if the state has power to grant recognition to a religion, it has also the power to suppress other religions and religious opinions. And that is more power than can safely be entrusted to it, power enough to pervert the ends for which genuinely republican government is instituted.

As to one of the arguments put forth by the friends of establishment, that it is needed to help religion—this, says Madison, is unhistorical nonsense. Consider the history of the Christian church. At what point in its development was Christianity at its purest and most vigorous—before or after Constantine? In fact it flourished in "the ages prior to its incorporation with Civil policy," and this in spite of prodigious resistance to its growth.

On the other hand, fifteen centuries of establishment have very nearly emaciated Christianity in those countries where one or another version of it has received official sanction. And if enacted, the Virginia assessment bill—which Madison regards as in effect an establishment of religion—would actually obstruct the progress of Christianity. It would make Virginia little different from those heathen countries that seek to shut out the light of Christian revelation, for "instead of levelling as far as possible, every obstacle to the victorious progress of truth, the Bill with an ignoble and unchristian timidity would circumscribe it, with a wall of defence, against the encroachments of error." That wall would frighten away potential converts to Christianity. Benefit religion? Establishment destroys it.

Prelude to Tyranny

Now if religion is better off without direct government support, then government itself need not rest on an official religious foundation. For if government is helped by healthy religion, and if religion is healthiest when unbridled by the state, then government ought for its own sake to leave it be. It should not, in Madison's words, "employ Religion as an engine of Civil policy." To do so would be "an unhallowed perversion of the means of salvation."

In fine, legal establishments of religion plunge a people into spiritual or political tyranny. "In no instance have they been seen the guardians of the liberties of the people." A just government (and to Madison "just" means republican} "will be best supported by protecting every citizen in the enjoyment of his Religion with the same equal hand which protects his person and his property; by neither invading the equal rights of any Sect, nor suffering any Sect to invade those of another."

It is important to grasp what Madison is saying here. He is saying that republican government does itself a favor when it relaxes the political control of religion in society—an assertion that would have shocked Machiavelli, if anything could. Government interference will destroy genuine religion and thereby thwart the supposed purpose for interfering in the first place, which is to aid religion and thus republican government. But relax the controls and religion can prosper; and, as Machiavelli himself would say, when religion prospers the state prospers.

Madison's fellow Virginians sided with him in the debate against Machiavelli, for popular pressure brought on defeat of the assessment measure. But when the General Assembly proceeded to enact in 1786 Jefferson's bill for complete religious liberty, lamentations went up elsewhere, especially over New England. By disestablishing religion, declared one northern critic, the Virginia legislators have crushed "the most powerful seeds of that very virtue it must be supposed they wish to see flourish in the state they represent."[16]

But had they? Years later, when a correspondent asked Madison about the state of religion and morals in Virginia, Madison replied that, contrary to some reports, religion had not been blown to pieces by disestablishment. The number of denominations had multiplied and, despite failure of the assessment bill to pass, knowledge of the Christian religion had increased:

> Religious instruction is now diffused throughout the community by preachers of every sect with almost equal zeal. . . . The qualifications of the preachers, too among the new sects where there was the greatest deficiency, are understood to be improving. . . . The civil government, though bereft of everything like an associated hierarchy, possesses the requisite stability and performs its functions with complete

success; whilst the number, the industry, and the morality of the priesthood, and the devotion of the people have been manifestly increased by the total separation of the church from the state.[17]

A prejudiced appraisal? Possibly. But such evidence as survives seems to support Madison. We know, for instance, that among Baptists in the James River settlements there commenced in 1785, the year of the assessment's defeat, a revival that lasted well into the 1790s and spread throughout Virginia to other dissenting sects. Even the old Anglican-Episcopal Church appears to have profited in the long run from disestablishment.[18]

Nor did the nation in general fail to profit from Virginia's experience. Largely at Madison's instigation, religious liberty became a constitutional (and republican) principle with passage of the First Amendment, so that Tocqueville, the astute French observer who visited America in the 1830s, could write:

> For most people in the United States religion, too, is republican, for the truths of the other world are held subject to private judgment, just as in politics the care for men's temporal interests is left to the good sense of all. Each man is allowed to choose freely the path that will lead him to heaven, just as the law recognizes each citizen's right to choose his own government.[19]

Such freedom, Tocqueville believed, had animated religion in America, causing it to hold "quiet sway" over the country while in Europe the progress of secular social revolution was sweeping away established churches in its fury.

Unanswered Questions

All this doesn't answer the question of what happens to republican virtue when religion decays of its own accord, when republican Christians, for instance, lose their "first love" and lapse into vice and folly. Nor does it answer a second question implied, perhaps, in the first: Does history turn in cycles, making the rise and decline of religion, and hence of republican government, inevitable? Personally this writer sees few things inevitable in a world where the great conditioning reality is man's freedom of will. But let the philosophers grapple with that one.

The truth that Madison taught us, the thing which ought by now to be burned into our brains, is that republican government can do nothing to help religion except to guard jealously the *freedom* of religion. And, in the final analysis, as Madison showed, that is much. Whatever becomes of the American Republic in the years ahead, let us do our best to see that Madison's answer to Machiavelli is never forgotten.

---

1. Machiavelli, *Discourses,* in *The Prince and the Discourses* (New York: Modern Library, 1940), p. 148.

2. *Ibid.,* pp. 145–148.

3. *Plutarch 's Lives,* trans. John Dryden, rev. A. H. Clough, 5 vols. (Boston: Little, Brown and Co., 1910), 1:137.

4. *Discourses,* p. 158.

5. *Ibid.,* pp. 153–154.

6. *Ibid.,* p. 150.

7. *Ibid.,* pp. 148–149.

8. See Lily Ross Taylor, *Party Politics in the Age of Caesar* (Berkeley and Los Angeles: University of California Press, 1961), pp. 76–97.

9. *Discourses,* p. 285.

10. See, e.g., Rousseau's chapter "Concerning Civil Religion" in *The Social Contract,* trans. Willmoore Kendall (Chicago: Henry Regnery Co.,

1954), pp. 148–162. On Harrington see Perez Zagorin, A *History of Political Thought in the English Revolution* (London: Routledge and Kegan Paul, 1954), p. 141.

11. Charleston *S.C. and American Gazette,* 21 January 1779, quoted in Gordon S. Wood, *The Creation of the American Republic, 1776–1787* (Chapel Hill: University of North Carolina Press, 1969), p. 417.

12. Mason to Patrick Henry, 6 May 1783, in *The Papers of George Mason,* Robert A. Rutland, ed., 3 vols. (Chapel Hill: University of North Carolina Press, 1970), 2:770.

13. The Massachusetts Constitution of 1780, in *The Popular Sources of Authority,* ed. Oscar and Mary Handlin (Cambridge: Harvard University Press, Belknap Press, 1966), pp. 442–443.

14. Charles F. James, *Documentary History of the Struggle for Religious Liberty in Virginia* (New York: Da Capo Press, 1971), p. 129. On the religious controversy in Virginia see John M. Mecklin, *The Story of American Dissent* (New York: Harcourt, Brace and Co., 1934), pp. 264–283.

15. For full text see *The Complete Madison,* Saul K. Padover, ed. (New York: Harper and Brothers, 1953), pp. 299–306.

16. [John Swanwick], *Considerations on an Act of the Legislature of Virginia, Entitled an Act for the Establishment of Religious Freedom* (Philadelphia, 1786), p. 6, quoted in Wood, *Creation of the American Republic,* p. 427n.

17. Madison to Robert Walsh, 2 March 1819, in *The Writings of James Madison,* ed. Gaillard Hunt, 9 vols. (New York: G. P. Putnam's Sons, 1908), 8:430–432. Spelling and punctuation updated here.

18. See James, *Documentary History,* pp. 147–149; William Henry Foote, *Sketches of Virginia,* new ed. (Richmond, Va.: John Knox Press, 1966), pp. 348, 412–429; George MacLaren Brydon, *Virginia's Mother Church,* 2 vols. (Philadelphia: Church Historical Society, 1952), 2:506–507.

19. Tocqueville, *Democracy in America,* J. P. Mayer, ed.; George Lawrence, trans. (Garden City, N.Y.: Doubleday Anchor Books, 1969), p. 397. For a classic essay on separation of church and state, and how that principle prospered American government and religion in the early days of the Republic, see *ibid.,* pp. 294–301.

George Washington on Liberty and Order

Clarence B. Carson

There are truths to which the passage of time and the gaining of new experience add luster and vitality. So it has been, for me at least, with those contained in Washington's Farewell Address. With each new reading of it, I have been impressed anew with the relevance of so much that he had to say to our own time. Often, too, I discover some new theme or emphasis that I had not been aware of earlier. Undoubtedly, these different impressions arise in part from the richness of the material but also may be conditioned by my particular interests at a given time. At any rate, the theme of liberty and order stood out for me in my latest reading of the Farewell Address. It seemed to me that all the parts fitted together into a whole within the framework of this theme.

Before getting into that, however, it may be of some aid to place the address in a much broader historical frame. Some observations about liberty and order more generally will help to set the stage for his remarks.

Thoughtful men may differ about the desirability of liberty, but they rarely do about the necessity for order. Also, nations, kingdoms, and empires have differed much more over the extent of liberty within them than of the degree of order, over long periods of time anyway. They have ranged from the most compulsive tyrannies to ones in which

---

This essay appeared in the February 1983 issue of *The Freeman*.

considerable liberty prevails. By contrast, all governments are to a greater or lesser extent devoted to maintaining order. But there are great differences of belief, persuasion, and practice as to how order is to be maintained and the proper role of government in doing so. It is the differences on this that largely determine the extent of liberty in a country.

There have been, and are, countries in which those in power believe that government must act to impose order in every nook and cranny of society. The active principle in this, if principle it be, is that if government does not impose order then disorder and chaos will prevail. Thomas Hobbes, English philosopher in the seventeenth century, expressed this view with clarity and force. He declared that if men were permitted to act according "to their particular judgments and particular appetites, they can expect thereby no defense, nor protection against a common enemy, nor against the injuries of one another." There must be a power over them, he said, and the way to get that power is "to confer all their power and strength upon one man, or upon one assembly of men, that may reduce all their wills . . . unto one will. . . . For by this authority, given him by every particular man in the commonwealth, he hath the use of so much power and strength conferred on him, that by terror thereof, he is enabled to perform the wills of them all. . . ."

A view similar to this of what was necessary to order and how it could be achieved, as well as the role of government in it, was widespread in Europe in the seventeenth century. It was an age of royal absolutism, of claims about the Divine right of kings, and of the assertion of government power to direct the lives of peoples. England had an established church; no others were tolerated. All were required to attend its services, contribute to its support, and have most of the great events of life celebrated or recorded in it. The church officials censored publications, licensed schools, and kept watch over the doings of the people.

Mercantilism

Economic life was circumscribed and controlled by the government under a system most commonly known as mercantilism. The government controlled exports and imports, gave subsidies, bounties, and grants to encourage certain undertakings, prohibited others, gave patents, charters, and other forms of monopolies to individuals and companies, enforced craft regulations, and maintained much power over the lands of the realm. Harsh penalties were imposed for every sort of offense from blasphemy to treason. Evidence abounded that government was making massive efforts to impose order. As for liberties, they had most commonly to be asserted against the grain of the prevailing system.

So, too, in the twentieth century, the dominant view of those in power in many lands is that government must impose an all-encompassing order upon the peoples under its sway. At its farthest reaches, this view achieves its fruition in the totalitarian state, with its direct control over all the media of communication, every aspect of the economy, over education, over such religion as is permitted, over work and over play.

In other lands, where this bent toward state-compelled order has been moderated thus far—has been kept from going so far—it evinces itself in government intervention in the economy, the thrust of regulation into many realms, in redistribution of the wealth, in controls over education, medicine, charity, and hundreds of other areas. The ideologies supporting this pervasive government power differ in many particular respects from those that supported seventeenth-century government power, but the notion that government must impose an order else chaos and disorder will prevail is common to both. Extensive liberty can hardly be reconciled with such compulsive orders.

That George Washington held a view on how to maintain order and the proper role of government in sharp contrast to those described above is manifest in his life and works. Moreover, a seismic change in outlook, both in England and America and over much of Europe, had taken place between the time when Hobbes had penned his *Leviathan* and the founding of the United States. A major aspect of that change was a shift from the emphasis upon a government order imposed on men toward individual liberty and responsibility. The shift sparked in many Americans an awareness of the danger of government both to liberty and to order. At the root of this shift was a different conception of the origin and nature of order.

Belief in a Natural Order

George Washington and his contemporaries were imbued with a strong belief in a natural order. Order, in their view, was not something that could be arbitrarily contrived and imposed by man. The foundations of order, they held, are in the frame of the universe, in the laws that govern it, in the nature of man and his faculty of reason, and in the principles of relationships by which constructive activities can take place. At best, men can only act in accord with and imitate the order that is given.

The belief in a natural law and natural order was not

new to the eighteenth century, of course; it had been around since the ancient Greeks and Romans, at least. But it had come to the forefront in the century before the founding of the United States as a result both of vigorous efforts to revive it and of many scientific and philosophical formulations of it.

Newton had persuasively set forth in mathematical terms the laws governing the course of the heavenly bodies. Thinkers were getting impressive results in their searches for the laws and principles governing all sorts of relationships. What struck so many in that age was the idea of proportion, balance, harmony, and order resident in the natural tendencies of the world about them. Most marvelous of all, at least to many, this order was consonant with human liberty. Rather than frustrating man in the use of his faculties for his benefit (and for the commonweal as well), the natural order provided means for him to do so most effectively. The foundations of liberty in this belief in a natural order were in the natural rights doctrine.

In his Farewell Address, Washington did not expand upon or elaborate on the theme of liberty. Although the word "liberty" occurs several times in the document, it plays mainly a supportive role in what he has to say. The attachment to liberty is assumed, a given if you will, upon which to hinge his arguments. Washington said as much himself: "Interwoven as is the love of liberty with every ligament of your hearts, no recommendation of mine is necessary to fortify or confirm the attachment." But, he says, from first one angle then another, if you would have liberty you must support those things on which it depends.

For example, in recommending a united support for the general government, he declared: "This Government, the off-spring of our own choice, . . . adopted upon full investigation and mature deliberation, completely free in its principles, in the distribution of its powers, uniting security with energy, and containing within itself a provision for its own amendment, has a just claim to your confidence and support." To clinch the argument, he says that these "are duties enjoined by the fundamental maxims of true liberty." In arguing against the involvement of Americans in foreign intrigues, he says that by doing so "they will avoid the necessity of those overgrown military establishments which, under any form of government, are inauspicious to liberty. . . ."

A Sense of Order

The word "liberty" occurs frequently throughout the address, but by my fairly careful count the word "order" occurs only once. Even that instance is insignificant, however, for the word is used in a phrase, as "in order to" do something or other. It occurs at one other point as part of the word "disorders," which, while more significant, is hardly proof of a theme. Yet a sense of order pervades the whole document. It is there in the cadences of the sentences, in the matching of phrase with phrase, in the balance of one tendency against another, in the thrust toward discovering a common bond by piling up references to particular interests. It is clear, if one reads between the lines, that there is an order for men's lives, an order for nations, an order for relations among nations, an order by which parts belong to a whole, and an order by which balance and harmony can be maintained. Government is not the origin of this order, but it is necessary to the maintenance of it, even as it is ever a potential threat to it. Government is made necessary by the bent in man to disrupt order.

The two main sources of disorder to which Washington alludes are these. First, there are those passions in men which incline them to pursue their own particular and partisan designs at the expense of the well-being of others. Washington called it the spirit of party, but we might understand it better as partisanship for causes. (He had in mind the dangers of this to the stability of government, but it does no violence to his idea to apply it to individuals as well as groups.) "This spirit," he said, "unfortunately, is inseparable from our nature, having its roots in the strongest passions of the human mind." Among the dangers of these partisan passions, he declared, are these: "It serves always to distract the public councils and enfeeble the public administration. It agitates the community with ill-founded jealousies and false alarms; kindles the animosity of one part against another; foments occasionally riot and insurrection. It opens the door to foreign influence and corruption. . . . Thus the policy and will of one country are subjected to the policy and will of another."

The other source of disorder, to which Washington alludes, is "that love of power and proneness to abuse it which predominates in the human heart. . . ." It is this power hunger which makes government dangerous, for it prompts those who govern to overstep the bounds of their authority. "The spirit of encroachment," Washington pointed out, "tends to consolidate the powers of all the departments in one, and thus to create, whatever the form of government, a real despotism."

Advice and Counsel

The body of the Farewell Address is devoted to advice and counsel about how to conduct the government so as to maintain order and preserve liberty, and to warnings about holding in check those partisan tendencies and the bent toward consolidating power which endanger them. The following were his main points: (1) Maintain the union; (2) Keep the principles of the Constitution intact; (3) Preserve national independence; (4) Buttress policy and behavior with religion and morality; (5) Cherish the public credit; and (6) Follow peaceful policies toward all nations. These general principles are not nearly so revealing, however, as his particular recommendations and the arguments he used to support them.

The main device Washington employed to support his advice to maintain the union was to invoke those things the people had in common: the name American, their struggles for independence, their common beliefs, and their common interest. He surveyed the continent, from a mountaintop as it were, and ticked off how north and south, east and west, were bound together.

"The *North*," he said, "in an unrestrained intercourse with the *South*, protected by the equal laws of a common government, finds in the production of the latter great . . . resources of maritime and commercial enterprise and precious materials of manufacturing industry. The *South,* in the same intercourse . . . sees its agriculture grow and commerce expand. . . . The *East,* in a like intercourse with the *West,* already finds . . . a valuable vent for the commodities which it brings from abroad or manufactures at home. The *West* derives from the *East* supplies requisite to its growth and comfort." This was an economic order which had its roots in the diversities of the regions. Washington warned against the rise of factions seeking to use political power for partisan ends that might disrupt the union and disturb the existing order.

Preserve the Constitution

Washington's concern for preserving the Constitution intact was motivated by the belief that a balance had been incorporated in it, a balance in which the national and state government checked one another, and the branches held one another in check. "The necessity of reciprocal checks in the exercise of political power," he declared, "by dividing and distributing it . . . has been evinced by experiments ancient and modern. . . ." "Liberty itself," he pointed out, "will find in such a government with powers properly distributed and adjusted, its surest guardian." He warned against two things in particular. One was the "spirit of innovation upon its principles." The other was "change by usurpation" of power. That was not to say that the Constitution was perfect as it stood in 1796. But if something needed correction, it should be "by an amendment in the way which the Constitution designates." No man or body of men should assume the power to do so, "for though this in one instance may be the instrument of good, it is the customary weapon by which free governments are destroyed."

Washington hoped that the United States would follow an independent course in world affairs, that it would lend its weight toward an order in which peace would be the norm, but that it would not become entangled with other nations in the quest for power and dominance. His distrust of government did not end at the water's edge, for he believed that foreign governments would, if they could, use the United States for their own ends. He warned "Against the insidious wiles of foreign influence," for "(I conjure you to believe me, fellow-citizens) the jealousy of a free people ought to be *constantly* awake, since history and experience prove that foreign influence is one of the most baneful foes of republican government." Underlying these fears was the belief that in the nature of things, in the natural order, each nation pursues its own interests. Hence, "There can be no greater error than to expect or calculate upon real favors from nation to nation." He cautioned against constant preference for one nation and opposition to others. "It is our true policy," Washington said, "to steer clear of permanent alliances with any portion of the foreign world. . . ."

Religion and Morality

The first President had some other recommendations on foreign policy, but before discussing them, it would be best, as he did, to refer to the role of religion and morality. The belief in a natural order, the hope that the American political system had been shaped in accord with it, was not sufficient, in Washington's opinion, to assure the working or continuation of order among men. Man is a creature of unruly passions, as already noted, and the necessary corrective to these is religion and morality.

"It is substantially true," Washington commented, "that virtue or morality is a necessary spring of popular government." And, "Of all the dispositions and habits which lead to political prosperity, religion and morality are indispensable supports. In vain would that man claim the tribute of patriotism who should labor to subvert these great pillars of human happiness. . . . A volume could not trace all their connections with private and public felicity." Moreover, "let us with caution indulge the supposition that morality can be maintained without religion."

These remarks preceded both his advice on public credit and on peaceful relations with other nations. On cherishing the public credit, he said: "One method of preserving it is to use it as sparingly as possible . . ." Washington expected that there would be occasions for extraordinary expenses, making war came to mind, when it might be necessary for the government to borrow money. But he warned against the "accumulation of debt," declaring that the way to avoid this was "not only by shunning occasions of expense, but by vigorous exertions in time of peace to discharge the debts which unavoidable wars have occasioned." That way, it should be possible to avoid "ungenerously throwing upon posterity the burthen which we ourselves ought to bear." Washington thought his countrymen might be the more inclined to follow these policies if they would keep in mind "that toward the payment of debts there must be revenue; that to have revenue there must be taxes; that no taxes can be devised which are not more or less inconvenient and unpleasant. . . ." Not everyone may find the balanced formulations of eighteenth-century sentences pleasant, but it must be admitted that the logic in the above is impressive.

At any rate, the principles discussed in the above two paragraphs provided the framework for his recommendations for maintaining peaceful relations with other nations. To that end, Washington advised this: "Observe good faith and justice toward all nations. Cultivate peace and harmony with all. Religion and morality enjoin this conduct. And can it be that good policy does not equally enjoin it." Above all, "The great rule of conduct for us in regard to foreign nations is, in extending our commercial relations to have with them as little *political* connection as possible."

Any extended political connections—permanent alliances, for example—could only embroil the United States in the conflicts among other nations. Otherwise, "Harmony, liberal intercourse with all nations are recommended by policy, humanity, and interest. But even our commercial policy should hold an equal and impartial hand, neither seeking nor granting exclusive favors or preferences; con-

sulting the natural course of things; diffusing and diversi-
fying by gentle means the streams of commerce, but forcing
nothing. . . ." That is surely the natural order for trade, and
a plausible hope for peace to those who knew of, when they
had not experienced, the devastating mercantile wars
resulting from the use of force in national commerce.

A Farewell Message of Timeless Truths on Liberty and Order

George Washington reckoned that he had devoted the
better part of forty-five years to the service of his country
when he retired. He was an unabashed patriot, proud to be
called an American, a sturdy friend of the union, and none
knew better than he the struggles out of which the United
States had been born. He was a man of his time, as are all
mortal men, spoke in the phraseology of times past, yet in
his Farewell Address he touched upon and elaborated
some timeless truths. Further experience has served only to
confirm the validity of many of his recommendations.

His thoughts on unity, on the love of power, on the
impact of partisan strife, on the importance of focusing on
our common interests, on avoiding entanglements with
other nations, on religion and morality, on the public credit,
and on freedom of trade have worn well when they have
been observed, and have brought suffering by their neglect.
The terror and tyranny of this century, the slave labor
camps and barbed wired borders of nations with their fet-
tered peoples prove once again that liberty depends upon
order, and that if order is not founded upon and in accord
with an underlying order it will tend to be nothing more
than the will of the tyrant.

John Witherspoon:
"Animated Son of Liberty"

Robert A. Peterson

On July 4, 1776, the Declaration of Independence lay on the table of Independence Hall in Philadelphia. Two days earlier, Richard Henry Lee's resolution for independence had been adopted, and now the time was at hand when each delegate would put pen to paper, thus committing his life, his fortune, and his sacred honor to a future darkened by clouds of war. If their bid for liberty failed, those who signed would be the first to be hung from a British noose.

Sensing the urgency of the moment, John Witherspoon of New Jersey rose to speak:

> There is a tide in the affairs of men, a nick of time. We perceive it now before us. To hesitate is to consent to our own slavery. That noble instrument upon your table, which ensures immortality to its author, should be subscribed this very morning by every pen in this house. He that will not respond to its accents and strain every nerve to carry into effect its provisions is unworthy the name of freeman. For my own part, of property I have some, of reputation more. That reputation is staked, that property is

Mr. Peterson is headmaster of the Pilgrim Academy, Egg Harbor City, New Jersey. This essay appeared in the December 1985 issue of *The Freeman*.

pledged, on the issue of this contest; and although these gray hairs must soon descend into the sepulchre, I would infinitely rather that they descend thither by the hand of the executioner than desert at this crisis the sacred cause of my country.[1]

Witherspoon's words gave voice to the sentiments of the majority of delegates, and on July 4, America declared her independence.

In his philosophy of freedom, Witherspoon was one of the most consistent of the Founding Fathers. Leaving no realm of thought untouched, all knowledge was his province as he discussed money, political economy, philosophy, and education, all in relation to Whig principles of liberty. His articles and teachings on the nature of money foreshadowed the discoveries of the Austrian school of economics in the nineteenth century, and contributed to making the Constitution a "hard-money document"— a fact that has been forgotten by modern politicians.

His Influence on Others

Witherspoon never led an army into battle, nor did he run for high national office after the war. Yet his influence was such that in his role as President of the College of New Jersey (now Princeton) he helped to educate a generation of leaders for the new nation. His students included James Madison, the young Aaron Burr, Henry and Charles Lee of Virginia, and the poets Philip Freneau and Hugh Brackenridge. Of his former students 10 became cabinet officers, 6 were members of the Continental Congress, 39 became Congressmen, and 21 sat in the Senate. His graduates included 12 governors, and when the General Assembly of the Presbyterian Church in America met in 1789, 52 of the 188 delegates had studied under Witherspoon. The limited-government philosophy of most of these men was due in large measure to Witherspoon's influence.[2]

Born in Scotland in 1723, Witherspoon was reared on stories of the Scottish Covenanters who in years past had stood for both religious and political liberty. In due time he was sent to the grammar school at Haddington, and later entered Edinburgh University at the age of fourteen.

Witherspoon received his education in Scotland at a time when the air was filled with the kind of thinking that led to Adam Smith's *Wealth of Nations.* Indeed, Witherspoon and Smith were contemporaries, and in 1776 both would strike an important blow for liberty—Witherspoon with the signing of the Declaration on one side of the Atlantic, and Smith with his publication of the *Wealth of Nations* on the other. Witherspoon spoke out for political liberty, while Smith took a stand against mercantilism and for economic liberty. Freedom is all of a piece, and the work of these two Scotsmen complemented and supported one another. Political freedom and economic freedom go hand in hand—you cannot have one without the other.

Witherspoon received his M.A. in 1743, and spent the next two decades serving as a parish minister in the Church of Scotland. During this period of his life he developed a reputation for being the champion of the "Popular Party," which stood against patronage and pluralism in the Church of Scotland. His fame continued to grow in both Scotland and America, and so, when an opening occurred for the presidency of Princeton, Witherspoon's name was brought up and approved by the trustees. After careful negotiations and some pleading by Princeton alumnus Benjamin Rush, who was studying medicine in Edinburgh, Witherspoon accepted the call.[3]

Arriving in America in 1766, Witherspoon plunged into his new task with vigor. One of his first jobs was to get the college on a sound financial footing. Unlike many college administrators today, who go begging at the public trough, Witherspoon could not appeal for federal aid. Princeton was totally supported by tuitions and voluntary contributions. Within two years, Witherspoon's fund-raising efforts (even George Washington contributed) brought Princeton back from the brink of bankruptcy.

Educational Reform

After laying a sound foundation for school finances, Witherspoon turned his attention to educational reform. He was the first to use the lecture method at Princeton. Previously, instructors had assigned readings and then quizzed their students in class. He also set up a grammar school, authored several works on child-rearing, introduced modern languages into the college curriculum, and taught a course on moral philosophy. Witherspoon's activities at Princeton were brought to an abrupt halt by the outbreak of the War for Independence. Like most Americans, Witherspoon was at first slow to embrace the cause of independence, hoping instead for a reconciliation of the two countries based on the restoration of full English rights for the colonials—in particular, the right of their own little parliaments to tax them and make their laws, under the overall jurisdiction of the king.

Witherspoon grew increasingly concerned, however, with the attempt of the British to install an Anglican bishop over the American colonies.[4] He viewed this as the first step toward an ecclesiastical tyranny over the colonies, of which the Quebec Act was also a part (the Quebec Act extended French law, which meant no trial by jury, and Roman Catholicism into the Ohio Valley). Witherspoon understood that religious liberty—man's freedom to own his conscience—was inextricably intertwined with political and economic liberty: "There is not a single instance in history," he wrote, "in which civil liberty was lost, and religious liberty preserved entire. If, therefore, we yield up our temporal property, we at the same time deliver the conscience into bondage."[5]

When hostilities broke out, and continued for about a year with no end in sight, Witherspoon felt that it was his duty to set forth the issue from the pulpit. In what is perhaps his most celebrated sermon, "The Dominion of Providence Over the Passions of Men," Witherspoon said:

> ... the cause in which America is now in arms, is the cause of justice, of liberty, and of human nature. So far as we have hitherto proceeded, I am satisfied that the confederacy of the colonies has not been the effect of pride, resentment, or sedition, but of a deep and general conviction that our civil and religious liberties, and consequently in a great measure the temporal and eternal happiness of us and our posterity, depended on the issue.[6]

Witherspoon went on to say that Americans would need "pure manners," "bravery," "economy," and "frugality" if they wanted to win their independence.

Limited Government

In his concept of political economy, Witherspoon believed that good government was limited government, wherein "faction" checked "faction" so that no person or group of persons could gain unlimited power. Thus, he believed in a system of checks and balances—a system that found its way into the United States Constitution through the influence of one of his favorite students, James Madison.[7] Ashbel Green, who would follow in Witherspoon's steps as a president of Princeton, said that the aging statesman approved of the Constitution "as embracing principles and carrying into effect measures, which he had long advocated, as essential to the preservation of the liberties, and the promotion of the peace and prosperity of the country."[8]

Witherspoon put his views on civil government into practice when he served in Congress from 1776 to 1782. Always active, he served on over one hundred committees and preached to members of the Continental Congress on Sundays while in Philadelphia. The British showed that they realized the significance of Witherspoon's contribution when they burned him in effigy along with George Washington during the occupation of New York City.

The war left Nassau Hall in ruins, as the British particularly singled out Presbyterian institutions for destruction. Undaunted, Witherspoon left the Continental Congress in 1782 to rebuild his beloved Princeton. He still found time to comment on the problems which confronted the new nation—particularly economic problems. An economist, or moral philosopher, of the first rank and an advocate of hard money, Witherspoon had seen firsthand the effects of the inflationary "Continentals." In his "Essay on Money," which in many ways presaged the writings of the Austrian school of economics, Witherspoon wrote:

> I observe that to arm such bills with the authority of the state, and make them legal tender in all payments is an absurdity so great, that it is not easy to speak with propriety upon it . . . It has been found, by the experience of ages, that money must have a standard of value, and if any prince or state debase the metal below the standard, it is utterly impossible to make it succeed. Why will you make a law to oblige men to take money when it is offered them? Are there any who refuse it when it is good? If it is necessary to force them, does not this system produce a most ludicrous inversion of the nature of things?[9]

Witherspoon was also mindful of the tremendous productive capacity of the free society, not only in the physical realm but in the other fields of human action as well. In a textbook he wrote for his students, he concluded: "What then is the advantage of civil liberty? I suppose it chiefly consists in its tendency to put in motion all the human powers. Therefore it promotes industry, and in this respect happiness—produces every latent quality, and improves the human mind.—Liberty is the nurse of riches, literature, and heroism."[10]

Contracts Are Important

The contract, so essential to capitalism, also loomed large in Witherspoon's thought: "Contracts are absolutely necessary in social life. Every transaction almost may be considered as a contract, either more or less explicit."[11] And in what constituted an intellectual "end run" around the classical economists, Witherspoon touched upon the discovery that value is essentially subjective, determined not by the amount of labor that goes into a product or by government decree, but by individuals freely acting in the marketplace. "Nothing has any real value unless it be of some use in human life, or perhaps we may say, unless it is supposed to be of use, and so becomes the object of human desire. . . ."[12]

Besides writing, Witherspoon spent his last years building up Princeton and his church. Two accidents left him blind the last two years of his life. His light spent, he continued to preach and teach, relying upon the vast store of knowledge that he had husbanded away through years of diligent study.

At the age of seventy-one, having crammed several careers into one lifetime, Witherspoon passed away and was buried in the President's Lot at Princeton. Two hundred years later, Witherspoon's great contributions in helping to lay the foundations of American freedom are still only darkly understood. There have been those in the past, however, who have recognized the magnitude of Witherspoon's life and thought. John Adams, for instance, noted in his diary that Witherspoon was "as hearty a friend as any of the Natives—an animated Son of Liberty."[13] One of his students, Philip Freneau, wrote:

> His words still vibrate on my ear,
> His precepts, solemn and severe,
> Alarmed the vicious and the base,
> To virtue gave the loveliest face
> That humankind can wear.[14]

It was through the influence of men like John Witherspoon that a new nation gained a constitution that repudiated interventionism, fiat currency, and embraced the idea of hard money. He was a pastor, educator, statesman, economist, and political theorist. He was, and still remains, "an animated Son of Liberty."

---

1. John Witherspoon, quoted in Charles Augustus Briggs, *American Presbyterianism* (New York: Charles Scribner's Sons, 1885), p. 351.

2. Charles G. Osgood, *Lights in Nassau Hall* (Princeton: Princeton University Press, 1951), pp. 12–13.

3. Lyman H. Butterfield, *John Witherspoon Comes to America* (Princeton: Princeton University Library, 1953).

4. Carl Bridenbaugh, *Mitre and Sceptre: Transatlantic Faiths, Ideas, Personalities, and Politics 1689–1775* (New York: Oxford University Press, 1962).

5. John Witherspoon, *The Works of John Witherspoon*, 9 vols. (Edinburgh: 1804–1805) Vol. ii, pp. 202–203.

6. *Ibid.*

7. James H. Smylie, "Madison and Witherspoon: Theological Roots of American Political Thought," *The Princeton University Library Chronicle*, Vol. xxii, No. 3 (Spring, 1961), MS, Presbyterian Historical Society.

8. Ashbel Green, quoted in Smylie, p. 130.

9. Works, Vol. iv, p. 223.

10. John Witherspoon, *An Annotated Edition of Lectures on Moral Philosophy*, Jack Scott, ed. (Newark, Del.: University of Delaware Press, 1982), p. 147.

11. *Lectures on Moral Philosophy*, p. 168.

12. *Lectures on Moral Philosophy*, p. 178.

13. Martha Lou Stohlman, *John Witherspoon: Parson, Politician, Patriot* (Philadelphia: The Westminster Press, 1976), p. 15.

14. Philip Freneau, quoted in Mary Weatherspoon Bowden, *Philip Freneau* (Boston: Twayne Pub., 1976), p. 17.

Education in Colonial America

Robert A. Peterson

One of the main objections people have to getting government out of the education business and turning it over to the free market is that "it simply would not get the job done." This type of thinking is due, in large measure, to what one historian called "a parochialism in time,"[1] i.e., a limited view of an issue for lack of historical perspective. Having served the twelve-year sentence in government-controlled schools, most Americans view our present public school system as the measure of all things in education. Yet for two hundred years in American history, from the mid-1600s to the mid-1800s, public schools as we know them today were virtually nonexistent, and the educational needs of America were met by the free market. In these two centuries, America produced several generations of highly skilled and literate men and women who laid the foundation for a nation dedicated to the principles of freedom and self-government.

The private system of education in which our forefathers were educated included home, school, church, voluntary associations such as library companies and philosophical societies, circulating libraries, apprenticeships, and private study. It was a system supported primarily by those who bought the services of education, and by private benefactors. All was done without compulsion. Although there

This essay appeared in the September 1983 issue of *The Freeman*.

was a veneer of government involvement in some colonies, such as in Puritan Massachusetts, early American education was essentially based on the principle of voluntarism.[2]

Dr. Lawrence A. Cremin, distinguished scholar in the field of education, has said that during the colonial period the Bible was "the single most important cultural influence in the lives of Anglo-Americans."[3]

Thus, the cornerstone of early American education was the belief that "children are an heritage from the Lord."[4] Parents believed that it was their responsibility to not only teach them how to make a living, but also how to live. As our forefathers searched their Bibles, they found that the function of government was to protect life and property.[5] Education was not a responsibility of the civil government.

Education Began in the Home and the Fields

Education in early America began in the home at the mother's knee, and often ended in the cornfield or barn by the father's side. The task of teaching reading usually fell to the mother, and since paper was in short supply, she would trace the letters of the alphabet in the ashes and dust by the fireplace.[6] The child learned the alphabet and then how to sound out words. Then a book was placed in the child's hands, usually the Bible. As many passages were familiar to him, having heard them at church or at family devotions, he would soon master the skill of reading. The Bible was supplemented by other good books such as *Pilgrim's Progress* by John Bunyan, *The New England Primer*, and Isaac Watts' *Divine Songs*. From volumes like these, our founding fathers and their generation learned the values that laid the foundation for free enterprise. In "Against Idleness and

Mischief," for example, they learned individual responsibility before God in the realm of work and learning.[7]

How doth the busy little bee
  Improve each shining hour,
And gather honey all the day
  From every opening flower.

How skillfully she builds her cell,
  How neat she spreads the wax
And labours hard to store it well
  With the sweet food she makes.

In works of labour, or of skill,
  I would be busy too;
For Satan finds some mischief still
  For idle hands to do.

In books, or work, or healthful play
  Let my first years be passed;
That I may give for every day
  Some good account at last.

Armed with love, common sense, and a nearby woodshed, colonial mothers often achieved more than our modern-day elementary schools with their federally funded programs and education specialists. These colonial mothers used simple, time-tested methods of instruction mixed with plain, old-fashioned hard work. Children were not ruined by educational experiments developed in the ivory towers of academe. The introduction to a reading primer from the early nineteenth century testifies to the importance of home instruction.[8] It says: "The author cannot but hope that this book will enable many a mother or aunt, or elder brother or sister, or perhaps a beloved grandmother, by the family fireside, to go through in a pleasant and sure way with the art of preparing the child for his first school days."

Home education was so common in America that most children knew how to read before they entered school. As Ralph Walker has pointed out, "Children were often taught to read at home before they were subjected to the rigours of school. In middle-class families, where the mother would be expected to be literate, this was considered part of her duties."[9]

Without ever spending a dime of tax money, or without ever consulting a host of bureaucrats, psychologists, and specialists, children in early America learned the basic academic skills of reading, writing, and ciphering necessary for getting along in society. Even in Boston, the capital city of the colony in which the government had the greatest hand, children were taught to read at home. Samuel Eliot Morison, in his excellent study on education in colonial New England, says:[10]

> Boston offers a curious problem. The grammar (Boston Latin) school was the only public school down to 1684, when a writing school was established; and it is probable that only children who already read were admitted to that. . . . they must have learned to read somehow, since there is no evidence of unusual illiteracy in the town. And a Boston bookseller's stock in 1700 includes no less than eleven dozen spellers and sixty-one dozen primers.

The answer to this supposed problem is simple. The books were bought by parents, and illiteracy was absent because parents taught their children how to read outside of a formal school setting. Coupled with the vocational skills children learned from their parents, home education met the demands of the free market. For many, formal schooling was simply unnecessary. The fine education they received at home and on the farm held them in good stead for the rest of their lives, and was supplemented with Bible reading and almanacs like Franklin's *Poor Richard's*.

Some of our forefathers desired more education than they could receive at home. Thus, grammar and secondary schools grew up all along the Atlantic seaboard, particularly near the centers of population, such as Boston and Philadelphia. In New England, many of these schools were started by colonial governments, but were supported and controlled by the local townspeople.

In the Middle Colonies there was even less government intervention. In Pennsylvania, a compulsory education law was passed in 1683, but it was never strictly enforced.[11] Nevertheless, many schools were set up simply as a response to consumer demand. Philadelphia, which by 1776 had become second only to London as the chief city in the British Empire, had a school for every need and interest. Quakers, Philadelphia's first inhabitants, laid the foundation for an educational system that still thrives in America. Because of their emphasis on learning, an illiterate Quaker child was a contradiction in terms. Other religious groups set up schools in the Middle Colonies. The Scottish Presbyterians, the Moravians, the Lutherans, and Anglicans all had their own schools. In addition to these church-related schools, private schoolmasters, entrepreneurs in their own right, established hundreds of schools.

Historical records, which are by no means complete, reveal that over one hundred and twenty-five private schoolmasters advertised their services in Philadelphia newspapers between 1740 and 1776. Instruction was offered in Latin, Greek, mathematics, surveying, navigation, accounting, bookkeeping, science, English, and contemporary foreign languages.[12] Incompetent and inefficient teachers were soon eliminated, since they were not subsidized by the State or protected by a guild or union. Teachers who satisfied their customers by providing good services prospered. One schoolmaster, Andrew Porter, a mathematics teacher, had over one hundred students enrolled in 1776. The fees the students paid enabled him to provide for a family of seven.[13]

In the Philadelphia Area

Philadelphia also had many fine evening schools. In 1767, there were at least sixteen evening schools, catering mostly to the needs of Philadelphia's hard-working German population. For the most part, the curriculum of these schools was confined to the teaching of English and vocations.[14] There were also schools for women, blacks, and the poor. Anthony Benezet, a leader in colonial educational thought, pioneered in the education for women and Negroes. The provision of education for the poor was a favorite Quaker philanthropy. As one historian has pointed out, "the poor, both Quaker and non-Quaker, were allowed to attend without paying fees."[15]

In the countryside around Philadelphia, German immigrants maintained many of their own schools. By 1776, at least sixteen schools were being conducted by the Mennonites in Eastern Pennsylvania. Christopher Dock, who made several notable contributions to the science of pedagogy, taught in one of these schools for many years. Eastern Pennsylvanians, as well as New Jerseyans and Marylanders, sometimes sent their children to Philadelphia to further their education, where there were several boarding schools, both for girls and boys.

In the Southern colonies, government had, for all practical purposes, no hand at all in education. In Virginia, education was considered to be no business of the State. The educational needs of the young in the South were taken care of in "old-field" schools. "Old-field" schools were buildings erected in abandoned fields that were too full of rocks or too overcultivated for farm use. It was in such a school that George Washington received his early education. The Southern Colonies' educational needs were also taken care of by using private tutors, or by sending their sons north or across the Atlantic to the mother country.

Colonial Colleges

A college education is something that very few of our forefathers wanted or needed. As a matter of fact, most of them were unimpressed by degrees or a university accent. They judged men by their character and by their experience. Moreover, many of our founding fathers, such as George Washington, Patrick Henry, and Ben Franklin, did quite well without a college education. Yet for those who so desired it, usually young men aspiring to enter the ministry, university training was available. Unlike England, where the government had given Cambridge and Oxford a monopoly on the granting of degrees,[16] there were nine colleges from which to choose.

Although some of the colonial colleges were started by

colonial governments, it would be misleading to think of them as statist institutions in the modern sense.[17] Once chartered, the colleges were neither funded nor supported by the state. Harvard was established with a grant from the Massachusetts General Court, yet voluntary contributions took over to keep the institution alive. John Harvard left the college a legacy of 800 pounds and his library of 400 books. "College corn," donated by the people of the Bay Colony, maintained the young scholars for many years.[18] Provision was also made for poor students, as Harvard developed one of the first work-study programs.[19] And when Harvard sought to build a new building in 1674, donations were solicited from the people of Massachusetts. Despite the delays caused by King Philip's War, the hall was completed in 1677 at almost no cost to the taxpayer.[20]

New Jersey was the only colony that had two colleges, the College of New Jersey (Princeton) and Queens (Rutgers). The Log College, the predecessor of Princeton, was founded when Nathaniel Irwin left one thousand dollars to William Tennant to found a seminary.[21] Queens grew out of a small class held by the Dutch revivalist, John Frelinghuyson.[22] Despite occasional hard times, neither college bowed to civil government for financial assistance. As Frederick Rudolph has observed, "neither the college at Princeton nor its later rival at New Brunswick ever received any financial support from the state. . . ."[23] Indeed, John Witherspoon, Princeton's sixth president, was apparently proud of the fact that his institution was independent of government control. In an advertisement addressed to the British settlers in the West Indies, Witherspoon wrote: "The College of New Jersey is altogether independent. It hath received no favor from Government but the charter, by the particular friendship of a person now deceased."[24]

Based on the principle of freedom, Princeton under Witherspoon produced some of America's most "animated Sons of Liberty." Many of Princeton's graduates, standing firmly in the Whig tradition of limited government, helped lay the legal and constitutional foundations for our Republic. James Madison, the Father of the Constitution, was a Princeton graduate.

Libraries

In addition to formal schooling in elementary and secondary schools, colleges, and universities, early America had many other institutions that made it possible for people to either get an education or supplement their previous training. Conceivably, an individual who never attended school could receive an excellent education by using libraries, building and consulting his own library, and by joining a society for mutual improvement. In colonial America, all of these were possible.

Consumer demand brought into existence a large number of libraries. Unlike anything in the Old Country, where libraries were open only to scholars, churchmen, or government officials, these libraries were rarely supported by government funds. In Europe, church libraries were supported by tax money as well, for they were a part of an established church. In America, church libraries, like the churches themselves, were supported primarily by voluntarism.

The first non-private, non-church libraries in America were maintained by membership fees, called subscriptions or shares, and by gifts of books and money from private benefactors interested in education. The most famous of these libraries was Franklin and Logan's Library Company in Philadelphia, which set the pattern and provided much of the inspiration for libraries throughout the colonies.[25] The membership fee for these subscription libraries varied from twenty or thirty pounds to as little as fifteen shillings a year. The Association Library, a library formed by a group of Quaker artisans, cost twenty shillings to join.[26]

Soon libraries became the objects of private philanthropy, and it became possible for even the poorest citizens to borrow books. Sometimes the membership fee was completely waived for an individual if he showed intellectual promise and character.[27]

Entrepreneurs, seeing an opportunity to make a profit from colonial Americans' desire for self-improvement, provided new services and innovative ways to sell or rent printed matter. One new business that developed was that of the circulating library. In 1767, Lewis Nicola established one of the first such businesses in the City of Brotherly Love. The library was open daily, and customers, by depositing five pounds and paying three dollars a year, could withdraw one book at a time. Nicola apparently prospered, for two years later he moved his business to Society Hill, enlarged his library, and reduced his prices to compete with other circulating libraries.[28] Judging from the titles in these libraries,[29] colonial Americans could receive an excellent education completely outside of the schoolroom. For colonial Americans who believed in individual responsibility, self-government, and self-improvement, this was not an uncommon course of study. Most lawyers, for example, were self-educated.

Sermons as Educational Tools

The sermon was also an excellent educational experience for our colonial forefathers. Sunday morning was a time to hear the latest news and see old friends and neighbors. But it was also an opportunity for many to sit under a man of God who had spent many hours preparing for a two-, three-, or even four-hour sermon. Many a colonial pastor, such as Jonathan Edwards, spent eight to twelve hours daily studying, praying over, and researching his sermon. Unlike sermons on the frontier in the mid-nineteenth century, colonial sermons were filled with the fruits of years of study. They were geared not only to the emotions and will, but also to the intellect.

As Daniel Boorstin has pointed out, the sermon was one of the chief literary forms in colonial America.[30] Realizing this, listeners followed sermons closely, took mental notes, and usually discussed the sermon with the family on Sunday afternoon. Anne Hutchinson's discussions, which later resulted in the Antinomian Controversy, were merely typical of thousands of discussions which took place in the homes of colonial America. Most discussions, however, were not as controversial as those which took place in the Hutchinson home.

Thus, without ever attending a college or seminary, a churchgoer in colonial America could gain an intimate knowledge of Bible doctrine, church history, and classical literature. Questions raised by the sermon could be answered by the pastor or by the books in the church libraries that were springing up all over America. Often a sermon was later published and listeners could review what they had heard on Sunday morning.

The first Sunday Schools also developed in this period. Unlike their modern-day counterparts, colonial Sunday Schools not only taught Bible but also the rudiments of reading and writing. These Sunday Schools often catered to the poorest members of society.

Modern historians have discounted the importance of

the colonial church as an educational institution, citing the low percentage of colonial Americans on surviving church membership rolls. What these historians fail to realize, however, is that unlike most churches today, colonial churches took membership seriously. Requirements for becoming a church member were much higher in those days, and many people attended church without officially joining. Other sources indicate that church attendance was high in the colonial period. Thus, many of our forefathers partook not only of the spiritual blessing of their local churches, but the educational blessings as well.

Philosophical Societies

Another educational institution that developed in colonial America was the philosophical society. One of the most famous of these was Franklin's Junto, where men would gather to read and discuss papers they had written on all sorts of topics and issues.[31] Another society was called The Literary Republic. This society opened in the bookbindery of George Rineholt in 1764 in Philadelphia. Here, artisans, tradesmen, and common laborers met to discuss logic, jurisprudence, religion, science, and moral philosophy (economics).[32]

Itinerant lecturers, not unlike the Greek philosophers of the Hellenistic period, rented halls and advertised their lectures in local papers. One such lecturer, Joseph Cunningham, offered a series of lectures on the "History and Laws of England" for a little over a pound.[33]

By 1776, when America finally declared its independence, a tradition had been established and voluntarism in education was the rule. Our founding fathers, who had been educated in this tradition, did not think in terms of government-controlled education. Accordingly, when the delegates gathered in Philadelphia to write a Constitution for the new nation, education was considered to be outside the jurisdiction of the civil government, particularly the national government. Madison, in his notes on the Convention, recorded that there was some talk of giving the federal legislature the power to establish a national university at the future capital. But the proposal was easily defeated, for as Boorstin has pointed out, "the Founding Fathers supported the local institutions which had sprung up all over the country."[34] A principle had been established in America that was not to be deviated from until the mid-nineteenth century. Even as late as 1860, there were only 300 public schools as compared to 6,000 private academies.[35]

A Highly Literate Populace

The results of colonial America's free-market system of education were impressive indeed. Almost no tax money was spent on education, yet education was available to almost anyone who wanted it, including the poor. No government subsidies were given, and inefficient institutions either improved or went out of business. Competition guaranteed that scarce educational resources would be allocated properly. The educational institutions that prospered produced a generation of articulate Americans who could grapple with the complex problems of self-government. *The Federalist Papers,* which are seldom read or understood today, even in our universities, were written for and read by the common man. Literacy rates were as high or higher than they are today.[36] A study conducted in 1800 by DuPont de Nemours revealed that only four in a thousand Americans were unable to read and write legibly.[37] Various accounts from colonial America support these statistics. In 1772, Jacob Duche, the Chaplain of Congress, later turned Tory, wrote:

> The poorest labourer upon the shore of Delaware thinks himself entitled to deliver his sentiments in matters of religion or politics with as much freedom as the gentleman or scholar. . . . Such is the prevailing taste for books of every kind, that almost every man is a reader; and by pronouncing sentence, right or wrong, upon the various publications that come in his way, puts himself upon a level, in point of knowledge, with their several authors.[38]

Franklin, too, testified to the efficiency of the colonial educational system. According to Franklin, the North American libraries alone "have improved the general conversation of Americans, made the common tradesmen and farmers as intelligent as most gentlemen from other countries, and perhaps have contributed in some degree to the stand so generally made throughout the colonies in defense of their privileges."[39]

The experience of colonial America clearly supports the idea that the market, if allowed to operate freely, could meet the educational needs of modern-day America. In the nineteenth century, the Duke of Wellington remarked that "the Battle of Waterloo was won on the playing fields of Eton and Cambridge." Today, the battle between freedom and statism is being fought in America's schools. Those of us who believe in Constitutional government would do well to promote the principle of competition, pluralism, and government nonintervention in education. Years ago, Abraham Lincoln said, "The philosophy of the classroom will be the philosophy of the government in the next generation."

---

1. Bertrand Russell, quoted in: Tim Dowley, ed., *The History of Christianity* (Grand Rapids: Wm. B. Eerdman's Pub. Co., 1977), p. 2.

2. Clarence B. Carson has emphasized this point in his *The American Tradition* (Irvington-on-Hudson, N.Y.: The Foundation for Economic Education, Inc., 1964).

3. Lawrence A. Cremin, *American Education: The Colonial Experience, 1607–1789* (New York, Evanston, and London: Harper and Row, 1970), p. 40.

4. *Psalms* 127:3.

5. *Romans* 13.

6. Elizabeth McEachern Wells, *Divine Songs by Isaac Watts* (Fairfax, Va.: Thoburn Press, 1975), p. ii.

7. *Ibid.,* p. 42.

8. Eric Sloane, *The Little Red Schoolhouse* (Garden City, New York: Doubleday and Company, Inc., 1972), p. 3.

9. Ralph Walker, "Old Readers," in *Early American Life,* October 1980, p. 54.

10. Samuel Eliot Morison, *The Intellectual Life of New England* (Ithaca: Cornell University Press, 1965), pp. 71, 72.

11. Carson, p. 152.

12. Louis B. Wright, *The Cultural Life of the American Colonies* (New York: Harper and Row Pub., Inc., 1957), p. 108.

13. *Ibid.*

14. Wright, p. 109.

15. Carl and Jessica Bridenbaugh, *Rebels and Gentlemen* (New York: Oxford University Press, 1982), p. 36.

16. *Ibid.,* p. 39.

17. Frederick Rudolph, *The American College and University* (New York: Random House, A Vintage Book, 1962), pp. 15–16.

18. Morison, p. 39.

19. Morison, p. 37.

20. Morison, p. 39.

21. Archibald Alexander, *The Log College* (London: Banner of Truth Trust, 1968; first published, 1851), pp. 14–22.

22. William H. S. Demarest, *A History of Rutgers College,* 1766–1924 (Princeton: Princeton University Press, 1924), p. 45.

23. Rudolph, p. 15.

24. John Witherspoon, "Address to the Inhabitants of Jamaica and Other West-India Islands, in Behalf of the College of New Jersey," *Essays upon Important Subjects,* Vol. III (Edinburgh, 1805), pp. 312–318, 328–330.

25. Max Farrand, ed., *The Autobiography of Benjamin Franklin* (Berkeley, Cal., 1949), p. 86.

26. Bridenbaugh, p. 87.

27. Bridenbaugh, p. 99.

28. Bridenbaugh, p. 91.

29. Wright, pp. 126–133.

30. Daniel Boorstin, *The Americans: The Colonial Experience* (New York: Random House, Vintage Books, 1958), pp. 10–14.

31. This later became, of course, the American Philosophical Society.

32. Bridenbaugh, pp. 64–65.

33. Bridenbaugh, p. 65.

34. Boorstin, p. 183.

35. Richard C. Wade, *et al.,* A *History of the United States with Selected Readings,* Vol. I (Boston: Houghton Mifflin Co., 1966, 1971), p. 398.

36. Rousas John Rushdoony, *The Messianic Character of American Education* (Nutley, N.J.: The Craig Press, 1963, 1979), p. 330.

37. *Ibid.*

38. Bridenbaugh, p. 99.

39. Farrand, p. 86.

Reasserting the Spirit of '76

Wesley H. Hillendahl

A fresh spirit of change is in the air. It has swept into the Office of President a man who, as the Governor of California, has shown his dedication to the principles of limited government. It has carried into ascendancy in the halls of Congress men who by their records have demonstrated their commitment to support constitutional principles which were designed to protect individual liberty.

Let us seek the roots of that spirit. Perhaps we may find the key to curing what the late Dean Clarence Manion termed "Cancer in the Constitution."[1]

An examination of the Declaration of Independence will produce several important clues: "(Men) are endowed by their Creator with certain unalienable rights . . . among these are life, liberty and the pursuit of happiness." ". . . to secure these rights governments are instituted . . . deriving their just powers from the consent of the governed." Government is to be founded on principles and its powers organized in such form "most likely to effect safety and happiness."

Men capable of expressing thoughts such as these had of necessity developed an inbred sense of self-reliance. They were God-fearing, Bible-reading people who were accustomed to taking responsibility for their own actions.

The late Mr. Hillendahl was a banker and long-time member of FEE's Board of Trustees. This essay appeared in the March 1981 issue of *The Freeman*.

Whence would they likely receive guidance for these ideas of liberty? We know they invariably looked to the Bible as the source of inspiration and direction. So let us follow their steps.

James, the president of the church at Jerusalem, was eloquent in translating the spirit of the Old Testament law into Christianity. In Chapter 1:25 he wrote: "But whoever looks into the perfect law of liberty and abides in it is not merely a hearer of the word which can be forgotten, but a doer of the work, and this man shall be blessed in his labor."[2] In Chapter 2:11, James admonished those who have broken the commandments: "You have become a transgressor of the law . . . so speak and act as men who are to be judged by the law of liberty."[3] This clearly denotes that individuals are to be held responsible for their choices and actions. Irresponsible actions are to be judged accordingly.

Paul wrote from Corinth encouraging the Galatians to maintain Christian liberty. Chapter 5:1, "Stand firm therefore in the liberty with which Christ has made us free, and be not harnessed again under the yoke of servitude." In *Romans* 8:21 we find that servitude is the bondage of corruption. Then in *Galatians* Chapter 5:13 and 14, "For my brethren you have been called to liberty, only do not use your liberty for an occasion to the things of the flesh, but by love serve one another. For the whole law is fulfilled in one saying that is: You shall love your neighbor as yourself." Underlying liberty is freedom of choice. We are admonished to make only responsible choices. Our actions should focus on service rather than on the accumulation of wealth as an end in itself. To live within the laws of the Commandments also includes the prohibition of making laws which institutionalize greed, envy, lust, or coveting of property. So herein is the spirit of the law.

The Purpose of Law

As to the purpose of law, we may turn to the great English judge, Sir William Blackstone, who said "The principal aim of society is to protect individuals in the enjoyment of those absolute rights which were vested in them by the immutable laws of nature. . . . The first and primary end of human laws is to maintain and regulate those 'absolute' rights of individuals."[4] The Frenchman, Frederic Bastiat, in his pamphlet on *The Law* wrote: "We hold from God the gift which includes all others. This gift is life—physical, intellectual and moral life. . . . Life, faculties, production—in other words, individuality, liberty, property—this is man. And in spite of the cunning of artful political leaders, these three gifts from God precede all human legislation, and are superior to it.

"Life, liberty and property do not exist because men have made laws. On the contrary, it was the fact that life, liberty, and property existed beforehand that caused men to make laws in the first place. . . . The law is the organization of the natural right of lawful defense. It is the substitution of a common force for individual forces. And this common force is to do only what the individual forces have a natural and lawful right to do; to protect persons, liberties, and properties; and to maintain the right of each, and to cause justice to reign over us all."[5]

Constitutional Law—Power to the People

In the United States Constitution we find a codification of the Biblical laws. It provided for the protection of life, liberty, property, and the pursuit of happiness. It provided for the freedom of choice of individuals with implied self-responsibility for their actions, and the protection of individuals against those who would abridge or infringe those rights. A society wherein individuals are free to choose requires a government supported willingly by the consent of the governed. Individuals who choose to be free must be willing to support laws which protect the rights of all others who choose to be free. This constitutes a free and open society wherein each can choose to serve God and mankind in the ways of his own choice, free from the will of others.

At the same time, the men who drafted the Constitution accepted the fact that individuals are corruptible. They are subject to temptation; they can be envious, and greedy; they may steal, or covet property. As someone has said, each man has his price, and it is indeed a rare individual who is totally incorruptible, given the opportunity to gain power. So their principal concern was how to develop a legal framework that would prevent corruptible individuals or groups from acquiring power to infringe on the rights of other individuals. The key word is power. The division of power, fragmentation of power, and the checks and balances of power extend through the entire fabric of the Constitution. A horizontal division of power was provided in the form of legislative, executive, and judicial separation. A vertical division of power appears in the form of the federal, state, and local governments. The goal was to limit opportunities to concentrate powers taken from the people.

Limiting the Government

The Bill of Rights includes a set of specific "thou shalt nots" which were designed to constrain the federal government from infringing on specific individual rights. In substance, the Constitution is a document which was designed to hold in chains the powers and authority of the federal government along with those who would use government to further their own ends.

For such a system to survive requires a continual effort toward maintaining the distribution and balance of power at all times. During a speech in Ireland on July 10, 1790, John Curran warned, "The condition upon which God hath given liberty to man is eternal vigilance."

The guarantees of "freedom to"—to choose, to try and to fail—can only be made under a government which is restricted from interfering with individual choices. In contrast, the constitution of the Soviet Union and the United Nations charter are vehicles of unlimited power. Their goals of "freedom from"—from war, disease, want, unemployment and the like—can only be enforced by an unlimited central authority and bureaucracy.

Being aware that neither the Constitution nor statutory law can ever change the nature of man, nor force him to be what he cannot or will not be, we may ask how successful were the framers of the Constitution. We live in an imperfect world. It is an imperfect Constitution, and we are imperfect individuals. Yet for nearly two centuries with freedom of opportunity the people of the United States increased their standard of living more rapidly than did those of any other nation in the world. Given the choice, the acid test is whether one would rather live in the United States or somewhere else in the world. The vast influx of legal and illegal aliens speaks for itself.

The Problems of Government—Man Was Made Vain

Yet we are troubled today; inflation, unemployment, economic instability, housing shortages, high taxes, high interest rates, are but a few of our problems. How do the conditions underlying the problems of today compare with the concerns and grievances of the Founding Fathers? Let's look again at the Declaration of Independence. The signers were concerned about "relinquishing the rights of representation in the legislature." Today we are concerned about centralized government and administrative law.

In 1776 they were concerned about being "exposed to dangers of invasion from without and convulsions from within." Increasing numbers are concerned about our defense posture today and the problems of internal unrest.

They complained that "judges were dependent on the will (of the King) for tenure of their offices." Today's judges are political appointees who, to a significant extent, legislate according to their ideologies rather than seek precedent for decisions.

The Founders were concerned about "a multitude of new offices," and we are concerned about burgeoning bureaucracy.

They were concerned about "imposing taxes without our consent." Who isn't concerned today about high taxes, consent or otherwise?

They were concerned about "deprived . . . benefits of trial by jury." Today administrative law has gone a long way to the same end, and has altered fundamentally the forms of government.

They complained about exciting "domestic insurrections among us." Today who is not concerned about crime and personal safety? The very survival of our system is threatened by the encroachment of a totalitarian ideology.

Are we not faced again today with the problems of 200 years ago? We are in fact encountering an ageless collision with a destructive ideology. Paul wrote in his letter to the

Romans 8:20,21, "For man was made subject to vanity . . ." (Definitions of vanity include, "inflated pride of one's self," or "emptiness, worthlessness." We may ponder the significance of this polarity of meaning.) "For man was made subject to vanity, not willingly, but by reason of him who gave him free will in the hope that he would choose rightly. Because man himself shall be delivered from the bondage of corruption into the glorious liberty of the Children of God."

Or perhaps more clearly, man (of) himself shall be delivered . . . Man only by his own choice of responsible thoughts and actions can achieve the soul growth that is required to achieve grace, and entrance into the Kingdom of God.

But in fact, has he chosen "rightly"? In spite of the commandment "Thou shalt not covet thy neighbor's property," we have permitted laws to be passed which, taken all together, confiscate almost half of our neighbor's property via taxes in the vain concept of doing good. These vain thoughts manifest in a number of syndromes:

• The "welfare" syndrome which enforces the privilege of the few at the expense of the rights of the individuals who constitute the body politic.

• The "free lunch" syndrome which looks on dollars sent from Washington as free. If we don't get them, someone else will.

• The "meddling in the affairs of others" syndrome in which individuals feel compelled to attempt to solve the problems of others rather than minding their own business and concentrating on solving their own problems.

• Similarly, the "let George do it" syndrome considers today's problems to be too complex to be solved equitably at the state or local level—they must be sent to Washington.

• The "exploitation" syndrome in which the producers in society are held to have victimized those less stationed. Therefore the producers must be chained with regulations and their ill-gotten profits must be taxed away.

• The "victims of society" syndrome maintains that criminals are the innocent victims of society—they cannot be held responsible for their crimes or misdeeds; therefore they must be pampered and "rehabilitated" rather than punished, while many live in fear that they may be the next victims.

• Finally, the "homogenized milk" syndrome which is destroying all natural affinity groups and is forcing all people to live and work together on the basis of a "social adjustment" formula of equality based on race, color, creed, or whether one fancies dogs, cats, horses, or white rats.

These syndromes are all manifestations of an ideology that is anathema to liberty. They reflect the attitude of those who lack faith in the ability of each individual to solve his or her own problems; hence, a forced redistribution of society is necessary to overcome maladjustments.

The thermometer of a redistributive society is what? Inflation. Inflation is a measure of the maldistribution of wealth via government—no more, no less. The underlying motivating forces and the mechanics of inflation are complex and widely misunderstood. Yet no one in good conscience can deny the necessity to help those who are in a condition of misfortune. However, today much redistributed wealth is going to those who have established vested positions of privilege. The consequence is that regardless of how legitimate a given cause may be, the total burden of aggregate causes on the nation has exceeded the carrying capacity of its productive resources to the point where inflation is an unavoidable condition. The problem goes far deeper than any transient federal administration, its roots extend back through decades. Inflation is the manifestation of vain thoughts and ideas applied cumulatively since the Civil War. It represents the misapplication of free will and an accumulation of a vast number of wrong choices.

The Redistribution of Power

What have been the mechanics of change wherein these false doctrines have gained ascendancy?

Dr. Cornelius Cotter, Professor of Political Science at the University of Wisconsin, appeared before a special Senate committee in April, 1973.[6] He remarked: "You know, Senator Mathias, it has been said—and, I think wisely so—that if the United States ever developed into a totalitarian state we would not know it. We would not know that it had happened. It would be all so gradual, the ritualism would all be retained as a facade to disguise what had happened. Most people in the United States, in official position, would continue to do the sorts of things that they are doing now. The changes would have all been so subtle although so fundamental that people generally would be unaware."

Senator Church responded, "That is the way it happened in Rome, is it not?"

Dr. Cotter: "Indeed."

Senator Mathias: "No Roman was more deferential than Augustus."

Dr. Cotter: "Exactly."

Senator Church: "And kept the Senate happy, although the Senate had lost its power."

So this age-old collision of ideas is producing very subtle changes in the power structure of the United States. The mechanism of change involves power, its balance and the

concentration. Four simultaneous flows have been under-
way for a century: (1) Power from the Congress to the Executive Branch, (2) power from the Congress to the Supreme
Court, (3) power from the states to the federal government,
and (4) power from individuals to the government.

Judicial Abuses

Let's examine some of these flows of power. First, the
Supreme Court. The Bill of Rights expressly forbids the federal government to interfere with the fundamental personal
liberties of individuals in this society. That's clear enough.
As an outfall of the Civil War, the 14th Amendment was
adopted in 1868. This amendment forbids the states to
interfere with the rights of the people. However, it had a
devious intent, namely to give Congress control over the
people of the South. But in 1873 the Supreme Court
thwarted that intent in the "Slaughterhouse Cases." For
half a century an ideal situation prevailed in which both the
federal government and the states were constrained by the
Constitution and its amendments from interfering with the
liberties of the people.

However, in more recent years a subtle but profound
change has been effected by the Supreme Court. Dean
Clarence Manion wrote, ". . . . For the 32 years of service
together on the Supreme Court, Justices Black and Douglas
have been repetitiously citing each other as authority for a
gross and gratuitous misconstruction of the First and 14th
Amendments."[7]

"The accumulation of these malignant constitutional
misconstructions of the first eight amendments with the
14th has placed a cancer near the heart of our constitu-

tional system which is proliferated with each successive term of the United States Supreme Court."[8] Essentially, today the Court has legislated its jurisdiction over the rights of people by effectively merging the Bill of Rights into the 14th Amendment and reversing its position in 1873.

The specific consequences of the Black and Douglas decision were highlighted in an editorial which appeared in the *San Diego Union:* "The United States Supreme Court has returned three more decisions drastically altering the pattern of American life.

"For more than 15 years now the Court has been steadily rewriting the laws and reinterpreting the Constitution to suit the ideological bias or judicial whims of its members . . .

"In recent days the Supreme Court has ridden over states' rights abolishing residency requirement for relief, sidestepped a ruling in a case of burning the American Flag, and placed further restrictions on law enforcement by freeing a convicted rapist because the police took his fingerprints in some legal hocus-pocus . . .

". . . Court majorities in those 15 years have returned more than 30 decisions . . . have brought about basic and often demoralizing changes in the fields of politics, criminal procedure, religion, race relations, subversion and communism, antitrust laws and obscenity.

"The Court has told the states how they are to portion their legislatures, granted avowed Communists the run of defense plants; made a criminal's confession almost impossible to use; approved even secondary school demonstrations against the South Vietnam war; banned prayers or reading of the Bible in public classrooms; ruled that passports cannot be withheld from Communists just because they are Communists; and held that deserters from the armed forces, even in wartime, cannot be stripped of citizenship. . . .

"In the notorious Keylishian case, a majority opinion held that a college professor may not be dismissed for teaching and advocating, in college, or anywhere, the overthrow of our government by force and violence . . .[9] The Court, once the ultimate in both prudence and jurisprudence, is now the darling of the liberal radicals; it has done for them what the Congress has refused to do."[10]

This is a most concise summary of the consequences of the Court's abrogation of states' rights and the jurisdiction of Congress.

Courts Take Charge as Congress Forfeits Control

At this point, the more perceptive will grasp the real issue which underlies the polarization of the Nation concerning the Equal Rights Amendment. Under the facade of women's rights, the real objective is to deliver the jurisdiction for defining the rights of all individuals into the hand of a Congress which has already defaulted its jurisdiction to the legislative whims of the Supreme Court. At the heart of the opposition to ERA are those who recognize its passage would give validity to the Supreme Court's abridgement of the Bill of Rights, and encourage further intrusions into the private affairs of individuals.

As a curtain over these actions, a myth has been erected which holds that Supreme Court decisions are the "Law of the Land." It presumes that once the Court takes a position on a case, every similar case would be adjudged that way. In actuality, each ruling is the "law of the case." It is possible for a court, made up of the same or different justices, to arrive at a different interpretation if it were to rule on a similar case.

Under a second myth, the prevailing belief is that Congress has no control over the Supreme Court, hence, Congress has no way to redress the sorties of the Court into the legislative arena. Such an alleged lack of control is far from fact. Congress enacted the first Federal Judiciary Act in 1789 and this act has been employed to apply its unquestioned constitutional power over the jurisdiction of all federal courts.

The Congress by a wide margin recently voted to deny the Supreme Court the right to spend appropriated funds to conduct hearings into school busing cases, in effect, denying the court jurisdiction.

Dean Clarence Manion of Notre Dame held that a major step will be taken toward rectifying the consequences of the Court's unconstitutional decisions when the Congress restricts, abolishes or controls selected types of appellate jurisdiction of both the Supreme Court and all other federal courts.[11] A federal court system comprised mainly of judges and justices who are committed to upholding the original tenets underlying the Constitution, can do a great deal to curb the judicial misuses and excesses which have prevailed in recent years.

Legislative Abuses

For many decades the Supreme Court routinely struck down as unconstitutional various acts passed by Congress which infringed on the Bill of Rights. However, over the last two decades the Congress, taking its cue from the Black-Douglas Supreme Court decisions, has enacted a number of bills which have intruded ever-increasingly into those rights which were originally held to be out of bounds. These intrusions are being felt by the public in their opportunities for employment, work environment, on the highway, in the air, while shopping and banking, in schools, among family relations and in the home. While obviously accomplishing some benefits, the bulk of this legislation has been undertaken in response to the highly vocal, sometimes rowdy, pressure of special-interest groups. In the main, these intrusions have caused vast numbers of people to become outraged, resentful, and rebellious.

In its attempts to legislate social justice and equality, the Congress has cut to the core of the mores of the incredibly complex but generally balanced and tolerant American society.

The wisdom of those who insisted on including the Bill of Rights in the Constitution is gradually seeping into the subconscience of all but the most hardheaded advocates of reform by coercion. It would be a wise Congress indeed that undertook to reverse or modify these unconstitutional intrusions which prior congresses have made over the years.

Executive Abuses

The scope of the powers of the executive branch has been expanded enormously, particularly in recent years. Authority of the office of the President has increased while departments, commissions, boards, and agencies have proliferated.

Professor Cotter and Professor J. M. Smith determined that the powers entrusted by Congress to the Executive Branch can be grouped in four categories: (1) powers over persons, (2) powers to acquire property, (3) powers to regulate property, and (4) control of communications.[12]

Executive Orders: The President normally employs Executive Orders to implement the efficient conduct of the daily routines of the office.[13] However, several presidents have employed Executive Orders to conduct international relations and to effect legislation.

For example, President Roosevelt used an Executive Order in 1933 to establish diplomatic relationships with the Communist regime in Russia at a time when it was unlikely that such action by Congress would have been supported by a consensus of the people.

Under the pressure of time, the President has employed emergency orders properly in the declaration of national emergencies. However, one would believe that matters as basic as the legal framework for the conduct of government under such national emergencies would be given extensive examination by the Congress in the process of passing suitable laws. Such is not the case.

President John F. Kennedy issued a series of Executive Orders in 1962 which established a comprehensive legal framework to deal with any national emergency as defined by the President or the Congress.[14] On its face, this would appear to have constituted an unwarranted intrusion into the legislative process.

On October 11, 1966, President Lyndon Johnson issued Executive Order 11310 which continued the process by transferring the authority granted under the emergency orders from the Office of Emergency Planning to the Department of Justice.

President Richard Nixon also gave attention to updating the emergency orders while in office.

Early in the 1970s Congress became sufficiently concerned about the existence of national emergencies that the Senate established a Special Committee on the Termination of the National Emergency.[15] This led in 1976 to the passage of the National Emergencies Act.[16] This act terminated all existing declared emergencies and established procedures and limits for the declaration of future national emergencies.

The matter took on new impetus when, on July 20, 1979, President Jimmy Carter issued two new Executive Orders:

(1) E.O. 12148 Federal Emergency Management, which authorized a thorough overhaul of both civil and war emergency procedures and placed them under a newly created Federal Emergency Management Council.

(2) E.O. 12149 Federal Regional Councils, which established councils for ten standard federal regions, their principal function being to implement federal programs.

Taken separately or together these Executive Orders provide wide-ranging ramifications when analyzed from the point of view of the powers delegated to these Councils. While these structures may be thought of as logical provisions for the implementation of federal policy, increasing numbers of states are taking the position that Regional Councils constitute a major intrusion into their autonomy.[17]

Such widespread reaction would lead one to conclude that a deep rift has developed in the power structure as a consequence of the thrust underlying these Executive Orders. As a consequence of these and other Executive Orders, a broad review by Congress of their use and abuses should lead to establishing guidelines which define appropriate uses of Executive Orders by the Executive Branch.

Administrative Law: The myriad of statutes, regulations, and codes by which the various departments and bureaus of government administer their operations under the

Executive Branch constitute administrative law. In large part they are established to implement details of the broad language of the acts of Congress. These regulations are essential to the smooth and orderly functioning of government.

Nevertheless, the structure of departments which combines executive, legislative, and enforcement or judicial functions, provides a concentration of power and authority which lends itself to potential bureaucratic abuses. Among many possible examples, congressional hearings have revealed that the detailed statutes developed in administering the Occupational Safety and Health Act (OSHA) went far beyond the intent of the act, and provided the basis for executive abuses and deliberate harassment, in particular of small business. Many are aware of instances in which the Antitrust Division of the Justice Department, using the charge of conspiracy and restraint of trade, has imposed fines and/or jail sentences though the accused firms and their officers were innocent. These firms chose to make payment under a plea of *nolo contendere* because the legal fees required to establish their innocence would exceed the fine.

Administered properly, government agencies should facilitate trade and commerce, and protect the various interests of the people. At best, administrative law can only regulate, prohibit, or constrain individuals or groups from imposing on the rights of others. However, in increasing numbers of cases the bureaucracy has gone far beyond its legitimate functions. One may find dozens of magazine and newspaper articles reciting wasteful or counter-productive bureaucratic activities, and arrogant abuses of power. Today the friction and costs to society of the bureaucracy have reached destructive proportions. These excesses must be brought again under control. The implementation of reforms is too broad a subject to address here. A comprehensive report by the Heritage Foundation[18] has recommended a broad platform of reforms to President-Elect Reagan "to roll back big government." Included are specific recommendations concerning Executive Orders and administrative law. Implementation of these recommendations should go a long way in restoring a proper balance of power.

Revitalizing the American Dream

The foregoing are but a few examples of the restructuring of power which has been achieved during the last century. They have been selected to illustrate the vast departure from the spirit in which the Constitution was written some 200 years ago. As a consequence, people in all walks of life—both the providers and the recipients of government aid—are hurting as they have never hurt before. The thermometer—inflation—shows that the waters of our economic and political environment are approaching the boiling point. Not one amongst us is immune to the heat.

In the face of these adversities, a new spirit is emerging in the land. The new religious revival extending from neighborhoods to nationwide television is a new expression of the old Spirit of '76. People are going back to basics. They are thinking, questioning, and organizing.[19]

The overwhelming choice by the electorate of a new administration dedicated to redressing these abuses of power is a manifestation of the revival of the spirit.

The retirement of many congressmen who have aided and abetted this misdirection of power, together with the election of other congressmen who affirm the original precepts of the Constitution are further manifestations of the spirit.

Yet this is only a beginning. We must not expect miracles from any administration, nor can any of us escape the painful process of readjustment. We are presently in a position to achieve a victory in this battle. But the foes in the ageless war for the minds of men are not to be easily vanquished. It will require years of unrelenting effort to overcome the damages which have been incurred by the Republic.

We know in our hearts that cold, impersonal welfare will never succeed loving charity. Government can never provide security to replace self-reliance. No government can accomplish those things we must do for ourselves if our souls and spirits are to expand. If we are to restore the American dream we must never again become complacent and allow ourselves to be overridden by those who are in a vain quest for false goals.

Let us again restore the balance between spiritual and material values. The institutions of church and state are inseparable, they are as inseparable as two ends of a rope, each is a manifestation of the spirit and substance of society.[20] We may recall that the spirit of liberty was heralded from every pulpit during our Revolutionary War. I maintain that Spirit of '76 has never really disappeared, we have simply allowed it to become encrusted with false doctrine.

Paul offered words of encouragement: "Stand firm therefore in liberty with which Christ has made us free. Be not harnessed again under the yoke of servitude. . . . the bondage of corruption." James urged us: "So speak and so act as men and women who are to be judged by the law of liberty." Let freedom-loving individuals prevail by reasserting the Spirit of '76.

1. Clarence E. Manion, *Cancer in the Constitution* (Shepherdsville, Ky.: Victor Publishing Company, 1972).

2. *Holy Bible,* trans. George M. Lamsa (Philadelphia: A. J. Holman, 1957). This version is translated into English from the Aramaic, the language of Jesus and is recognized for accuracy and clarity of expression.

3. The law of liberty within the context of Bible usage expresses freedom of choice with consequences. All thoughts and actions cause reactions for which we are to be held accountable. The law of liberty is the Christian counterpart of the Sanskrit term, *karma.*

4. James Mussatti, *The Constitution of the United States, Our Charter of Liberties* (Princeton: D. Van Nostrand Co., Inc., 1960), p. 9.

5. Frederic Bastiat, *The Law,* trans. Dean Russell (Irvington-on-Hudson, N.Y.: Foundation for Economic Education, 1950), pp. 5, 6, 7. *(The Law* was first published as a pamphlet in June 1850.)

6. U.S. Congress, Senate, Special Committee on the Termination of the National Emergency, *National Emergency, Part 1 Constitutional Questions Concerning Emergency Powers,* Hearings before the Special Committee of the Senate, 93rd Cong., 1st sess., April 11, 12, 1973, p. 29.

7. Manion, p. 33.

8. *Ibid.,* p. 35.

9. As a consequence of this Supreme Court decision, by 1975 an estimated 2,000 campus "radical economists" who "respect the point of view of Mao" and who believe in "a socialism of affluence" were members of the Union of Radical Political Economists. (*Los Angeles Times,* December 21, 1975).

10. *San Diego Union,* April 28, 1969.

11. Manion, p. 27.

12. C. P. Cotter and J. M. Smith, *Powers of the President During Crises* (Washington, D. C.: Public Affairs Press, 1960).

13. Executive Orders are issued by the President, reviewed by the Office of Legal Counsel and published in the Federal Register. They become law unless rescinded by Congress within a specified period of time.

14. Executive Orders including numbers 10995, 10997,10998, 10999 and 11000, 11001, 11002, 11003, 11004, 11005 and 11051 define procedures during war, attacks or other emergencies for executive control of communications, energy, food and farming, all modes of trans-

portation, civilian work brigades, health, education and welfare functions, housing, public storage and so on.

15. U.S. Congress, Senate, *National Emergency.*

16. *National Emergencies Act,* U.S. Code, vol. 50, sec. 1601- 51 (1976).

17. Extensive hearings on regional governance have been conducted by legislative committees in a score of states. The proceedings of these hearings appear in bulletins published by the Committee to Restore the Constitution, Inc., P.O. Box 986, Fort Collins, Colorado 80522.

18. Charles Heatherly, ed., *Mandate for Leadership* (Washington, D.C.: Heritage Foundation, 1980).

19. For an example of grass roots organization see "The Pro-Family Movement: A Special Report" in *Conservative Digest* 6 (May/June 1980).

20. Into the artfully contrived rift between church and state has been driven the wedge of Humanism. According to the book *The Assault on the Family,* "As a religion, Humanism demands the end of all religions that are God-oriented, and the abolition of the profit-motivated society, so that a world utopian state may be established which will dictate the distribution of the means of life for everyone." See "Our Last Opportunity" in *Don Bell Reports,* November 13, 1980.

Faith of Our Fathers

Clarence B. Carson

History, it has been said, is a seamless cloth. The thought is apt. You cannot clip a thread within it and attempt to extricate it without unraveling the whole. There have been efforts to tell the history of the United States with the role of religion either excised from it or altered within it. One common alteration occurs in those textbooks which claim that the Pilgrims and Puritans came to America for freedom of religion.

They did not. They came in order to be able to practice their religion. The difference is by no means merely a quibble. Freedom of religion, as it is now understood, is a secular concept. It is probably even more highly valued by those who have no religious faith than by active believers. To be able to practice one's faith is only of value to him who has a faith to practice. It is a sacred, not a secular, value. The Puritans at the time of settlement could no more conceive of the desirability of freedom of religion than Treasury officials today can conceive of the desirability of freedom of counterfeiting.

My point is that books on American history often either secularize religious values, treat them as alien, or leave them out of account. Yet, without these religious foundations there could have been no United States as it was and

This essay was published in the December 1976 issue of *The Freeman*.

is. There is no knowing American history without grasping its underpinnings in Judeo-Christian faith. America as it was and is cannot even be successfully imagined without the thread of faith woven into the cloth of history.

Biblically Based and Christian Settlement of America

American history cannot be imagined without the powerful evocative phrases of the King James Version of the Bible, or without the story of our origins in *Genesis:*

> In the beginning God created the heavens and the earth. The earth was without form, and void; and darkness was on the face of the deep. And the Spirit of God moved upon the face of the waters.
>
> *Genesis* 1:1–2.

Or, without the account of man's place in the creation:

> And God said, Let us make man in our image, after our likeness: and let them have dominion over the fish of the sea, and over the fowl of the air, and over the cattle, and over all the earth, and over every creeping thing that creepeth upon the earth.
>
> So God created man in his *own* image, in the image of God created he him; male and female created he them.
>
> *Genesis* 1:26–27.

The fundamental character of all proper law is revealed in the Ten Commandments. Though two of them do command appropriate affirmative action, the remainder are prohibitive in nature. They are brief, concise, and are readily understood. A United States without the Ten Commandments in its background would have been a United States without transcendent law upon which to build:

> 1. Thou shalt have no other gods before me.
> 2. Thou shalt not make unto thee any graven image.
> 3. Thou shalt not take the name of the Lord thy God in vain.
> 4. Remember the sabbath day, to keep it holy.
> 5. Honour thy father and thy mother.
> 6. Thou shalt not kill.
> 7. Thou shalt not commit adultery.
> 8. Thou shalt not steal.
> 9. Thou shalt not bear false witness against thy neighbor.
> 10. Thou shalt not covet.
>> Excerpted and numbered from *Exodus* 20: 3–17.

Most of those who settled in the New World were Christian, nominally or devoutly as the case might be. Their attitude toward life had been winnowed through and conditioned by the Christian perspective. This meant many things, but one of its meanings is never to be ignored by the historian: That good ultimately triumphs over evil, that life is not necessarily tragic but that it is potentially triumphant when it is in accord with God's will. America without the assurance of this Revelation could not have been as it has been:

> In the beginning was the Word, and the Word was with God, and the Word was God. He was in the beginning with God; all things were made through him, and without him was not anything made that

was made. In him was life, and the life was the light of men. The light shines in the darkness, and the darkness has not overcome it.

John 1:1–5 (RSV)

This assurance comes through in the beautiful promises of the Beatitudes:

Blessed are the poor in spirit, for theirs is the kingdom of heaven.

Blessed are those who mourn, for they shall be comforted.

Blessed are the meek, for they shall inherit the earth.

Blessed are those who hunger and thirst for righteousness, for they shall be satisfied.

Blessed are the merciful, for they shall obtain mercy.

Blessed are the pure in heart, for they shall see God.

Blessed are the peacemakers, for they shall be called the sons of God.

Blessed are those who are persecuted for righteousness' sake, for theirs is the kingdom of heaven.

Blessed are you when men revile you and persecute you and utter all kinds of evil against you falsely on my account.

Rejoice and be glad, for your reward is great in heaven, for so men persecuted the prophets who were before you.

Matthew 5: 3–11 (RSV)

Roman Catholicism

The Christian religion was for a thousand years of its history represented primarily by the Roman Catholic Church. Within that fold many doctrines were shaped and many great preachers and teachers held forth. While the Catholic Church was suspect to some of the Founders of the United States, it is nonetheless the case that the Faith of Our Fathers found many of its underpinnings in that faith. Here is a statement from the monastic ideal of the Middle Ages:

> This treasure, then, namely Christ, our God and Lord, who was made for us as both redeemer and reward, He Himself both the promiser and the prize, who is both the life of man and the eternity of the angels—this, I say, store away with diligent care in the recesses of your heart. On Him cast the anxiety of any care whatsoever. In Him delight through the discourse of zealous prayer. In Him refresh yourself by the nightly feasts of holy meditation. Let Him be your food, and your clothing no less. If it should happen that you lack anything of external convenience, do not be uncertain, do not despair of His true promise in which He said "Seek ye first the kingdom of God, and all things shall be added unto you. . . ."
>
> *Peter Damiani* (Eleventh Century)

Protestant Reformation

Even more, however, is the United States inconceivable without the Protestant Reformation. Most of the colonies were settled by one or more offshoots of this movement.

The emphasis upon reason, Scripture, and decision by the individual—hallmarks of the Reformation—was never more dramatically stated than by Martin Luther at the Diet of Worms in his refusal to recant:

> Since your Majesty and your lordships ask for a simple reply, I shall give you one without horns and without teeth; unless I am convinced by the evidence of Scriptures or by plain reason . . . I am bound by the Scriptures I have cited and my conscience is captive to the Word of God. I cannot and will not recant anything, for it is neither safe nor right to go against conscience. I can do no other.
>
> *Martin Luther* (Diet of Worms, 1521)

The tendency in Protestant lands, however, was to have one established church. Those who did not want such an establishment, or wanted a different one, were often persecuted in their home lands. Some of these sought refuge in America. The Pilgrims were the first of such English groups to do so. The character of the faith of one of their leaders, William Bradford, comes through in this selection from his writing:

> What could now sustain them but the Spirit of God and His grace? May not and ought not the children of these fathers rightly say: "Our fathers were Englishmen which came over this great ocean, and were ready to perish in this wilderness; but they cried unto the Lord, and He heard their voice and looked on their adversity," etc. "Let them therefore praise the Lord because he is good: and His mercies endure forever." Yea, let them which have been redeemed of

the Lord, shew how He hath delivered them from the hand of the oppressor. When they wandered in the desert wilderness out of the way, and found no city to dwell in, both hungry and thirsty, their soul was overwhelmed in them. Let them confess before the Lord his lovingkindness and His wonderful works before the sons of men.

William Bradford,
Of Plymouth Plantation.

The Great Awakening

At the outset, many of those who settled in the New World were divided from one another by religious differences. The fact that most of them were Protestant served at first more to divide than to unite them. Over the years, doctrinal antipathies moderated. Perhaps the single most important of the moderating influences was the Great Awakening. In the middle of the eighteenth century a great revival spread through the colonies. Though it did provoke some divisions within denominations, its tendency was to shift the emphasis from points of doctrine to the experience of conversion and a spiritual attitude toward life. Denominations continued to proliferate but their differences became more a matter of modes of organization and tastes as to ritual than of dogma and doctrine. The Great Awakening provided a widely shared evangelistic base for Protestant Christianity. The tenor of this evangelism appears in this excerpt from a sermon by Jonathan Edwards:

I invite you now to a better portion. There are better things provided for the sinful miserable children of men. There is a surer comfort and more durable peace: comfort that you may enjoy in a state of safety and on a sure foundation: a peace and rest that you may enjoy with reason and with your eyes wide open; having all your sins forgiven . . . ; being taken into God's family and made his children; and having good evidence that your names were written on the heart of Christ before the world was made. . . .

Jonathan Edwards

The God of Creation

In the great documents of the American Revolution there is often an explicit reliance upon natural law and an implicit underlying dependence on the inherited religious faith. The God of nature and the God revealed in Scripture was the same God. There were, however, differences in the interpretation of Scripture, differences which did not extend to the natural law. Hence, the appeal in the Declaration of Independence was to the God of Creation:

When in the Course of human events, it becomes necessary for one people to dissolve the political bands which have connected them with another, and to assume among the Powers of the earth, the separate and equal station to which the Laws of Nature and of Nature's God entitle them, a decent respect to the opinions of mankind requires that they should declare the causes which impel them to the separation.

We hold these truths to be self-evident, that all men are created equal, that they are endowed by their Creator with certain unalienable Rights, that

among these are Life, Liberty, and the Pursuit of
Happiness. . . .

Declaration of Independence, 1776

The practice of having a written constitution is American in origin. It was grounded in their British heritage and
colonial experience, but it was particularly informed by
their Christian and Protestant religion. The Founders were
people of the Book, the Bible, the recorded word. As Protes-
tants mainly, they attached an unusually high importance
to Scripture and to its careful exposition. It was, to them,
the highest authority. The United States Constitution
became for them, out of this tradition, the highest authority
within the country. It was written, precise, and was to be
carefully interpreted and observed.

A Subtle Parallel

One part of the Constitution has been especially revered
over the years. It is the first ten amendments, commonly
called the Bill of Rights. Some of its antecedents are generally understood to be the Magna Carta and the English Bill
of Rights. But its most profound antecedent is usually
ignored. It is more difficult than it may at first appear to
imagine that the First Ten Amendments have played the
role they have without the prior position of the Ten Commandments in the Judeo-Christian religion. It is not just
that each of them numbers ten, though they do. It is considerably more. They are similar in form. The Ten Commandments usually begin with "Thou shalt not." The first
Ten Amendments are equally prohibitive in their language:"Congress shall make no law . . . , No Soldier shall
. . . , shall not be violated . . . , Excessive bail shall not be

required . . . ," and so forth. More, the Ten Commandments forbid individuals to do acts that would be harmful to anyone. The First Ten Amendments forbid *government* to do acts arbitrarily detrimental to our life, liberty, and property. The Ten Commandments proceed from our Maker to us. The First Ten Amendments proceed from the makers of government to it. Can it be doubted that they draw subtle force from the parallel?

The Faith of Hamilton

The Founding Fathers were not particularly renowned for their piety. But the springs of religious faith often ran deep within them, to break forth only on extraordinary occasions. So it was with Alexander Hamilton. It was his fate to meet his death in a duel with Aaron Burr. Perhaps "fate" is the wrong word; he took a course which exposed him to such a death if Burr so chose. Hamilton believed that dueling was wrong and knew that it was against the law. Yet, when challenged he felt that he must participate. The last note to his wife written on the night before the duel contained these thoughts, among others:

> . . . The scruples of a Christian have determined me to expose my own life to any extent, rather than subject myself to the guilt of taking the life of another. This much increases my hazards, and redoubles my pangs for you. But you had rather I should die innocent than live guilty. Heaven can preserve me, and I humbly hope will; but, in the contrary event, I charge you to remember that you are a Christian. God's will be done! The will of a merciful God must be good. . . .

On the day of the duel both Hamilton and Burr raised their pistols to the ready position on command. Burr then aimed and fired directly at Hamilton. Hamilton fired into the air, as he had said he would do. Hamilton died from the wounds inflicted on him. It is difficult to imagine America without men devoted to principles founded upon their faith.

Washington's Farewell

Nor should we imagine an America without the guidance of Washington's Farewell Address. Nor would that address have been the same without its references to religious underpinnings:

> Of all the dispositions and habits which lead to political prosperity, religion and morality are indispensable supports. In vain would that man claim the tribute of patriotism who should labor to subvert these great pillars of human happiness—these firmest props of the duties of men and citizens. The mere politician, equally with the pious man, ought to respect and cherish them. A volume would not trace all their connections with private and public felicity. Let it simply be asked, Where is the security for property, for reputation, for life, if the sense of religious obligation *desert* the oaths which are instruments of investigation in courts of justice? And let us with caution indulge the supposition that morality can be maintained without religion. Whatever may be conceded to the influence of refined education on minds of peculiar structure, reason and experience

both forbid us to expect that national morality can prevail in exclusion of religious principle.

George Washington, *Farewell Address*

But, then, the United States of America could hardly be conceived without the Faith of Our Fathers.

II. A BIBLICAL VIEW

Jeremiah's Job

Gary North

Sooner or later, those who are interested in the philosophy of liberty run across Albert J. Nock's essay, "Isaiah's Job." Taking as an example two Old Testament prophets, Isaiah and Elijah, Nock makes at least two important points. *First,* until society seems to be disintegrating around our ears, not many people are going to listen to a critic who comes in the name of principled action. The masses want to get all the benefits of principled action, but they also want to continue to follow their unprincipled ways. They want the fruits but not the roots of morality. Therefore, they refuse to listen to prophets. *Second,* Nock pointed out, the prophet Elijah was convinced that he was the last of the faithful, or what Nock calls the Remnant. Not so, God told the prophet; He had kept seven thousand others from the rot of the day.

Elijah had no idea that there were this many faithful people left. He had not seen any of them. He had heard no reports of them. Yet here was God, telling him that they were out there. Thus, Nock concludes, it does no good to count heads. The people whose heads are available for counting are not the ones you ought to be interested in. Whether or not people listen is irrelevant; the important thing is that the prophet makes the message clear and

Dr. North is president of the Institute for Christian Economics in Tyler, Texas. This essay appeared in the March 1978 issue of *The Freeman.*

consistent. He is not to water down the truth for the sake of mass appeal.

Nock's essay helps those of us who are used to the idea that we should measure our success by the number of people we convince. We are "scalphunters," when we ought to be prophets. The prophets were not supposed to give the message out in order to win lots of public support. On the contrary, they were supposed to give the message for the sake of truth. They were to witness to a generation which would not respond to the message. The truth was therefore its own justification. Those who were supposed to hear, namely, the Remnant, would get the message, one way or the other. They were the people who counted. Lesson: the people who count can't be counted. Not by prophets, anyway.

A Sad Message

The main trouble I have with Nock's essay is that he excluded another very important prophet. That prophet was Jeremiah. He was a contemporary of Isaiah, and God gave him virtually the same message. He was told to go to the highest leaders in the land, to the average man in the street, and to everyone in between, and proclaim the message. He was to tell them that they were in violation of basic moral law in everything they did, and that if they did not turn away from their false beliefs and wicked practices, they would see their society totally devastated. In this respect, Jeremiah's task was not fundamentally different from Isaiah's.

Nevertheless, there were some differences. Jeremiah also wrote (or dictated) a book. He was not content to preach an unpleasant message to skeptical and hostile people. He wanted to record the results of their unwillingness to listen. His thoughts are preserved in the saddest book in the Bible, the Book of *Lamentations.* Though he knew in advance that the masses would reject his message, he also knew that there would be great suffering in Israel because of their stiffnecked response. Furthermore, the Remnant would pay the same price in the short run. They, too, would be carried off into captivity. They, too, would lose their possessions and die in a foreign land. They would not be protected from disaster just because they happened to be decent people who were not immersed in the practices of their day. He wrote these words in response to the coming of the predicted judgment: "Mine eye runneth down with rivers of water for the destruction of the daughter of my people" (*Lam.* 3:48). He knew that their punishment was well deserved, yet he was also a part of them. The destruction was so great that not a glimmer of hope appears in the whole book.

What are we to conclude? That everything is hopeless? That no one will listen, ever, to the truth? That every society will eventually be ripe for judgment, and that this collapse will allow no one to escape? Is it useless, historically speaking, to serve in the Remnant? Are we forever to be ground down in the millstones of history?

One key incident in Jeremiah's life gives us the answer. It appears in the 32nd chapter of *Jeremiah,* a much-neglected passage. The Babylonians (Chaldeans) have besieged Jerusalem. There was little doubt in anyone's mind that the city would fall to the invaders. God told Jeremiah that in the midst of this crisis, his cousin would approach him and make him an offer. He would offer Jeremiah the right, as a relative, to buy a particular field which was in the cousin's side of the family. Sure enough, the cousin arrived with just this offer. The cousin was "playing it smart." He was selling off a field that was about to fall into the hands of the enemy, and in exchange he would be given silver, a highly liquid, easily concealed, transportable form of capital—an international currency. Not bad for him, since all he would be giving up would be a piece of ground that the enemy would probably take over anyway.

Long-Range Planning

What were God's instructions to Jeremiah? *Buy the field.* So Jeremiah took his silver, and witnesses, and balances (honest money), and they made the transaction. Then Jeremiah instructed Baruch, a scribe, to record the evidence. (It may be that Jeremiah was illiterate, as were most men of his day.) Baruch was told by Jeremiah to put the evidences of the sale into an earthen vessel for long-term storage. "For thus saith the Lord of hosts, the God of Israel; Houses and fields and vineyards shall be possessed again in this land" (32:15).

God explained His purposes at the end of the chapter. Yes, the city would fall. Yes, the people would go into captivity. Yes, their sins had brought this upon them. But this is not the end of the story. "Behold, I will gather them out of all countries, whither I have driven them in mine anger, and in my fury, and in great wrath; and I will bring them again unto this place, and I will cause them to dwell safely: And they shall be my people, and I will be their God" (32:37–38). It doesn't stop there, either: "Like as I have brought all this great evil upon this people, so will I bring upon them all the good that I have promised them. And fields shall be bought in this land, whereof ye say, It is desolate without man or beast; it is given into the hand of the Chaldeans" (32:42–43).

What was God's message to Jeremiah? *There is hope for the long run for those who are faithful to His message.* There will eventually come a day when truth will out, when law will reign supreme, when men will buy and sell, when contracts will be honored. "Men shall buy fields for money, and sub-scribe evidences, and seal them, and take witnesses in the land of Benjamin, and in the places about Jerusalem, and in the cities of Judah, and in the cities of the mountains, and in the cities of the valley, and in the cities of the south: for I will cause their captivity to return, saith the Lord" (32:44). In other words, business will return because the law of God will be understood and honored.

God had told them that they would be in captivity for seventy years. It would be long enough to make certain that Jeremiah would not be coming back to claim his field. Yet there was hope nonetheless. The prophet is not to imagine that all good things will come in his own day. He is not to be a short-term optimist. He is not to conclude that his words will turn everything around, making him the hero of the hour. He is told to look at the long run, to preach in the short run, and to go about his normal business. Plan for the future. Buy and sell. Continue to speak out when times are opportune. Tell anyone who will listen of the coming judg-ment, but remind them also that all is not lost forever just because everything seems to be lost today.

The Job Is to Be Honest

The prophet's job is to be honest. He must face the laws of reality. If bad principles lead to bad actions, then bad consequences will surely follow. These laws of reality cannot be underestimated. In fact, it is the prophet's task to reaffirm their validity by his message. He pulls no punches. Things are not "fairly bad" if morality is ignored or laughed at. Things are terrible, and people should understand this. Still, there is hope. Men can change their minds. The prophet knows that in "good" times, rebellious people usually don't change their minds. In fact, that most reluctant of prophets, Jonah, was so startled when the city of Nineveh repented that he pouted that the promised judgment never came, making him look like an idiot—an attitude which God reproached. But in the days of Elijah, Isaiah, and Jeremiah, the pragmatists of Israel were not about to turn back to the moral laws which had provided their prosperity. It would take seven decades of captivity to bring them, or rather their children and grandchildren, back to the truth.

Invest long-term, God told Jeremiah. Invest as if all were not lost. Invest as if your message, eventually, will bear fruit. Invest in the face of despair, when everyone is running scared. Invest for the benefit of your children and grandchildren. Invest as if everything doesn't depend on the prophet, since prophets, being men, are not omniscient or omnipotent. Invest as if moral law will one day be respected. Keep plugging away, even if you yourself will never live to see the people return to their senses and return to their land. Don't minimize the extent of the destruction. Don't rejoice at the plight of your enemies. Don't despair at the fact that the Remnant is caught in the whirlpool of destruction. Shed tears if you must, but most important, keep records. Plan for the future. Never give an inch.

A prophet is no Pollyanna, no Dr. Pangloss. He faces reality. Reality is his calling in life. To tell people things are terrible when they think everything is fine, and to offer hope when they think everything is lost. To tell the truth, whatever the cost, and not to let short-term considerations blur one's vision. The Remnant is there. The Remnant will survive. Eventually, the Remnant will become the masses, since truth will out. But until that day, for which all prophets should rejoice, despite the fact that few will see its dawning, the prophet must do his best to understand reality and present it in the most effective way he knows how. That is Jeremiah's job.

Ezekiel's Job

Ridgway K. Foley, Jr.

Basic distinctions often prove elusive. Whether by virtue of inattention, human resistance, lack of comprehension, or some indefinable perversity of life, we human beings often fail to grasp and act upon the most central differences both of concept and deed. As a result, all manner of disappointing and disturbing events take place, inasmuch as one misstep at the outset of a journey can foreordain an unexpected destination.

Consider one such essential distinction: personal belief and action premised upon a set moral code versus the coercive imposition of one's moral strictures upon another, unwilling human being. The dissimilarity is fundamental and not particularly obscure; yet, the blurring and commingling of these two very different precepts (and their attendant activities) have vexed men and women across time.

Ezekiel provides insights into this common and perplexing situation. Of course, it is not "with it" to relate modern problems to some old fellow who lived long ago and far away; in the skeptical and intolerant climate of today, so lacking in the civility of open thought, it just does not meet the modern dictates of intellectual exclusivity to refer to the Bible, to Christianity, or to any traditional religion—particularly one with established attitudes of "right"

Mr. Foley lives in Prescott, Arizona, and practices law in Portland, Oregon, with Greene & Markley, P.C. This essay appeared in the September 1990 issue of *The Freeman*.

and "wrong." Yet the Book of *Ezekiel* lays a firm foundation from which all of us, no matter our religious persuasion, may investigate the differences between proper belief and proper respect for the beliefs of others. After all, the essence of the human condition remains unchanged despite the passage of centuries.

Recall the backdrop of history. The Jewish people received the gift of insight into the very marrow of the individual—the ability to choose, to evaluate, and to select among alternatives, and in so doing to affect not only the actor's destiny but also the course of a lineal world history: " . . . I have set before thee this day life and good, and death and evil. . . . I have set before you life and death, blessing and cursing: therefore choose life, that both thou and thy seed shall live. . . ."(*Deut.* 30:15,19)

These ancient men and women displayed the same features and failings as we do. At times they made venal, undesirable, and unwise choices, and as a result suffered the inexorable consequences which flowed from their conduct. As a nation, ancient Israel waxed and waned: Things worked out well when the people adhered to the Decalogue, and bad times followed their evil exploits. God endowed men with freedom, even the freedom to forsake Him and to choose wrongly, for freedom necessarily entails the freedom to fail. Although the ineluctable law of cause-and-consequence foretold unpleasant sequels from inappropriate acts, the Jews of old seemed hell-bent on the eternal folly of trying to beat the house.

Now and then, when the Hebrew nation deviated sufficiently from the proper standard of behavior, God sent a prophet, a man assigned to remind His flock of the rules of the game and to warn them of the inevitable lunacy of trying to avoid responsibility for their wickedness. Sometimes the body politic listened; more often, the people ignored, joshed, or abused the prophet.

Enter Ezekiel

Ezekiel was one of the major prophets, a chap God called forth 26 centuries ago during one of those troubled times for Israel. Prophets were role players; they were given a part to play without a thought of the consequences. They spoke to largely hostile audiences. They faced uncomfortable, and sometimes dangerous, situations. They forsook popularity, credibility, status, and wealth. In return, they knew that somewhere, somehow, a dutiful Remnant[1] would hear and heed the words they uttered as God's intermediary.[2] Ezekiel fit right into this tapestry of history and role of prophet. God instructed him and he, in turn, carried the message to those of the multitude who chose to listen. And, it is that critical message recorded in *Ezekiel* 33:1–11 which edifies us specifically as to the dichotomy between personal commitment and coerced orthodoxy.

Ezekiel 33:1–11 imparts threefold tidings. First, God tells His people "I have sent thee a watchman" (*Ezek.* 33:7) and He outlines the obligations of the watchman. Second, He advises the Remnant of the duties laid upon those who hear His watchman. Third—and most saliently for our present purpose—He answers the ageless inquiry of the listeners, "How should we then live?" (*Ezek.* 33:10)

How should we then live? Distinguish between the encompassed relativism of a humanistic "man is the measure of all things" precept and an understanding that imperfect individuals will profess different beliefs. It is one thing to ascertain for oneself how the moral life is to be lived; it is quite another matter to impose that particular view upon an unwilling neighbor. The Christian may think it great folly for each man to live according to his internal moral code oblivious to God's law ("ye shall be as gods," *Gen.* 3:5), or "each individual's innate sense of truth and justice"; does this profession of faith necessarily or properly vest in the practicing Christian the right to compel all others to accept his creed? Or rather, doesn't the modern theocrat—be he religious, atheistic or agnostic—confuse subjective value with moral absolutes?

Thus, the Remnant through Ezekiel asked God, "How should we then live?" and received a simple and direct mandate: "As I live, saith the Lord." (*Ezek.* 33:11) Yet, simple declarations may cloak deeper lessons. Surely, reflective men and women in the sixth century before Christ, as now, wondered how the Lord did live. And, for the Jew of 2,600 years ago, as for the Christian in the late twentieth century, the answer appears in the recorded reports of eyewitnesses to history.[3]

God's Answers

God often provided sound answers to this secondary inquiry (How does the Lord live?) for Old Testament followers. For example, in the entire passage from Deuteronomy abstracted heretofore, God directed His people to follow His statutes and laws (see *Deut.* 30:15–19), a message often repeated but seldom heeded. He condensed His rules of conduct in the Decalogue (*Ex.* 20:1–17), a precise summary not dissimilar from the essential teachings of most of the world's great religions, and not wholly unlike the alleged inbred "innate moral sense" so popularly presupposed in current lore to reside in all individuals.

Somehow, the content of these simple yet exact rules of

order either escaped most folks or suffered the serious ame-lioration of convenience. Hebraic law became burden-somely formal and uselessly coercive, smothering the essence in arid dust. People became baffled: How did God live? Was it as some neighbor declared? Or according to the local prophet, general, or rabbi? Couldn't these restrictive commandments be modified just a bit to fit a particular case which coincidentally happened to be of personal interest to the inquirer? Didn't modern times mandate more modern and less archaic solutions? And so the waxing and waning of the Old Testament travails continued unabated long after Ezekiel departed.

For the Christian, a remarkable and unprecedented event occurred 2,000 years ago: God answered the sec-ondary inquiry (How does the Lord live?) in a unique and direct way. God became Incarnate, sending His Son in the form of a man, to live among witnesses, to encounter and suffer the range of human events and emotions and, inci-dentally, to show us just how the Lord does live.

In the examination of Jesus' life, set against the back-drop of the Old Testament law, we see not only how the Lord lives but also the stark distinction between principled personal belief and the mandate to respect the beliefs (no matter how dissimilar or possibly erroneous) of others. Simply put, Jesus lived a life of pristine purity: He adhered to the essence of the Ten Commandments and eschewed sin and evil. He built no monuments to His reign; He assembled no mighty army to strike down the soldiers of Satan; He accepted no patronage; He granted no special favors; He left no estate of substance. In short, Jesus lived quite unlike any human being, ruler or ruled, in all of human history.

Did Jesus ever force anyone to believe, to chant His

praise, to recite His creed, to follow Him? Did He ever box the ears of an unreceptive and hooting audience and charge them to "be Christians and do exactly as I say and do or I'll whomp you"? Did He ever ostracize or humiliate those who declined His offers? There is absolutely *no* evidence of such behavior.

Peter presents the perfect counterpoint, the epitome of demonstrative evidence. Once Peter figures out who his Master is he immediately suggests building a grand temple (*Matt.* 17:4–9); he admonishes Jesus that He must avoid His trip to Jerusalem and His destiny on the cross (*Mark* 8:31–33); and, in the garden, he slices off the ear of the servant of the high priest (*Matt.* 26:51–52). In every instance, Peter's actions earn stern rebukes, for Peter behaves as men do, not as the Lord does.

Abundant Lessons

Layers of lessons abound in the Lord's answer to Ezekiel's question, and each layer offers guidance for believer and nonbeliever alike.

First, Ezekiel and his counterparts must adhere to principle in a sea of challenge, doubt, and seduction. Absolutes in the form of correct choices and proper principles do exist; consequences flow from all choices, results that must be endured, events that beget future choices. Selection between alternatives may be made randomly, thoughtlessly, malevolently, or may rest upon the basis of the actor's understanding of, and adherence to, fundamental principle. The principled individual is charged to live scrupulously, to make the right choice at each and every opportunity, be he Christian or Jew, atheist or agnostic; the distinction exists in the standard.

When the moral individual refuses to soften this quest for perfection, he is often met with derision, enticement, or compulsion. In this regard, scant differences separate the doctrinaire libertarian and the overzealous Christian. There appears a natural human tendency to challenge the beliefs of others, first through shunning and scorn, last by force and fraud. Those most inflexible in principle seem to suffer the greatest assaults, possibly because the traducers implicitly recognize the propriety of the upright and seek to wrench them down to their level.

Disorderly man occupies an orderly sphere and setting. Gifted with the power to choose, flawed mankind necessarily makes poor choices on occasion, for freedom encompasses the power and the right to be wrong. The Christian is called only to be a faithful steward, not a perfect one. Perfection is our goal; it is not within our grasp. A sentry at Buckingham House, two-and-one-quarter centuries back, put it artfully: "But, Sir, if GOD was to make the world today, it would be crooked again tomorrow."[4] Intolerance of human failings—of self or others—often eclipses the quest for betterment; this inherent intolerance leads directly to the second layer of understanding and the dichotomy between principle and force.

Second, then, Jesus' answer to Ezekiel's inquiry aptly illustrates the difference between holding and practicing a belief and demanding adherence by others to that ideal. While men are flawed, God is not; yet Jesus did not command obedience to His banner although He knew it to be true. Nor should men. Indeed, since men—unlike God—do not inevitably *know* that they hold proper principles and exhibit correct behavior, they ought not compel others to accept and adopt a possibly flawed precept.

Ample manifestations of the impermissible blurring of principle and command appear upon reflection: the religious zealot who seizes the machinery of government, establishes a state religion *de facto* or *de jure*, enacts blue laws, and orders compulsory chapel; the arid libertarian who, intolerant of any suggestion that others might reach similar results from dissimilar bases, mocks his Christian counterpart out of the discussion; the well-meaning sophisticate concerned about the homeless, the young, the irascible, or the disabled, who induces the county commission to use tax revenues to pay for shelters and rehabilitation centers; the illiberal liberal who concocts false testimony concerning, and selectively applies state legal sanctions against, disliked religious persons or groups who hear a different voice and dare to speak out. Sadly, the list appears endless: For religious and agnostic alike, the concept of "witness" has all too often transmuted proper belief and the quest for moral excellence into an evil charade replete with clever rationalizations, as each individual seeks to impose his agenda upon all others, to limit the discussion to prescribed topics, and to foreordain all solutions, hence circumscribing human action with his own finite boundaries in the name of his "truth."

Third, Ezekiel reveals the role assigned to the committed: They are called to be watchmen (*Ezek.* 33:1–10). Watchmen perform specific tasks: They search out the truth, live out the truth, and speak out the truth, in order that others may hear and assimilate. No one expects a watchman to battle those about him. Watchmen cry out; they sound the tocsin; they raise the alarm; but Ezekiel does not suggest that the watchman's obligations include compelling anyone to believe, to profess, or to act in any discrete manner.

Instead, God's watchmen provide knowledge and opportunity, a palpable form of due process, to any and all who choose to consider the message.

The watchman directive applies to the nonreligious believer by a parity of reasoning. Leonard E. Read devoted many of his adult years to the study and explication of the appropriate methodology of freedom. He repeatedly reminded his readers and listeners that one who truly espouses the freedom philosophy could not coerce others to adopt those premises, since to attempt to do so would constitute the most startling contradiction in terms. He admonished us that the "end preexists in the means," "the bloom preexists in the rose." If we improve our own self and live according to right precepts, others will observe and be drawn to the proper path by the flame of attraction. Leonard Read's adjurations do not differ in essence from God's admonition to Ezekiel and echoed in *Matthew* 16:5 to "Let your light so shine before men, that they may see your good works, and glorify your Father which is in Heaven."

In this fashion, the *Ezekiel* passage makes it manifest that committed individuals are duty-bound to honor their commitment, but they are not to coerce others to follow their opinions or mimic their precepts. They should seek the truth, follow the right, improve the self, and never stray from fundamental principle. In the timeless truth of the redoubtable F. A. Harper, "A principle can be broken, but it cannot be bent." Concomitantly, committed men and women should attract others by the light of their words and the propriety of their deeds, never by the exercise of compulsion, aggression, fraud, manipulation, or malevolence—with or without the sanction of the state.

Further, Ezekiel offers us a fourth lesson. Those who hear the watchman must heed his warning or suffer the ineluctable consequences. Remember, one need not accept or act favorably upon a warning, but God makes it clear that the listener disregards the sound of the tocsin at his own peril. Once more, this passage accords with the fundamentals of freedom. Force and freedom are inimical: Freedom includes the freedom to fail, to make choices that seem wrong to legions of observers, to act meanly or intolerantly or foolishly, to go against the crowd. The essence of man resides in his power to make meaningful choices that will affect not only his life but also the lives of others here and hereafter. Deprivation of this power of creative choice, for whatever reason, not only limits that man's array of selections but also diminishes him as a person. "To enslave" is much too light and lax a verb to describe such oppression, for the person restricted is thereby lessened as a human being, stunted in his potential, and cut down in his moral growth.

God's watchman must speak out fearlessly and his listeners must act accordingly, or both will suffer inevitable consequences of their respective breaches of duty. But nowhere does the message provide that disagreeing men should either thwart the warning or forestall the reaction by destructive means. Just so the observant nonbeliever may deny the existence of the law of gravity, but when he leaps from an airplane without a parachute he pays the inexorable price for his sincere if incorrect intellectual position.

Limiting Human Action

What limits then restrain human action? The rules and order of the universe and the civil sanctions against aggression. The nature of man and the consequential constraints of the world permit growth but preclude perfection. The civil or positive law—no less than the essential Biblical code—ought to deter and punish the employment of fraud and the initiation of aggression; after all, if Ezekiel demonstrates that proper belief does not include the coercive imposition of that belief upon an unwilling other, the lesson must also implicitly disparage the use of force for lesser purposes as well.

Most compulsion develops facially as a quest for "good" and as an affray against evil. B wishes to protect A from his folly. B "knows" that he knows better what ought to be done under the circumstances by virtue of his expertise, his beliefs, or his prominence, so he substitutes his moral, aesthetic, political, or economic judgment for that of his fellows. After all, if left to their own devices and desires, "they will make bad choices." On the surface, B's outward clamor is always for good, justice, and protection. In fact, the Bs of the world seek glory, patronage, and power, and their conduct displays the most heinous intolerance and cant. Those who seek to "do good" by coercive means accomplish great evil by depriving their subjects of their primary human trait. These dictators great and small live as men do, not as God.

Commitment to Christianity and to the free society are one and the same. The sole difference of note lies in the choices made by freely choosing individuals once all recognize the fundamental difference between commitment to principle and the use of compulsion to impose that principle upon others.

---

1. See, for example, *Isaiah* 1:9; *Nehemiah* 1:3.
2. Albert Jay Nock, "Isaiah's Job," available as a reprint from The Foundation for Economic Education, Irvington-on-Hudson, New York.

3. It is confusing and amusing to consider the reluctance of some individuals to credit the notable—if not inspired— eyewitness accounts of ancient men and women, when those same individuals voraciously grasp as gospel the silly and demonstrably unsupported reports of modern ideologues and charlatans. For further insight, consider G. K. Chesterton, *The Everlasting Man* (New York: Dodd, Mead & Company, 1925), and Charles Mackay, *Extraordinary Popular Delusions and the Madness of Crowds* (London: Richard Bentley, 1841).

4. James Boswell, *Boswell's London Journal,* edited by Frederick A. Pottle (New York: McGraw-Hill, 1950), entry of December 22, 1762, p. 100.

The Road to Jericho

Hal Watkins

One of the most famous stories Jesus told is the parable of the Good Samaritan as recorded in *Luke* 10:25–37. It concerns a tragic incident on the road from Jericho to Jerusalem, a distance of about 20 miles. Part of the road was very steep and rugged; some of it was quite smooth. It illustrates the common road over which all of us must travel; sometimes it is steep and rugged, and other times it is quite smooth. It's every man's road.

A number of characters appear on the Jericho road, just as they do on the road of life. By examining them we will be able to identify with some of them and perhaps learn some lessons.

The first to demand our attention is the lone man. By common consent the road was open to the public, so this lone man had every right to be on it without fear or hindrance. Each of us has a God-given right to travel the road of life without being hindered or molested. Even though we enjoy various types of companionship along the way, in a sense we are traveling the road of life alone. We will be influenced more or less by family, church, school, co-workers, business, government, and some predators, but the final decisions, for the most part, devolve on each of us individually.

The Reverend Mr. Watkins, editor and publisher of *The Printed Preacher*, wrote this article for the June 1978 issue of *The Freeman*.

As a lone man I have a right to expect non-threatening treatment from all my fellowmen. If any other man finds himself in a circumstance where he feels he must act toward me, he should do only that which helps rather than hinders. This, of course, is also my obligation toward him. A lone man (woman or child) is vulnerable to harm of various kinds, and also to help.

The next characters to appear in this drama of life are the cruel men, the robbers who recognized no God but their animalistic desires. They took advantage of the lone man, stealing his goods, his time and his well-being. The motivation in the hearts of these men was the Satanic principle that "might makes right," or "what's yours is mine—if I can get it." Such evil men add nothing of value to the lives of the people they contact along the way, but they will take everything they can get by fair means or foul. Their own advantage is their only consideration. They wound, bruise, and rob. It may be money, reputation, or even characters—they don't care.

The thieves in the parable probably ambushed the lone man as he came around a blind corner, but some of their counterparts are more sophisticated or subtle in our day. They might feign distress along the freeway, beg a ride to the next town and rob the benefactor en route. Or, they might put out a plea in favor of the "disadvantaged" and ask the government for help, but since the government has nothing to give, it must first steal the funds from its taxpayers. This might even involve a conspiracy between those desiring the aid, the group pleading their cause and the government agents (legislators, etc.). The whole problem may become difficult to sort out, trying to determine just who are the sincere agents and who are the thieves. But the apparent difficulty should not be allowed to obscure the problem: the lone man *has* been robbed; his freedom and his very life have been threatened. In what we like to call a "free society," can we shrug it off by saying that each man will have to hire his own army or police force? Perhaps we would do better to examine a system that threatens and crushes the individual and rewards thieves and their accomplices.

On the road of life, within the framework of a "Christian" society, there surely must be some protection for the lone man from the depredations of thieves, the "minus" men who would live solely at the expense of others.

On the road to Jericho there were also other men, selfish men who saw the plight of the abused traveler but had no concern for him or the problem. They were religious men too, but their religion—at least as they practiced it—did not consider the misfortunes or even the rights of their fellow human being. They, of course, would never steal from a lone traveler in the manner practiced by the bandits, but they didn't want to get involved. "Tough experience for the poor devil. Should have known better than to be traveling alone. Hope someone moves him off the road."

True Christianity is in the world today, but there are many counterfeits. Many of the alleged followers of Christ occasionally express concern for the plunder taking place along the road of life, but they don't lift a finger to expose or solve the problem. The New Testament writer, James, is quite blunt in his description of them: "To him therefore that knoweth to do good, and doeth it not, to him it is sin" (4:17). The attitude of these "zero" men is: "We were not robbed, so it's no concern of ours. What we have we will keep."

Fortunately, on the road to Jericho, there came another man who was not a disappointment but rather a delightful surprise. He had a pure Christian philosophy: "What is mine is yours, and in your misfortune I will share it." He gave of himself and his means. He was the compassionate, unselfish man. This type is also on the road of life today. Not only would he steal nothing from his fellows, but he adds much to their general welfare.

The Good Samaritan did not wait beside the stricken traveler until another victim came along, beat and plunder him, then give the proceeds to the first victim. He was not a first-century Robin Hood who robbed others to help the poor, but he gave of his own means. He didn't run for political office as a cover to conduct his robbery "legally," then give to the poor. Jesus certainly pictured him as a *concerned* man, one who was not content to pass by on the other side as though nothing had happened. He saw a fellow human being in distress, and he visualized himself as part of the solution to the problem. This was a mandate from his conscience to DO SOMETHING. He was not a "minus" man, or even a "zero" man. He was a "plus" man. And Jesus forced his hearer to admit that the Samaritan was motivated by love.

Within the Christian context we are not here to wound, crush, rob, or even to ignore. We are here to heal, lift, encourage and contribute of our talent and energy to the end that others too may, if they so desire, enjoy the same blessings we have. This truth has been around long enough to be axiomatic, and Jesus said, "Ye shall know the truth, and the truth shall make you free" (*John* 8:32).

What the Bible Says
About Big Government

James C. Patrick

Evidence is mounting that government programs fail to accomplish all that their advocates had promised. After dipping for a while, crime statistics are climbing again. Confidence in the institution of government has sagged. Some people wonder whether government has bitten off more than it can chew. They suspect that Henry Hazlitt came close to the mark when he wrote, "The more things a government undertakes to do, the fewer things it can do competently."[1]

What do the Hebrew and Christian scriptures have to say on the subject of government power and functions? News reports about clergymen's public statements and actions often reveal the men of the cloth on the side of big government—favoring more handouts, more intervention, more regulation. Does the Bible support that position? Or should the clergy take a closer look at what the scriptures disclose? Answers to these questions could be illuminating.

First, however, just what is government? Some of the thinkers who helped lift Western civilization into the modern era had pondered the question deeply but it is doubtful

Mr. Patrick, a retired banker and Chamber of Commerce executive, resides in Decatur, Illinois. This article is reprinted from the March 1976 issue of *The Freeman*.

that most people ever gave it a thought, either then or now. A look at what students of the subject have written should provide an answer.

The Essence of Big Government

In a stark cemetery at Mansfield, Missouri, stand two identical gravestones side by side, separated by about six feet of sod. Carved in large letters in the brown granite of one is the name Wilder, of the other, Lane. One marks the graves of Almanzo James and Laura Ingalls Wilder, the second the grave of their daughter, Rose Wilder Lane. Almanzo Wilder died in 1949 at the age of ninety-two. His wife lived till 1957 when she was ninety. Rose was almost eighty-two when she died in 1968.

A mile east of Mansfield on a pleasant hillside rests the modest white frame house that Almanzo Wilder built for Laura at the turn of the century, using building materials produced on the farm. Here Rose grew to womanhood and here in 1932 her mother began to write the "Little House" books that have charmed a generation of Americans with their picture of pioneer life in the second half of the nineteenth century and have now been adapted for television. Drawing on a descriptive talent developed as a girl when she served as the eyes for her scarlet-fever-blinded sister, Laura wrote the series of books in longhand on tablet paper, using both sides of the sheet to avoid waste and writing with a pencil.

Rose, too, became a writer and her best-known book, *Let the Hurricane Roar,* is in part a retelling in fiction of the pioneer experiences of her mother's family. But her most influential book is *The Discovery of Freedom,* published in 1943. It takes nothing from Rose Wilder Lane to point out that the book reflects viewpoints and attitudes that are evident in her mother's writing.

The Discovery of Freedom was the inspiration for Henry Grady Weaver's *The Mainspring of Human Progress*, described by Leonard Read, President of the Foundation for Economic Education, as probably the best introduction to freedom ideas available in a single volume. *Mainspring* has multiplied the outreach and the influence of Rose Wilder Lane's thought.

Today and for two generations there has been abroad in the land a naive faith in government as the solution to all problems —a belief in the ability of legislation to satisfy any need. Events in the last decade, when that trust reached its zenith in the Great Society programs, have dealt several stinging blows to the faith but it had become so deeply ingrained that it yields slowly to opposing evidence.

Weaver and Mrs. Lane did not share the popular belief. Instead, they took a very different view which Rose Wilder Lane expressed in these words: "What they (men in government) have is the use of force—command of the police and the army. Government, The State is always a use of force . . .[2] and "Buck" Weaver wrote, "In the last analysis, and stripped of all the furbelows, government is nothing more than a legal monopoly of the use of physical force— by persons upon persons."[3]

What Authorities Say

Although most Americans today seem never to have thought of it, this idea was not new. Numerous other writers, representing differing shades in the political spectrum, have expressed a similar view, both before and since Mrs. Lane and "Buck" Weaver wrote.

"The civil law . . . is the force of the commonwealth, engaged to protect the lives, liberties, and possessions of those who live according to its laws, and has power to take away life, liberty, or goods from him who disobeys." (John Locke)

"Government is not reason, it is not eloquence—it is force. Like fire it is a dangerous servant and a fearful master . . ." (George Washington)

"Law is the common force organized to act as an obstacle to injustice." (Frederic Bastiat)

" . . . penal sanction . . . is the essence of law . . ." (John Stuart Mill)

"The essential characteristic of all government, whatever its form, is authority. . . . Government, in its last analysis, is organized force." (Woodrow Wilson)

"The state belongs to the sphere of coercion. It would be madness to renounce coercion, particularly in the epoch of the dictatorship of the proletariat." (Nikolai Lenin)

"A government may be freely chosen, but it is still not all of us. It is some men vested with authority over other men." And democracy ". . . is a name for a particular set of conditions under which the right to coerce others is acquired and held."[4] (Charles Frankel)

"The State is the party that always accompanies its proposals by coercion, and backs them by force."[5] (Charles A. Reich)

It should come as no surprise to students of the Bible that the scriptures analyzed the ultimate nature of government much earlier than any of the writers cited. Christians sometimes wonder what Jesus had to say about the role of government, and theologians normally reply that he said very little on the subject. The principal relevant statement recorded in the gospels is his response to a question as to whether it was proper to pay the head tax imposed by Rome. The tax amounted to about twenty-five cents a person and was regarded as a mark of servitude to Rome.

In ancient times the authority of a ruler was symbolized by the circulation of his coinage and coins bearing the ruler's image were considered his property, in the final analysis.[6] When Jesus requested that his questioners show him one of the coins used to pay the tax, a coin was brought and he asked, "Whose likeness and inscription is this?" They replied that it was Caesar's. Jesus then said, "Render therefore to Caesar the things that are Caesar's, and to God the things that are God's." The account is told in *Matthew* 22 and in parallels in the gospel according to *Mark* and according to *Luke*.

While Jesus said little about the power of government and what government should or should not do, two other New Testament writers came down solidly on the side of respect for the civil authorities and obedience to law. One of these was the Apostle Paul. Of Paul a respected New Testament scholar wrote a few years ago, "It is evident from many allusions in his writings, that the thought of Rome had strongly affected his imagination. He associated the great city with all that was most august in earthly power. He believed that it had been divinely appointed to maintain order and peace among the contending races."[7]

In his letter to the Romans, St. Paul offered the following admonition: "Let every person be subject to the governing authorities. For there is no authority except from God, and those that exist have been instituted by God."

Pay your taxes and give respect and honor to whom they are due, said Paul. Conduct yourself properly and you will have no reason to fear an official. "But if you do wrong, be afraid, for he does not bear the sword in vain."[8]

And St. Peter wrote:

> Be subject for the Lord's sake to every human insti-
> tution, whether it be to the emperor as supreme, or
> to governors as sent by him to punish those who do
> wrong and to praise those who do right. For it is
> God's will that by doing right you should put to
> silence the ignorance of foolish men. Live as free
> men, yet without using your freedom as a pretext for
> evil; but live as servants of God. Honor all men.
> Love the brotherhood. Fear God. Honor the
> emperor.[9]

The statements are brief because the writers were not
primarily concerned for man's relation with the authorities
but for his relation with God and his fellow man. But the
statements are definite. And they provided the scriptural
foundation for what some students have considered Martin
Luther's exaggerated reverence for the State. Luther's attitude supplied the philosophical substructure for the
authoritarian character German governments have displayed more than once.

"When studied with any degree of thoroughness, the
economic problem will be found to run into the political
problem," wrote Irving Babbitt, "the political problem
into the philosophical problem, and the philosophical
problem itself to be almost indissolubly bound up at last
with the religious problem."[10] In short, what we believe or
do not believe about man and about God determines what
kind of society we will have and how our society will govern itself.

While there is support for paying taxes, obedience to
law, and respect for civil authority in the New Testament,

no detailed analysis of the nature of government or the proper functions of government is to be found there. There is, however, ample guidance for the individual conduct of government officials. They are human beings, so they will be fair, as all humans should be. They will deal justly with the people. Tax collectors will not steal because nobody should steal.

Another Biblical View

In the Old Testament, the writer of the books of *I Samuel* and *II Samuel* draws a definite contrast between limited government and the all-powerful State. The writer of the two books drew on earlier sources, some of which probably went back as far as 1000 B.C. or earlier and all of which had been completed by about 600 B.C.[11] For generations the Jewish people had been led by officials called Judges, of whom at least one, Deborah, was a woman. Best known of the judges to modern readers is Gideon, because his name is carried by the organization recognized for its practice of distributing Bibles in hotels and motels. The judges combined civil, military, and religious functions in their office. They led the Jewish people in battle against their enemies, settled questions of law, administered justice in disputes between individuals, and functioned as priests and prophets. To the enemies of Israel they often showed no quarter and in some of their judicial decisions they may have been arbitrary but their leadership of their own people was apparently rather mild. The writer of the book of Judges reports, in chapter 17 and again in his concluding verse, *Judges* 21:25, "In those days there was no king in Israel; every man did what was right in his own eyes."[11]

Gideon did not even want to be king. After he had led

the men of Israel successfully against their enemies, they asked him to rule over them but he replied, "I will not rule over you, and my son will not rule over you; the Lord will rule over you."[12]

After the death of Gideon one of his sons, Abimelech, seized power briefly and killed all of his brothers except one, the youngest, Jotham, who hid himself and escaped. When Jotham was told what his brother had done, he related a parable, recorded in *Judges* 9, about the trees going forth to anoint a king over themselves. The olive tree, the fig tree, and the vine all declined to abandon their productive pursuits to become king, so the trees then turned to the bramble and the bramble accepted.

The Worst on Top

In *The Road to Serfdom*, Professor Friedrich A. Hayek, for somewhat different reasons from those cited in Jotham's parable, reached a conclusion that resembles the parable of the trees and the bramble. Professor Hayek describes how kakistocracy arises in a chapter entitled, "Why the Worst Get on Top."[13]

Samuel was the last of the series of prophet-judges. He administered justice in his own city of Ramah, a few miles north of Jerusalem, and traveled a judicial circuit that took him annually to Bethel, Gilgal, and Mizpah. When senility approached, Samuel made his two sons judges but the scripture records that they lacked their father's honorable character and "turned aside after gain . . . took bribes and perverted justice."[14]

The Jewish people were still engaged in the prolonged effort to conquer the land they had occupied. Recurring wars threatened their security. Such enemies as the

Philistines were better organized and better equipped than the people of Israel who retained their loose tribal structure and had not yet fully abandoned the nomadic life. So the elders of Israel came to Samuel with a request: "Behold, you are old and your sons do not walk in your ways; now appoint for us a king to govern us like all the nations."

The request displeased Samuel, and he prayed to the Lord who admonished Samuel to heed their request, "for they have not rejected you, but they have rejected me. . . ." But Samuel was directed to tell them what it would be like to have a king. He did so in words recorded in *I Samuel* 8:

> These will be the ways of the king who will reign over you: He will take your sons and appoint them to his chariots and to be his horsemen, and to run before his chariots; and he will appoint for himself commanders of thousands and commanders of fifties, and some to plow his ground and to reap his harvest, and to make his implements of war and the equipment of his chariots. He will take your daughters to be perfumers and cooks and bakers. He will take the best of your fields and vineyards and olive orchards and give them to his servants. He will take the tenth of your grain and of your vineyards and give it to his officers and to his servants. He will take your menservants and maidservants, and the best of your cattle and your asses, and put them to his work. He will take the tenth of your flocks, and you shall be his slaves. And in that day you will cry out because of your king, whom you have chosen for yourselves. . . .

The people refused to listen to Samuel, however, and insisted that they wanted a king to govern them and fight their battles. Their wishes prevailed. They got big government.

The king who was selected was Saul, of the tribe of Benjamin. Many years before, when Moses explained to the people of Israel the law that he had delivered to them, he told them what kind of person to choose as king when the time came. His counsel is recorded in *Deuteronomy* 17:

> When you come to the land which the Lord your God gives you, and you possess it and dwell in it, and then say, "I will set a king over me, like all the nations that are round about me"; you may indeed set as king over you him whom the Lord your God will choose. One from among your brethren you shall set as king over you; you may not put a foreigner over you, who is not your brother. Only he must not multiply horses for himself, or cause the people to return to Egypt in order to multiply horses, since the Lord has said to you, "You shall never return that way again." And he shall not multiply wives for himself, lest his heart turn away; nor shall he greatly multiply for himself silver and gold.

In a book based on his research at the Hoover Institution on War, Revolution and Peace of Stanford University, Alvin Rabushka wrote, "Governments take resources from the public but use them to maximize their own welfare."[15] Both Moses and Samuel recognized this propensity and warned about it. To modern taxpayers the tenth part of their grain and vineyards and flocks, that Samuel said the king would require, must appear mild indeed but in time the burden became onerous to the people. Samuel's prophecy that one day they would cry out because of their king was not realized immediately. Then, as now, persons with the vision to foretell the consequences of certain popular choices and actions could only tell *what* would occur as a result, not *when it* would occur.

David and Solomon

David succeeded Saul as king, united the people of Israel under his rule, defeated their enemies, pushed the borders of his domain south to the Gulf of Aqaba, an arm of the Red Sea, and by treaty with vassals extended his control north and eastward to the Euphrates River.[16]

Thrusting aside an attempt of an older brother to become king, Solomon followed David, his father, on the throne. His reign was marked by lavish construction programs and public works projects. An extensive bureaucracy was established to man the elaborate governmental structure Solomon created. Twelve administrative regions were defined and each was to provide the taxes and other resources to support the king and his government for one month of each year. Solomon took as one of his wives a daughter of the Egyptian Pharaoh and built her a luxurious residence. He also built a temple at Jerusalem to be the center of worship for the entire nation. He was described as having "wisdom and understanding beyond measure, and largeness of mind like the sand on the seashore. . . ."[17] At the same time, however, the scripture speaks repeatedly of Solomon's use of forced labor and it tells of the hundreds of wives and concubines that he took. History casts doubt on the wisdom of a ruler who burdens his people with oppressive taxation and encumbers them with the upkeep of a sprawling bureaucracy and a parasitic court.

Like the Roman Catholic popes of the fifteenth and sixteenth centuries, Solomon mulcted the people of the resources to build imposing structures and create works of art.[18] The popes left great paintings and sculpture, as Solomon left a temple that stood for four centuries, but the exactions of the popes brought schism to the Church and those of Solomon brought rebellion in the kingdom when his son, Rehoboam, succeeded him.

After the death of Solomon the people who assembled for the coronation of Rehoboam came to the new king with a plea: "Your father made our yoke heavy. Now therefore lighten the hard service of your father and his heavy yoke upon us, and we will serve you." Rehoboam sent them away for three days while he consulted first with the elders who had advised his father and then with his youthful associates. In the end he rejected the counsel of the elders that he accede to the people's wishes. Instead he took the advice of his contemporaries and when the people returned for his answer, he told them, "My father made your yoke heavy, but I will add to your yoke; my father chastised you with whips, but I will chastise you with scorpions." Their appeal rejected, the people cried out, "To your tents, 0 Israel!" And the historian records in *I Kings* 12, "So Israel has been in rebellion against the house of David to this day."

The scriptures say that Saul and David and Solomon each reigned for forty years. So one hundred twenty years passed, or approximately four generations, from the time when the people abandoned limited government until the time when their descendents did "cry out" because of the king they had chosen. By 600 B.C. or earlier the people of Israel had learned, however, that government is indeed force—a dangerous servant and a fearful master.

The Role for Government

If government is force, as the serious students of the subject have agreed, what kinds of things should government do? The answer is obvious: Government should do those things that can be properly done by the use of force. The question follows: What are the proper uses of force among responsible adults?

Nobody has answered that question more clearly than the nineteenth century French statesman, Frederic Bastiat: "Every individual has the right to use force for lawful self-defense. It is for this reason that the collective force—which is only the organized combination of the individual forces—may lawfully be used for the same purpose; and it cannot be used legitimately for any other purpose."[19]

Government, therefore, is to be used to defend, to protect, to prevent violence, fraud, and other predatory acts. Other endeavors are to be left to the initiative and the choices of people acting voluntarily, either jointly or as individuals. In short, government should do what the judges of Israel did. Beyond that every man should do what is "right in his own eyes."

Obviously, that is not the direction Americans have been moving for the past two generations. Instead, as noted earlier, a naive faith that government can solve all problems has taken root and persists in spite of the repeated failures of government social programs. But it makes no difference that large numbers hold a wrong view. Right is not determined by majority vote. As Anatole France stated, "If fifty million people say a foolish thing, it is still a foolish thing." And Supreme Court Justice George Sutherland said, "A foolish law does not become a wise law because it is approved by a great many people."[20] Right, like truth, is usually discerned first by a minority, often in the beginning a minority of one.

Everybody Is Responsible

Everybody has a stake in preventing the unprincipled members of society from committing acts of violence or fraud upon peaceful persons, and should help pay a part of the cost of the police and defense mechanism necessary to protect people in their peaceful pursuits. Government is society's mechanism for protecting and defending; it properly collects taxes to pay for these services. But when it takes from some persons what belongs to them and gives it to other persons to whom it does not belong, government commits an act of plunder. One person who uses force or the threat of force to take from another what has been honestly earned or built or created, commits an immoral act and a crime. Two or more persons banding together do not acquire any moral rights that they did not have as individuals. When government provides benefits for one citizen at the expense of another by doing what the citizen himself cannot do without committing a crime, it performs an act of plunder.[21]

Not only is governmental plunder immoral, it reduces the general well-being of the people. It does so by taking away from some people what they have produced but are not permitted to use. It reduces well-being by distributing to other people what they have not been required to produce. Both the producers and the receivers are thus deprived of incentive. And government reduces the general well-being by creating an unproductive administrative bureaucracy to do the taking away and the distributing. Society needs the productivity of all its able members.

Shifted to producing goods and services that can be exchanged in the marketplace, the legions of bureaucrats could add materially to human well-being.

How is the situation to be corrected that has been allowed to develop? Rose Wilder Lane points the way: "The great English reform movement of the 19th century consisted wholly in repealing laws."[22] What is needed in the United States is to repeal laws, not to pass new ones. Repeal laws that vest some men with authority over other men. This is not to set the clock back, it is to set it right.[23]

As Samuel warned the people of Israel when they chose big government, various prophets have warned the people of America. Prophets can only tell *what* to expect, however, not *when* to expect it. More than a century of suffering passed before the people of Israel rose to throw off the yoke from their necks.

---

1. *Life and Death of the Welfare State,* (La Jolla, Cal.: La Jolla Rancho Press, 1968), p. 52.

2. *The Discovery of Freedom* (New York: Arno Press, 1972), p. 27.

3. *The Mainspring of Human Progress* (Irvington-on-Hudson, N.Y.: Foundation for Economic Education, 1953), p. 71.

4. Charles Frankel, *The Democratic Prospect* (New York: Harper & Row, 1964), p. 136 and p. 30.

5. Charles A. Reich, *The Greening of America* (New York: Bantam Books, 1971), p. 350.

6. *The Abingdon Bible Commentary* (New York and Nashville, Tenn.: Abingdon-Cokesbury Press, 1929), p. 988.

7. E. F. Scott, *The Literature of the New Testament* (New York: Columbia University Press, 1936), p. 156.

8. *Romans* 13:1–7. All scriptural quotations are from the Revised Standard Version of the Bible (New York: Thomas Nelson & Sons, 1952).

9. *I Peter* 2:13–17.

10. Quoted by Russell Kirk, *The Conservative Mind* (Chicago: Henry Regnery Company, 1960), p. 482.

11. Robert H. Pfeiffer, *Introduction to the Old Testament* (New York: Harper & Brothers, 1941), pp. 20–22.

12. *Judges* 8:23.

13. Friedrich A. Hayek, *The Road to Serfdom* (Chicago: The University of Chicago Press, 1944), Chapter X.

14. *I Samuel* 7:15–8:5.

15. Alvin Rabushka, *A Theory of Racial Harmony* (Columbia, S.C.: University of South Carolina Press, 1974), p. 93.

16. E. W. Heaton, *Solomon's New Men* (New York: Pica Press, 1974), Chapter 2.

17. *I Kings* 4:29.

18. Irving Stone, *The Agony and the Ecstasy* (New York: Doubleday & Company, 1961; Signet edition).

19. Frederic Bastiat, *The Law* (Irvington-on-Hudson, N.Y.: Foundation for Economic Education, 1956), p. 68.

20. Address as President of the American Bar Association, at the ABA annual meeting, Saratoga Springs, N.Y., September 4, 1917.

21. Bastiat, *op. cit.*, p. 21.

22. *Loc. cit.*, p. 239.

23. Wilhelm Roepke, *A Humane Economy* (Chicago: Henry Regnery Company, 1960), p. 88.

A Judeo-Christian Foundation

Hans F. Sennholz

Many voices in education and the media do not tire of denouncing and slandering the private-property order. They indict it for being heartless, merciless, cruel, inhuman, selfish, and exploitative, and, branding it "laissez-faire capitalism," condemn it roundly and loudly. Popular college textbooks of economics often set the tone. They devote many pages of friendly discussion to the writings of Karl Marx and other champions of socialism, but they dismiss, with a few lines of utter contempt, the ideas of "laissez-faire capitalism" and call its defenders ugly names (e.g., Paul Samuelson, *Economics,* all editions).

If capitalism nevertheless is alive and advancing in many parts of the world, the credit belongs not only to a few fearless defenders, but also to the visible failures and horrors of the command system and its economic and moral inadequacy. Despite all the slander and abuse that may be heaped on private property, its order offers more amenities of life even to its poorer members than the command system provides for its privileged members, and in contrast to the command system, it creates conditions of human existence that are most conducive to virtuous living and a moral order.

Dr. Sennholz is the President of The Foundation for Economic Education. This essay is an excerpt from his booklet, *Three Economic Commandments* (1990).

The private-property system rests on individual freedom, nonviolence, truthfulness, reliability, and cooperation. If everyone is free in his dealings with others, it is well nigh impossible to cheat, shortchange, or short-weight another. If customers and businessmen are free to choose, they are free to shun fraud and deception; goods and services must be satisfactory and priced right or they cannot be sold. A businessman who deceives his customers will lose them. If he mistreats his suppliers, they refuse to sell. If he abuses his workers, they will leave. It is in everyone's interest to be peaceful, honest, truthful, and cooperative.

Capitalism is no anarchism which rejects all forms of government for being oppressive and undesirable. The market order does not invite the strong to prey on the weak, employers to exploit their workers, and businessmen to gouge their customers. On the contrary, it is the only system that allocates to each member whatever he or she contributes to the production process. It alone provides the means for and gives wide range to all forms of charity, enabling man not only to satisfy his own desires, but also to assist other men in theirs. Yet its critics do not tire in charging that capitalism best serves selfish individuals ever searching for the greatest possible advantage. To the detractors, capitalism is synonymous with "maximizing profits," which they condemn as unrealistic and selfish.

This charge, too, misses the mark. In voluntary exchange, every individual prefers to buy the desired merchandise at the lowest possible price—unless he or she means to engage in charitable giving. Even rabbis, priests, and ministers choose to pay the lowest possible price for the automobile of their choice—unless they decide to make a gift to the dealer. They generally sell their old cars at the highest possible price—unless they choose to make a gift to the buyer. They seek to maximize their gains on the purchase or sale, which permits them to allocate the savings to the satisfaction of other needs.

A businessman is a man engaged in the production of economic goods and the rendering of economic services. He is the servant of consumers whose whims and wishes guide him in his production decisions. As they prefer to buy their goods in the most favorable market, so must he buy them at the lowest possible price. He cannot grant favors to suppliers at the expense of his customers; he cannot pay wages higher than those allowed by the buyers. If he does pay higher wages, he distributes his own property to his workers. In time, he is likely to face a bankruptcy judge who will dissolve his business. Surely, a businessman is free to spend his own income as he pleases. Motivated by various notions and impulses, he may buy his goods at a charity sale, paying higher prices, or sell his goods there for pennies or even give them away. His economic considerations do not differ from those of the rabbi, priest, and minister.

The private-property order is not lawless as its detractors so loudly proclaim. On the contrary, its very existence depends on honesty, integrity, and peaceful cooperation. Its bedrock is economic virtue. *Its complete and reliable guide on practical questions are the Ten Commandments, especially the second table with ethical standards for every area of life.* The second table is a solid foundation of all economic ease and comfort, and the guidepost to prosperity for all mankind. Even agnostics and atheists, Hindus, Buddhists, and Taoists, Confucianists and Shintoists who reject the first table governing man's relationship with God must live by the second table governing man's moral choices in his relationship with others, if they set out to thrive and multiply.

There is no other way, in this world of scarce resources and limited energy.[1]

The second table affirms the general principle of justice or righteousness for the organization of society. It is no command "to do good," but instead an order "to restrain evil." It does not propose a state that would create a good or great society, but directs man to abstain from evil. In order to avoid the bad, it merely says: abstain from coercion; do not commit adultery; do not lie; do not steal; do not covet. Aside from these admonitions, you are free to pursue your own interests.

The commandments call for a decent society that interacts voluntarily, a contract society rather than a coercive society, a peaceful society rather than a violent society. They do not elevate some men to be the rulers and lords over other men, nor do they commission some to manage the economic lives of others. On the contrary, the commandments set out to do very little—to restrain evil. Yet they accomplish so much by unleashing the creative energy of men fired on by their self-interest, but without harm to other men.

The private-property order rests on the solid foundation of the ethical commandments. It relies on the state and its instruments of force to restrain and punish the violators. It does not, however, call on the state to enforce the first table commanding man's relationship with God. (Thou shalt have no other gods before me; thou shalt not make any graven image; thou shalt not take the name of the Lord thy God in vain; remember the Sabbath day, to keep it holy.) Such an extension of the state would integrate or syndicate church and state. Government officials would reign supreme in the religious affairs of the people, denying religious freedom and generating bitter religious conflict, and church officials would labor to gain power over the state, or at least to exert great influence over the religious affairs of the state. The European experience with church and state affiliation throughout the centuries has been rather disheartening.

The state and its instruments of force receive their sole justification from their use and employment against antisocial individuals who would steal, rob, and otherwise disrupt the peaceful cooperation of society. As a guardian of the peace, the state is a very beneficial institution that deserves the support of every peaceful individual. Yet its coercive powers must be limited to the ethical commandments, the protection of which constitutes the very *raison d'être* and the first and only duty of the state.

Unfortunately, government never comes up to ideal standards. Governments the world over are enforcing some parts of the table while they sanction and even encourage the disregard of others. They may even lend their instruments of force to obvious violations of ethical laws, which puts every individual on the horns of a dilemma: if the policies of the state and the ethical commandments conflict with each other, what is he to do? Is he to obey the state or obey the commandments? Most people choose to obey the state because it readily and brutally enforces its laws. A few individuals who choose to live by God's commandments rather than man's unethical laws pay dearly for their defiance. They face armed sheriffs and jailers who unhesitatingly punish the resisters.

All ten commandments have a bearing on economic affairs;[2] three constitute the visible pillars of the private-property order: thou shalt not kill; thou shalt not steal; thou shalt not bear false witness. To violate any one of them is to do evil and do economic harm.

1. R. J. Rushdoony, *The Institutes of Biblical Law* (Nutley, N.J.: Craig Press, 1973); also *The Foundations of Social Order: Studies in the Creeds and Councils of the Early Church* (Fairfax, Va.: Thoburn Press, 1968; 1978); Gary North, *The Sinai Strategy* (Tyler, Tex.: Institute for Christian Economics, 1986); Lord John E.E.D. Acton, *Essays on Freedom and Power* (Boston, Mass.: Beacon Press, 1948); also *A Study in Conscience and Politics* (The University of Chicago Press, 1962); T. N. Carver, *Essays in Social Justice* (Harvard University Press, 1915); Gordon H. Clark, *A Christian View of Men and Things* (Grand Rapids, Mich.: Baker Book House, 1952).

2. The first commandment proclaims the sovereign power of God, who calls on man to submit to His law-order, including His eternal and inexorable laws of economics. The second commandment prohibits man from worshipping the works of man, especially the state and its institutions. The third commandment exhorts man to act judiciously and reverently in every area of life, including his economic life. The fourth commandment has numerous economic implications as to production and distribution, sabbath legislation, regulation, and enforcement. The fifth commandment exhorts children to honor their fathers and mothers—spiritually and financially—so that they may prosper for generations to come. The seventh commandment protects the family and safeguards social peace and economic productivity. Cf. R. J. Rushdoony, *The Institutes of Biblical Law, ibid.;* also *The Foundations of Social Order: Studies in the Creeds and Councils of the Early Church, ibid.;* Gary North, *The Sinai Strategy, ibid.*

III. THE RIGHTS OF MAN

Freedom, Morality, and Education

George C. Roche III

To fully appreciate the shortcomings of our present educational framework and face realistically the task of rebuilding it requires a careful and complete understanding of the concepts we value in society—a "thinking through" of our own first principles. What kind of educational goals do we really desire?

To Plato, proper education of the young consisted in helping them to form the correct mental habits for living by "the rule of right reason." But, how do we define right reason?

An important part of education centers on the attempts of society to transmit its culture to the rising generation. What are the accomplishments of past generations? What have been the goals and values by which society has lived? What guidelines should be available to the rising generation as it faces its own inevitable problems?

Still, education must be far more than the mere indoctrination of the young into the methods of the past. A hallmark of Western civilization is its educational focus upon the development of the individual's capacity to function as an individual, tempered by recognition of the common characteristics imposed upon all civilized communities by the unchanging aspects of human nature. In this sense, the

Dr. Roche is president of Hillsdale College. This article appeared in the November 1968 issue of *The Freeman*.

proper goal of education is everywhere the same: improve the individual as an individual, stressing the peculiar and unique attributes each has to develop, but also emphasizing the development of that "higher side" shared by all men when true to their nature. This educational goal might be described as the quest for "structured freedom," freedom for the individual to choose *within* a framework of values, values universal to *all* men simply because they are human beings.

A Framework of Values

Education in this best sense requires no elaborate paraphernalia. It is characterized, not by elaborate classrooms or scientific "methods," but by an emphasis upon the continuity and changelessness of the human condition. The effort to free the creative capacities of the individual, to allow him to become truly himself, must recognize the values which past generations have found to be liberating, asking that each new generation make the most of inherited values while striving to enrich that heritage. True education is society's attempt to enunciate certain ultimate values upon which individuals, and hence society, may safely build. The behavior of children toward their parents, toward their responsibilities, and even toward the learning process itself is closely tied to such a framework of values.

Thus, in the long run, the relationship we develop between teacher and pupil, the type of learning we encourage, the manner in which we organize our school systems, in short, the total meaning we give to the word "education," will finally be determined by our answers to certain key questions concerning ultimate values.

Those who built the Western World never questioned this continuity of our civilization nor attempted to pluck out the threads that run through its fabric. Ever since the Hebrews and Greeks made their great contributions to Western thought, it has been taken for granted that through the life of the mind man can transcend his physical being and reach new heights. Self-realization, discipline, loyalty, honor, and devotion are prevailing concepts in the literatures, philosophies, and moral precepts that have shaped and mirrored Western man for centuries.[1]

The necessity for such an underlying value system has been well established in the work of such eminent social critics of our age as C. S. Lewis and Richard Weaver. The case for such an underlying system must not depend upon the whims of debate with the relativistic, subjectivist spokesmen who today dominate so much of American education and thought. Those who hold that certain civilized values are worthy of transmission to the young, that some standards are acceptable and others are not, are on firm ground in their insistence that such values and standards must be the core of any meaningful educational framework.

Truth

The late C. S. Lewis, an urbane and untiring critic of the intellectual tendencies of the age, used the word *Tao* to convey the core of values and standards traditionally and universally accepted by men, in the Platonic, Aristotelian,

Stoic, Christian, and Oriental frameworks. The *Tao* assumes a fixed standard of principle and sentiment, an objective order to the universe, a higher value than a full stomach. As such, the *Tao* presupposes standards quite incompatible with the subjective, relativist suppositions of "modern" man. We are told by the relativists that the *Tao* must be set aside; the accumulated wisdom of centuries, the values of East as well as West, of Christian and non-Christian, the striving of the past to discover the higher side of man and man's conduct, must not stand in the path of "progress." Thus, the "revolt" of the "Now Generation."

Advances in technology account in part for the denial of our heritage. Since scientific and technological knowledge tends to accumulate (i.e., be subject to empirical verification as correct or incorrect, with the correct then added to the core of previously verified knowledge), many people assume that man's scientific progress means he has outgrown his past and has now become the master of his own fate. Moral questions are of a different order. Wisdom, not science or technology, points the way for progress here. For an individual to be inspired by the wisdom and moral rectitude of others, he must first make such wisdom his own. This is education in its finest sense.

Plato's "Rule of Right Reason"

To grasp the accumulated moral wisdom of the ages is to become habituated to such concerns and to their claims upon one's personal conduct. At that point, the rule of right reason, the goal which Plato set for education, becomes the guiding light of the individual.

This rule of right reason could provide the frame of reference so lacking in today's society. Many modern existentialists complain that the world is meaningless and absurd. It is not surprising that the world no longer has meaning for those who recognize none but materialistic values. The world of reason and freedom, the real world in which it matters a great deal what the individual chooses to do, is revealed only in the spiritual quality of man that so many moderns deny. It is this higher spiritual quality of the individual, evidenced in his creative capacity to choose, which alone can give meaning to life and transform the world of the individual. This is the recognition of those higher values that lead to Truth. Such an awareness on the part of the individual, such a rule of right reason, will be, in Berdyaev's words " . . . the triumph of the realm of spirit over that of Caesar. . . ." This triumph must be achieved anew by each individual as he strives for maturity . . . and his struggle for maturity constitutes the educative process.

A Higher Law

Despite our vaunted "modern breakthroughs in knowledge," it is doubtful that anyone now alive possesses more wisdom than a Plato, an Epictetus, a Paul, or an Augustine. Yet much of what passes for "education" in our time either denies this accumulation of past wisdom or belittles it in the eyes of the student. Truth, after all, is a measure of *what is*, a measure of an infinite realm within which the individual is constantly striving to improve his powers of perception. As the individual draws upon his heritage and applies self-discipline, he comes to recognize more and more of that truth and to understand it. The individual is thus able to find himself and his place in the universe, to become truly free, by recognizing a fixed truth, a definite right and wrong, not subject to change by human whim or political dictate. The individual can only be free when he serves a higher truth than political decree or unchecked appetite.

Such a definition of freedom in consonance with a higher law has its roots deep in the consciousness of civilized man.

> In early Hinduism that conduct in men which can be called good consists in conformity to, or almost participation in, the *Rta*—that great ritual or pattern of nature and supernature which is revealed alike in the cosmic order, the moral virtues, and the ceremonial of the temple. Righteousness, correctness, order, the *Rta*, is constantly identified with *satya* or truth, correspondence to reality. As Plato said that the Good was "beyond existence" and Wordsworth that through virtue the stars were strong, so the Indian masters say that the gods themselves are born of the *Rta* and obey it.
>
> The Chinese also speak of a great thing (the greatest thing) called the *Tao*. It is the reality beyond all predicates, the abyss that was before the Creator Himself. It is Nature, it is the Way, the Road. It is the Way in which the universe goes on, the Way in which things everlastingly emerge, stilly and tranquilly, into space and time. It is also the Way which every man should tread in imitation of that cosmic and super-cosmic progression, conforming all activities to that great exemplar. "In ritual," say the Analects, "it is harmony with Nature that is prized." The ancient Jews likewise praise the Law as being "true."[2]

Thus, the Christian insistence that man must order his affairs according to a higher law is far from unique. Such a view has been held in common by all civilized men. Our own early institutions of higher learning were deeply committed to the transmission of such a heritage. The nine colleges founded in America in the seventeenth and eighteenth centuries, (Harvard, Yale, Brown, Dartmouth, Columbia, Princeton, Pennsylvania, Rutgers, and William and Mary) were all of religious origin. Such was the early American view of education.

Human Freedom and the Soul of Man

There is a measure of truth in the Grand Inquisitor's assertion that many people do not wish to be free. Freedom can be painful, and someone like the Grand Inquisitor usually is at hand, quite willing to take over the chore of making decisions for others. Those civilizations which have prospered, however, have been peopled by those who appreciated the transcendent importance of their individuality and who valued the freedom necessary for its expression and fulfillment. "Education is not, as Bacon thought, a means of showing people how to get what they want; education is an exercise by means of which enough men, it is hoped, will learn to want what is worth having."

Education is an exercise by which men will learn to want what is worth having. This is a recurrent idea among Western thinkers. Aristotle wrote that the proper aim of education was to make the pupil like and dislike the proper things. Augustine defined the proper role of education as that which accorded to every object in the universe the kind and degree of love appropriate to it. In Plato's *Republic,* the well-educated youth is described as one . . .

who would see most clearly whatever was amiss in ill-made works of man or ill-grown works of nature, and with a just distaste would blame and hate the ugly even from his earliest years and would give delighted praise to beauty, receiving it into his soul and being nourished by it, so that he becomes a man of gentle heart. All this before he is of an age to reason; so that when Reason at length comes to him, then, bred as he has been, he will hold out his hands in welcome and recognize her because of the affinity he bears to her.

What is this higher side of human nature which can be cultivated, this higher side of man which will learn to want what is worth having? According to the standards of Western civilization, it is the human soul.

If we seek the prime root of all this, we are led to the acknowledgment of the full philosophical reality of that concept of the soul, so variegated in its connotations, which Aristotle described as the first principle of life in any organism and viewed as endowed with supramaterial intellect in man, and which Christianity revealed as the dwelling place of God and as made for eternal life. In the flesh and bones of man there exists a soul which is a spirit and which has a greater value than the whole physical universe. Dependent though we may be upon the lightest accidents of matter, the human person exists by the virtue of the existence of his soul, which dominates time and death. It is the spirit which is the root of personality.[4]

Our Choices Affect Our Lives

Some of those who espouse the idea of freedom are quick to declaim such terms as soul, God, or Higher Law, feeling that such "mysticism" denies the individual the capacity to freely choose since it binds him to a higher Authority. This is a groundless fear. In fact, the whole idea of a higher law and a God-given capacity for individual free choice only opens the door into a world in which man is constantly remaking the world as he modifies and expands his own horizons. It is precisely the fact that the soul of the individual derives from a higher order of nature that allows man to constantly remake the world and his own life according to his own understanding and his own perception. This is the source of the self-discipline which produces honor, integrity, courage, and the other attributes of civilized man. This is the source of the framework within which all meaningful, civilized choice takes place.

Still, the existentialists may be right about one point. It is true that man finds himself encased within a body and a material existence which he did not choose. It is also true that he finds himself limited by the ideas peculiar to his time. Even if he chooses to fight such ideas, the very nature of that choice and struggle is determined by the ideas he finds around him. This is why man is at once the molder and the molded, the actor and acted upon of history. We are all a part of an existential situation that is, and yet is not, of our own making. In a very real sense of the word, we are shaped by generations long past, yet have a role to play in the shaping process for generations to come. It is this capacity to choose, limited by the framework we have inherited, which man must come to understand and deal with if he is to be truly "educated."

> In principle, therefore, it does not matter whether one generation applauds the previous generation or hisses it—in either event, it carries the previous generation within itself. If the image were not so baroque, we might present the generations not horizontally but vertically, one on top of the other, like acrobats in the circus making a human tower. Rising one on the shoulders of another, he who is on top enjoys the sensation of dominating the rest; but he should also note that at the same time he is the prisoner of the others. This would serve to warn us that what has passed is not merely the past and nothing more, that we are not riding free in the air but standing on its shoulders, that we are in and of the past, a most definite past which continues the human trajectory up to the present moment, which could have been very different from what it was, but which, once having been, is irremediable—it is our present, in which, whether we like it or not, we thrash about like shipwrecked sailors.[5]

Unless he seeks only the freedom of shipwrecked sailors, freedom to drown in an existential sea, the individual desperately needs to recognize that his truly liberating capacity to choose is hinged upon a moral framework and certain civilized preconditions which at once limit and enhance his choice. It is this recognition that constitutes civilization.

Civilized Man

What is it then, that civilized man comes to value? One possible answer is given by Harold Gray, the creator of Little Orphan Annie and of the equally delightful Maw Green, Irish washerwoman and homey philosopher *par excellence.* In one of Gray's comic strips, he confronts Maw Green with a slobbering, unkempt, aggressive boob, who shouts, "I got rights, ain't I? I'm as good as any o' those big shots! *Nobody's* better'n *me*! I say all men are *born equal!* Ain't that right?"

Maw Green maintains her boundless good humor and agrees that all men are indeed born equal, but she turns aside to confide to the reader, "But thank Hiven a lot of folks outgrow it!"

Perhaps that civilizing task of "outgrowing it" is how the educative process can best help the individual. Yet in a time of collapsing standards, of "campus revolts," such a task for the educative process seems impossible of fulfillment. If so, Mario Savio and Mark Rudd may be samples of things to come, of tomorrow's torchbearers upon whom our civilization depends.

Surely, such a prospect is frightening to most of us. If we are to avoid such a fate, the underlying problem must be faced squarely: Does a proper definition of the nature of the universe and the nature and role of man within the universe presuppose the existence of a fixed standard of value, universally applicable to all men at all times? To accept such a view is to challenge directly the root assumption of the modern world . . . a world unwilling to accept the discipline inherent in such a fixed value system, a world finding self-congratulation in its illusory man-made heaven on earth, a heaven blending equal portions of subjectivism and relativism.

Man Must Be Free to Choose

There have been among us those men of intellect and integrity who have challenged the dominant mentality of the age, warning that man must be free to choose and yet properly instructed in the making of his choice. They have insisted that proper values can emerge and be defined by the passage of time and the accumulation of human experience. This accumulated wisdom, this framework of values, thus provides an enhancement of meaningful choice, not limiting but rather clarifying, the individual's power to decide. Such individual choice, plus the framework within which that choice takes place, is a reflection of higher values than society itself:

> Freedom of the human personality cannot be given by society, and by its source and nature it cannot depend upon society—it belongs to man himself, as a spiritual being. And society, unless it makes totalitarian claims, can only recognize this freedom. This basic truth about freedom was reflected in the doctrines of natural law, of the rights of man, independent of the state, of freedom, not only as freedom within society, but freedom from society with its limitless claims on man.[6]

To a maverick like Berdyaev, freedom was the key word, but even he admitted that man was a spiritual being and that nature had her own laws demanding respect from the individual as he made his choices.

Many others in the civilized tradition of individual freedom and a fixed moral framework have perceived that the individual must be not only free, but sufficiently educated in the proper values to permit intelligent choice. Albert Jay Nock, for instance, believed that

> . . . the Great Tradition would go on "because the forces of nature are on its side," and it had an invincible ally, "the self-preserving instinct of humanity." Men could forsake it, but come back to it they would. They had to, for their collective existence could not permanently go on without it. Whole societies might deny it, as America had done, substituting bread and buncombe, power and riches or expediency; "but in the end, they will find, as so many societies have already found, that they must return and seek the regenerative power of the Great Tradition, or lapse into decay and death."[7]

Nock was not alone in his insistence upon such standards for the education of future generations. He stood in the distinguished company of such men as Paul Elmer More, T. S. Eliot, C. S. Lewis, and Gilbert K. Chesterton, to name but a few of the defenders of the Great Tradition. These have been the civilized men of our age.

With Canon Bernard Iddings Bell, the distinguished Episcopal clergyman who saw so clearly the tendency of our times, we might ponder our future:

> I am quite sure that the trouble with us has been that we have not seriously and bravely put to ourselves the question, "What is man?" or, if and when we have asked it, we have usually been content with

answers too easy and too superficial. Most of us were trained to believe—and we have gone on the assumption ever since—that in order to be modern and intelligent and scholarly all that is required is to avoid asking "Why am I?" and immerse oneself in a vast detail of specialized study and in ceaseless activity. We have been so busy going ahead that we have lost any idea of where it is exactly that we are going or trying to go. This is, I do believe, the thing that has ruined the world in the last half century.[8]

We have lost our philosophic way in the educational community. We have often forgotten the moral necessity of freedom, and have usually forgotten the self-discipline which freedom must reflect if it is to function within the moral order. As parents, as human beings, as members of society, we must insist that our educational framework produce neither automatons nor hellions. The individual must be free to choose, yet must be provided with a framework of values within which meaningful, civilized choice can take place. That two-fold lesson must lie at the heart of any renaissance of American education.

---

1. Thomas Molnar, *The Future of Education*, p. 30.

2. C. S. Lewis, *The Abolition of Man*, pp. 27–28.

3. "Science and Human Freedom," *Manas*, February 28, 1968, p. 7.

4. Jacques Maritain, *Education at the Crossroads*, p. 8.

5. José Ortega y Gasset, *Man and Crisis*, pp. 53–54.

6. Nicholas Berdyaev, *The Realm of Spirit and The Realm of Caesar*, pp. 59–60.

7. Robert M. Crunden, *The Mind & Art of Albert Jay Nock*, p. 134.

8. Bernard Iddings Bell, *Crisis in Education*, p. 162.

Morals and Liberty

F. A. Harper

To many persons, the welfare state has become a symbol of morality and righteousness. This makes those who favor the welfare state appear to be the true architects of a better world; those who oppose it, immoral rascals who might be expected to rob banks or to do most anything in defiance of ethical conduct. But is this so? Is the banner of morality, when applied to the concept of the welfare state, one that is true or false?

Now what is the test of morality or immorality to be applied to the welfare state idea? I should like to pose five fundamental ethical concepts, as postulates, by which to test it. They are the ethical precepts found in the true Christian religion—true to its original foundations; and they are likewise found in other religious faiths, wherever and under whatever name these other religious concepts assist persons to perceive and practice the moral truths of human conduct.

After teaching at Cornell University for several years, Dr. Harper (1905–1973) joined the staff of The Foundation for Economic Education during its inaugural year of 1946. In 1961, he founded the Institute for Humane Studies, Inc., now located in Fairfax, Virginia. This article appeared in the July 1971 issue of *The Freeman*.

Moral Postulate No. 1

Economics and morals are both parts of one inseparable body of truth. They must, therefore, be in harmony with one another. What is right morally must also be right economically, and vice versa. Since morals are a guide to betterment and to self-protection, economic policies that violate moral truth, will, with certainty, cause degeneration and self-destruction.

This postulate may seem simple and self-evident. Yet many economists and others of my acquaintance, including one who was a most capable and admired teacher, presume to draw some kind of an impassable line of distinction between morals and economics. Such persons fail to test their economic concepts against their moral precepts. Some even scorn the moral base for testing economic concepts, as though it would somehow pollute their economic purity.

An unusually capable minister recently said that only a short time before, for the first time, he had come to realize the close connection and interharmony that exist between morals and economics. He had always tried to reserve one compartment for his religious thought and another separate one for his economic thought. "Fortunately," he said, in essence, "my economic thinking happened to be in harmony with my religious beliefs; but it frightens me now to realize the risk I was taking in ignoring the harmony that must exist between the two."

This viewpoint—that there is no necessary connection between morals and economics—is all too prevalent. It explains, I believe, why immoral economic acts are tolerated, if not actively promoted, by persons of high repute who otherwise may be considered to be persons of high moral standards.

Moral Postulate No. 2

There is a force in the universe which no mortal can alter. Neither you nor I nor any earthly potentate with all his laws and edicts can alter this rule of the universe, no matter how great one's popularity in his position of power. Some call this force God. Others call it Natural Law. Still others call it the Supernatural. But no matter how one may wish to name it, there is a force which rules without surrender to any mortal man or group of men—a force that is oblivious to anyone who presumes to elevate himself and his wishes above its rule.

This concept is the basis for all relationships of cause and consequence—all science—whether it be something already discovered or something yet to be discovered. Its scope includes phenomena such as those of physics and chemistry; it also includes those of human conduct. The so-called Law of Gravity is one expression of Natural Law. Scientific discovery means the unveiling to human perception of something that has always existed. If it had not existed prior to the discovery—even though we were ignorant of it—it could not have been there to be discovered. That is the meaning of the concept of Natural Law.

This view—there exists a Natural Law which rules over the affairs of human conduct—will be challenged by some who point out that man possesses the capacity for choice; that man's activity reflects a quality lacking in the chemistry of a stone and in the physical principle of the lever. But this trait of man—this capacity for choice—does not release him from the rule of cause and effect, which he can neither veto nor alter. What the capacity for choice means, instead, is that he is thereby enabled, by his own choice, to act either wisely or unwisely—that is, in either accord or discord with the truths of Natural Law. But once he has made his choice, the inviolate rule of cause and consequence takes over with an iron hand of justice, and renders unto the doer either a prize or a penalty, as the consequence of his choice.

It is important, at this point, to note that morality presumes the existence of choice. One cannot be truly moral except as there exists the option of being immoral, and except as he selects the moral rather than the immoral option. In the admirable words of Thomas Davidson: "That which is not free is not responsible, and that which is not responsible is not moral." This means that free choice is a prerequisite of morality.

If I surrender my freedom of choice to a ruler—by vote or otherwise—I am still subject to the superior rule of Natural Law or Moral Law. Although I am subservient to the ruler who orders me to violate truth, I must still pay the penalty for the evil or foolish acts in which I engage at his command.

Under this postulate—that there is a force in the universe which no mortal can alter—ignorance of Moral Law is no excuse to those who violate it, because Moral Law rules over the consequences of ignorance the same as over the consequences of wisdom. This is true whether the ignorance is accompanied by good intentions or not; whether it is carried out under the name of some religion or the welfare state or whatnot.

What, then, is the content of a basic moral code? What are the rules which, if followed, will better the condition of men?

Moral Postulate No. 3

The Golden Rule and the Decalogue, and their near equivalents in other great religions, provide the basic

moral codes for man's conduct. The Golden Rule and the Decalogue are basic moral guides having priority over all other considerations. It is these which have guided the conduct of man in all progressive civilizations. With their violation has come the downfall of individuals and civilizations.

Some may prefer as a moral code something like: "Do as God would have us do," or "Do as Jesus would have done." But such as these, alone, are not adequate guides to conduct unless they are explained further, or unless they serve as symbolic of a deeper specific meaning. What *would* God have us do? What *would* Jesus have done? Only by adding some guides such as the Golden Rule and the Ten Commandments can we know the answers to these questions.

The Golden Rule—the rule of refraining from imposing on others what I would not have them impose on me—means that moral conduct for one is moral conduct for another; that there is not one set of moral guides for Jones and another for Smith; that the concept of equality under Moral Law is a part of morality itself. This alone is held by many to be an adequate moral code. But in spite of its importance as part of the moral code of conduct in this respect, the Golden Rule is not, it seems to me, sufficient unto itself. It is no more sufficient than the mere admonition, "Do good," which leaves undefined what is good and what is evil. The murderer, who at the time of the crime felt justified in committing it, can quote the Golden Rule in self-defense: "If I had done what that so-and-so did, and had acted as he acted, I would consider it fair and proper for someone to murder me." And likewise the thief may argue that if he were like the one he has robbed, or if he were a bank harboring all those "ill-gotten gains," he would consider himself the proper object of robbery. Some claim that justification for the welfare state, too, is to be found in the Golden Rule. So, in addition to the Golden Rule, further rules are needed as guides for moral conduct.

The Decalogue embodies the needed guides on which the Golden Rule can function. But within the Ten Commandments, the two with which we shall be especially concerned herein are: (1) Thou shalt not steal. (2) Thou shalt not covet.

The Decalogue serves as a guide to moral conduct which, if violated, brings upon the violator a commensurate penalty. There may be other guides to moral conduct which one might wish to add to the Golden Rule and the Decalogue, as supplements or substitutes. But they serve as the basis on which others are built. Their essence, in one form or another, seems to run through all great religions. That, I believe, is not a happenstance, because if we embrace them as a guide to our conduct, our conduct will be both morally and economically sound.

This third postulate embodies what are judged to be the *principles* which should guide individual conduct as infallibly as the compass should guide the mariner. "Being practical" is a common popular guide to conduct; principles are scorned, if not forgotten. Those who scorn principles assert that it is foolish to concern ourselves with them; that it is hopeless to expect their complete adoption by everyone. But does this fact make a principle worthless? Are we to conclude that the moral code against murder is worthless because of its occasional violation? Or that the compass is worthless because not everyone pursues to the ultimate the direction which it indicates? Or that the law of gravity is made impractical or inoperative by someone walking off a cliff and meeting death because of his ignorance of this principle? No. A principle remains a principle in spite of its being ignored or violated—or even unknown. A principle, like a compass, gives one a better sense of direction, if he is wise enough to know and to follow its guidance.

Moral Postulate No. 4

Moral principles are not subject to compromise. The Golden Rule and the Decalogue, as representing moral principles, are precise and strict. They are not a code of convenience. A principle can be broken, but it cannot be bent.

If the Golden Rule and the Decalogue were to be accepted as a code of convenience, to be laid aside or modified whenever "necessity seems to justify it" (whenever, that is, one desires to act in violation of them), they would not then be serving as moral guides. A moral guide which is to be followed only when one would so conduct himself anyhow, in its absence, has no effect on his conduct, and is not a guide to him at all.

The unbending rule of a moral principle can be illustrated by some simple applications. According to one Commandment, it is wholly wrong to steal all your neighbor's cow; it is also wholly wrong to steal half your neighbor's cow, not half wrong to steal half your neighbor's cow. Robbing a bank is wrong in principle, whether the thief makes off with a million dollars or a hundred dollars or one cent. A person can rob a bank of half its money, but in the sense of moral principle there is no way to half rob a bank; you either rob it or you do not rob it.

In like manner, the law of gravity is precise and indivisible. One either acts in harmony with this law or he does not. There is no sense in saying that one has only half-observed the law of gravity if he falls off a cliff only half as high as another cliff off which he might have fallen.

Moral laws are strict. They rule without flexibility. They know not the language of man; they are not conversant with him in the sense of compassion. They employ no man-made devices like the suspended sentence—"Guilty" or "Not guilty" is the verdict of judgment by a moral principle.

As moral guides, the Golden Rule and the Decalogue are not evil and dangerous things, like a painkilling drug, to be taken in cautious moderation, if at all. Presuming them to be the basic guides of what is right and good for civilized man, one cannot overindulge in them. Good need not be practiced in moderation.

Moral Postulate No. 5

Good ends cannot be attained by evil means. As stated in the second postulate, there is a force controlling cause and consequence which no mortal can alter, in spite of any position of influence or power which he may hold. Cause and consequence are linked inseparably.

An evil begets an evil consequence; a good, a good consequence. Good intentions cannot alter this relationship. Nor can ignorance of the consequence change its form. Nor can words. For one to say, after committing an evil act, "I'm sorry, I made a mistake," changes not one iota the consequence of the act; repentance, at best, can serve only to prevent repetition of the evil act, and perhaps assure the repenter a more preferred place in a Hereafter. But repentance *alone* does not bring back to life a murdered person, nor return the loot to the one who was robbed. Nor does it, I believe, fully obliterate the scars of evil on the doer himself.

Nor does saying, "He told me to do it," change the consequence of an evil act into a good one. For an evildoer to assert, "But it was the law of my government, the decree of my ruler," fails to dethrone God or to frustrate the rule of Natural Law.

The belief that good ends are attainable through evil means is one of the most vicious concepts of the ages. The political blueprint, *The Prince,* written around the year 1500 by Machiavelli, outlined this notorious doctrine. And for the past century it has been part and parcel of the kit of tools used by the Marxian communist-socialists to mislead people. Its use probably is as old as the conflict between temptation and conscience, because it affords a seemingly rational and pleasant detour around the inconveniences of one's conscience.

We know how power-hungry persons have gained political control over others by claiming that they somehow possess a special dispensation from God to do good through the exercise of means which our moral code identifies as evil. Thus arises a multiple standard of morals. It is the device by which immoral persons attempt to discredit the Golden Rule and the Decalogue, and make them inoperative.

Yet if one will stop to ponder the question just a little, he must surely see the unimpeachable logic of this postulate: Good ends cannot be attained by evil means. This is because the end pre-exists in the means, just as in the biological field we know that the seed of continued likeness pre-exists in the parent. Likewise in the moral realm, there is a similar moral reproduction wherein like begets like. This precludes the possibility of evil means leading to good ends. Good begets good; evil, evil. Immoral means cannot beget a good end, any more than snakes can beget roses.

The concept of the welfare state can now be tested against the background of these five postulates: (1) Harmony exists between moral principles and wise economic practices. (2) There is a universal law of cause and effect, even in the areas of morals and economics. (3) A basic moral code exists in the form of the Golden Rule and the Decalogue. (4) These moral guides are of an uncompromising nature. (5) Good ends are attainable only through good means.

Moral Right to Private Property

Not all the Decalogue, as has been said, is directly relevant to the issue of the welfare state. Its program is an economic one, and the only parts of the moral code which are directly and specifically relevant are these: (1) Thou shalt not steal. (2) Thou shalt not covet.

Steal what? Covet what? Private property, of course. What else could I steal from you, or covet of what is yours? I cannot steal from you or covet what you do not own as private property. As Dr. D. Elton Trueblood has aptly said: "Stealing is evil because ownership is good." Thus we find that the individual's right to private property is an unstated assumption which underlies the Decalogue. Otherwise these two admonitions would be empty of either purpose or meaning.

The right to have and to hold private property is not to be confused with the recovery of stolen property. If someone steals your car, it is still—by this moral right—your car rather than his; and for you to repossess it is merely to bring its presence back into harmony with its ownership. The same reasoning applies to the recovery of equivalent value if the stolen item itself is no longer returnable; and it applies to the recompense for damage done to one's own property by trespass or other willful destruction of private property. These means of protecting the possession of private property, and its use, are part of the mechanisms used to protect the moral right to private property.

Another point of possible confusion has to do with coveting the private property of another. There is nothing morally wrong in the admiration of something that is the property of another. Such admiration may be a stimulus to work for the means with which to buy it, or one like it. The moral consideration embodied in this Commandment has to do with thoughts and acts leading to the violation of the other Commandment, though still short of actual theft.

The moral right to private property, therefore, is consistent with the moral codes of all the great religious beliefs. It is likely that a concept of this type was in the mind of David Hume, the moral philosopher, who believed that the right to own private property is the basis for the modern concept of justice in morals.

Nor is it surprising to discover that two of history's leading exponents of the welfare state concept found it necessary to denounce this moral code completely. Marx said: "Religion is the opium of the people." And Lenin said: "Any religious idea, any idea of a 'good God' . . . is an abominably nasty thing." Of course they would have to say these things about religious beliefs. This is because the moral code of these great religions, as we have seen, strikes at the very heart of their immoral economic scheme. Not only does their welfare state scheme deny the moral right to private property, but it also denies other underlying bases of the moral code, as we shall see.

Moral Right to Work and to Have

Stealing and coveting are condemned in the Decalogue as violations of the basic moral code. It follows, then, that the concepts of stealing and coveting presume the right to private property, which then automatically becomes an implied part of the basic moral code. But where does private property come from?

Private property comes from what one has saved out of what he has produced, or has earned as a productive employee of another person. One may also, of course, obtain private property through gifts and inheritances; but in the absence of theft, precluded by this moral code, gifts come from those who have produced or earned what is given. So the right of private property, and also the right to have whatever one has produced or earned, underlies the admonitions in the Decalogue about stealing and coveting. Nobody has the moral right to take by force from the producer anything he has produced or earned, for any purpose whatsoever—even for a good purpose, as he thinks of it.

If one is free to have what he has produced and earned, it then follows that he also has the moral right to be free to choose his work. He should be free to choose his work, that is, so long as he does not violate the moral code in doing so by using in his productive efforts the property of another person through theft or trespass. Otherwise he is free to work as he will, at what he will, and to change his work when he will. Nobody has the moral right to force him to work when he does not choose to do so, or to force him to remain idle when he wishes to work, or to force him to work at a certain job when he wishes to work at some other available job. The belief of the master that his judgment is superior to that of the slave or vassal, and that control is "for his own good," is not a moral justification for the idea of the welfare state.

We are told that some misdoings occurred in a Garden of Eden, which signify the evil in man. And I would concede that no mortal man is totally wise and good. But it is my belief that people generally, up and down the road, are intuitively and predominantly moral. By this I mean that if persons are confronted with a clear and simple decision involving basic morals, most of us will conduct ourselves morally. Most everyone, without being a learned scholar of moral philosophy, seems to have a sort of innate sense of what is right, and tends to do what is moral *unless and until he becomes confused by circumstances which obscure the moral issue that is involved.*

Immorality Is News

The content of many magazines and newspapers with widespread circulations would seem to contradict my belief that most people are moral most of the time. They headline impressive and unusual events on the seamy side of life, which might lead one to believe that these events are characteristic of everyday human affairs. It is to be noted, however, that their content is in sharp contrast to the local, hometown daily or weekly with its emphasis on the folksy reports of the comings and goings of friends. Why the difference? Those with large circulations find that the common denominator of news interest in their audience is events on the rare, seamy side of life; widely scattered millions are not interested in knowing that in Centerville, Sally attended Susie's birthday party last Tuesday. It is the rarity of evil conduct that makes it impressive news for millions. Papers report the event of yesterday's murder, theft, or assault, together with the name, address, age, marital status, religious affiliation, and other descriptive features of the guilty party because these are the events of the day that are unusual enough to be newsworthy. What would be the demand for a newspaper which published all the names and identifications of all the persons who yesterday failed to murder, steal, or assault? If it were as rare for persons to act morally as it is now rare for them to act immorally, the then rare instances of moral conduct would presumably become the news of the day. So we may conclude that evil is news because it is so rare; that being moral is not news because it is so prevalent.

But does not this still prove the dominance of evil in persons? Or, since magazines and newspapers print what finds a ready readership in the market, does not that prove the evilness of those who read of evil? I believe not. It is more like the millions who attend zoos, and view with fascination the monkeys and the snakes; these spectators are not themselves monkeys or snakes, nor do they want to be; they are merely expressing an interest in the unusual, without envy. Do not most of us read of a bank robbery or a fire without wishing to be robbers or arsonists?

What else dominates the newspaper space, and gives us our dominant impressions about the quality of persons outside our circle of immediate personal acquaintance? It is mostly about the problems of political power; about those who have power or are grasping for power, diluted with a little about those who are fighting against power. Lord Acton said: "Power tends to corrupt, and absolute power corrupts absolutely." This dictum seems to be true, as history has proved and is proving over and over again. So we can then translate it into a description of much of the news of the day: News is heavily loaded with items about persons who, as Lord Acton said, are either corrupt or are in the process of becoming more corrupt.

If one is not careful in exposing himself to the daily news—if he fails to keep his balance and forgets how it contrasts with all those persons who comprise his family, his neighbors, his business associates, and his friends—he is likely to conclude falsely that people are predominantly immoral. This poses a serious problem for historians and historical novelists to the extent that their source of information is the news of a former day—especially if they do not interpret it with caution.

To Steal or Not to Steal

As a means of specifically verifying my impression about the basic, intuitive morality of persons, I would pose this test of three questions:

1. Would you steal your neighbor's cow to provide for your present needs? Would you steal it for any need reasonably within your expectation or comprehension? It should be remembered that, instead of stealing his cow, you may explore with your neighbor the possible solution to your case of need; you might arrange to do some sort of work for him, or to borrow from him for later repayment, or perhaps even plead with him for an outright gift.

2. Would you steal your neighbor's cow to provide for a known case of another neighbor's need?

3. Would you try to induce a third party to do the stealing of the cow, to be given to this needy neighbor? And do you believe that you would likely succeed in inducing him to engage in the theft?

I believe that the almost universal answer to all these questions would be: "No." Yet the facts of the case are that all of us are participating in theft every day. How? By supporting the actions of the collective agent which does the stealing as part of the welfare state program already far advanced in the United States. By this device, Peter is robbed to "benefit" Paul, with the acquiescence if not the active support of all of us as taxpayers and citizens. We not only participate in the stealing—and share in the division of the loot—but as its victims we also meekly submit to the thievery.

Isn't it a strange thing that if you select any three fundamentally moral persons and combine them into a collective for the doing of good, they are liable at once to become three immoral persons in their collective activities? The moral principles with which they seem to be intuitively endowed are somehow lost in the confusing processes of the collective. None of the three would steal the cow from one of his fellow members as an individual, but collectively they all steal cows from each other. The reason is, I believe, that the welfare state—a confusing collective device which is believed by many to be moral and righteous—has been falsely labeled. This false label has caused the belief that the welfare state can do no wrong, that it cannot commit immoral acts, especially if those acts are approved or tolerated by more than half of the people, "democratically."

This sidetracking of moral conduct is like the belief of an earlier day: The king can do no wrong. In its place we have now substituted this belief: The majority can do no wrong. It is as though one were to assert that a sheep which has been killed by a pack of wolves is not really dead, provided that more than half of the wolves have participated in the killing. All these excuses for immoral conduct are, of course, nonsense. They are nonsense when tested against the basic moral code of the five postulates. Thievery is thievery, whether done by one person alone or by many in a pack—or by one who has been selected by the members of the pack as their agent.

"Thou Shalt Not Steal, Except. . . ."

It seems that wherever the welfare state is involved, the moral precept, "Thou shalt not steal," becomes altered to say: "Thou shalt not steal, except for what thou deemest to be a worthy cause, where thou thinkest that thou canst use the loot for a better purpose than wouldst the victim of the theft."

And the precept about covetousness, under the administration of the welfare state, seems to become: "Thou shalt not covet, except what thou wouldst have from thy neighbor who owns it."

Both of these alterations of the Decalogue result in complete abrogation of the two moral admonitions—theft and covetousness— which deal directly with economic matters. Not even the motto, "In God we trust," stamped by the government on money taken by force in violation of the Decalogue to pay for the various programs of the welfare state, can transform this immoral act into a moral one.

Herein lies the principal moral and economic danger facing us in these critical times: Many of us, albeit with good intentions but in a hurry to do good because of the urgency of the occasion, have become victims of moral schizophrenia. While we are good and righteous persons in our individual conduct in our home community and in our basic moral code, we have become thieves and coveters in the collective activities of the welfare state in which we participate and which many of us extol.

Typical of our times is what usually happens when there is a major catastrophe, destroying private property or injuring many persons. The news circulates, and generates widespread sympathy for the victims. So what is done about it? Through the mechanisms of the collective, the good intentions take the form of reaching into the other fellow's pocket for the money with which to make a gift. The Decalogue says, in effect: "Reach into your *own* pocket—not into your neighbor's pocket—to finance your acts of compassion; good cannot be done with the loot that comes from theft." The pickpocket, in other words, is a thief even though he puts the proceeds in the collection box on Sunday, or uses it to buy bread for the poor. Being an involuntary Good Samaritan is a contradiction in terms.

When thievery is resorted to for the means with which to do good, compassion is killed. Those who would do good with the loot then lose their capacity for self-reliance, the same as a thief's self-reliance atrophies rapidly when he subsists on food that is stolen. And those who are repeatedly robbed of their property simultaneously lose their capacity for compassion. The chronic victims of robbery are under great temptation to join the gang and share in the loot. They come to feel that the voluntary way of life will no longer suffice for needs; that to subsist, they must rob and be robbed. They abhor violence, of course, but approve of robbing by "peaceful means." It is this peculiar immoral distinction which many try to draw between the welfare state of Russia and that of Britain: The Russian brand of violence, they believe, is bad; that of Britain, good. This version of an altered Commandment would be: "Thou shalt not steal, except from nonresisting victims."

Under the welfare state, this process of theft has spread from its use in alleviating catastrophe, to anticipating catastrophe, to conjuring up catastrophe, to the "need" for luxuries for those who have them not. The acceptance of the practice of thus violating the Decalogue has become so widespread that if the Sermon on the Mount were to appear in our day in the form of an address or publication, it would most likely be scorned as "reactionary, and not objective on the realistic problems of the day." Forgotten, it seems, by many who so much admire Christ, is the fact that he did not resort to theft in acquiring the means of his material benefactions. Nor did he advocate theft for any purpose—even for those uses most dear to his beliefs.

Progress of Moral Decay

Violation of the two economic Commandments—theft and covetousness—under the program of the welfare state, will spread to the other Commandments; it will destroy faith in, and observance of, our entire basic moral code. We have seen this happen in many countries. It seems to have been happening here. We note how immorality, as tested by the two economic Commandments, has been spreading in high places. Moral decay has already spread to such an extent that violations of all other parts of the Decalogue, and of the Golden Rule, have become accepted as commonplace—even proper and worthy of emulation.

And what about the effectiveness of a crime investigation conducted under a welfare state government? We may question the presumed capability of such a government—as distinct from certain investigators who are admittedly moral individuals—to judge these moral issues. We may also question the wisdom of bothering to investigate the picayune amounts of private gambling, willingly engaged in by the participants with their own money, when untold billions are being taken from the people repeatedly by the investigating agent to finance its own immoral program. This is a certain loss, not even a gamble.

Once a right to collective looting has been substituted for the right of each person to have whatever he has produced, it is not at all surprising to find the official dispensers deciding that it is right for them to loot the loot—for a "worthy" purpose, of course. Then we have the loot used by the insiders to buy votes so that they may stay in power; we have political pork barrels and lobbying for the contents; we have political patronage for political loyalty—even for loyalty to immoral conduct; we have deep freezers and mink coats given to political or personal favorites, and bribes for the opportunity to do privileged business with those who hold and dispense the loot. Why not? If it is right to loot, it is also right to loot the loot. If the latter is wrong, so also is the former.

If we are to accept Lord Acton's axiom about the corrupting effect of power—and also the reasoning of Professor Hayek in his book *The Road to Serfdom*, about why the worst get to the top in a welfare state—then corruption and low moral standards in high political places should not be surprising. But when the citizens come more and more to laugh and joke about it, rather than to remove the crown of power and dismantle the throne, a nation is well on its way to moral rot, reminiscent of the fall of the Roman Empire and others.

Nor should we be surprised that there is some juvenile delinquency where adult delinquency is so rampant, and where the absence of any basic moral code among adults precludes even the possibility of their effectively teaching a moral code that will prevent delinquency in the young. If, as adults, we practice collective thievery through the welfare state, and advocate it as right and good, how can we question the logic of the youths who likewise form gangs and rob the candy store? If demonstration is the best teacher, we adults must start with the practice of morality ourselves, rather than hiring some presumed specialist to study the causes of similar conduct among the youngsters; their conduct is the symptom, not the disease.

Thievery and covetousness will persist and grow, and the basic morals of ourselves, our children, and our children's children will continue to deteriorate unless we destroy the virus of immorality that is embedded in the concept of the welfare state; unless we come to understand how the moral code of individual conduct must apply also to collective conduct, because the collective is composed solely of individuals. Moral individual conduct cannot persist in the face of collective immorality under the welfare state program. One side or the other of the double standard of morals will have to be surrendered.

Appendix: The Welfare State Idea

The concept of the welfare state appears in our everyday life in the form of a long list of labels and programs such as: Social Security; parity or fair prices; reasonable profits; the living wage; the TVA, MVA, CVA; federal aid to states, to education, to bankrupt corporations; and so on.

But all these names and details of the welfare state program tend only to obscure its essential nature. They are well-sounding labels for a laudable objective—the relief of distressing need, prevention of starvation, and the like. But how best is starvation and distress to be prevented? It is well, too, that prices, profits, and wages be fair and equitable. But what is to be the test of fairness and equity? Laudable objectives alone do not assure the success of any program; a fair appraisal of the program must include an analysis of the means of its attainment. The welfare state is a name that has been substituted as a more acceptable one for communism-socialism wherever, as in the United States, these names are in general disrepute.

The welfare state plan, viewed in full bloom of completeness, is one where the state prohibits the individual from having any right of choice in the conditions and place of his work; it takes ownership of the product of his labor; it prohibits private property. All these are done ostensibly to help those whose rights have been taken over by the welfare state.

But these characteristics of controlled employment and confiscation of income are not those used in promotion of the idea of the welfare state. What are usually advertised, instead, are the "benefits" of the welfare state—the grants of food and housing and whatnot—which the state "gives" to the people. But all these "benefits" are merely the other side of the forfeited rights to choose one's own occupation and to keep whatever one is able to produce. In the same sense that the welfare state grants benefits, the slave master grants to his slaves certain allotments of food and other economic goods. In fact, slavery might be described as just another form of welfare state, because of its likeness in restrictions and "benefits."

Yet the state, as such, produces nothing with which to supply these "benefits." Persons produce everything which the welfare state takes, before it gives some back as "benefits"; but in the process, the bureaucracy takes its cut. Only by thus confiscating what persons have produced can the welfare state "satisfy the needs of the people." So, the necessary and essential idea of the welfare state is to control the economic actions of the vassals of the state, to take from producers what they produce, and to prevent their ever being able to attain economic independence from the state and from their fellow men through ownership of property.

To whatever extent an individual is still allowed freedom in any of these respects while living under a government like the present one in the United States, then to that extent the development of the program of the welfare state is as yet not fully completed. Or perhaps it is an instance of a temporary grant of freedom by the welfare state such as when a master allows his slave a day off from work to spend as he likes; but the person who is permitted some freedom by the welfare state is still a vassal of that state just as a slave is still a slave on his day off from work.

The Idea of Equality

Jarret B. Wollstein

It is doubtful if any social concept in the entire history of man has been more fervently championed, more fiercely denounced, more misunderstood, more poorly defined, or more misrepresented than the idea of equality.

Many Christians proclaim all men "equal in the eyes of God." The United States was founded on the principle of "equality of rights." The basis of modern Western jurisprudence is "equality before the law." The rallying cry of the French Revolution was "Liberty, Equality, Fraternity." A central goal of communism and socialism is "economic equality." The American Civil Rights Movement seeks "equality of opportunity." And the modern women's movement champions "equal rights for women" and "equal pay for equal work."

While the meaning and compatibility of this multitude of "equalities" is far from clear, it is obvious that they do not all mean the same thing. Just what *does* equality mean?

What Is Equality?

For two things to be equal means for them to be identical in some respect. Thus if two trees are both precisely six feet tall, they are equal in height. If two men both earn pre-

Mr. Wollstein is a founder of the Society for Individual Liberty and author of *Society Without Coercion*. This article is reprinted from the April 1980 issue of *The Freeman*.

cisely $9,500 a year, they are equal in income. And if two people both have the same chance of winning a lottery, they have (in that respect) equality of opportunity.

However, while two things may be identical with respect to one or a limited number of attributes, no two physical objects can ever be identical with respect to *all* attributes. For example, all atoms differ in position, direction, and history. And all human beings differ with respect to anatomy, biochemistry, temperament, knowledge, skills, goals, virtue, and a thousand other characteristics.

Here we will primarily be concerned with three types of equality:

1. *Political equality,* a major goal of both the American and French revolutions, has *traditionally* meant equality of individual rights and equality of liberty. Stated simply, political equality means that the individual's right to life, liberty, and property is respected and that government abstains from conferring any special advantage or inflicting any special harm upon one individual (or group) in distinction to another. Clearly, political equality is at best only approximated and never exists completely.

2. *Economic equality* means in essence that people have the same income or total wealth.

3. *Social equality* generally means either (a) equality of social status, (b) equality of opportunity, or (c) equality of treatment. Social equality is also increasingly coming to mean (d) equality of achievement.

Equality and Liberty

A little reflection will quickly demonstrate that economic and social equality can only be achieved at the expense of political equality. Because people differ in ability, drive, intelligence, strength, and many other attributes it follows that, with liberty, people also will differ in achievement, status, income, and wealth. A talented singer will command a higher income than a ditchdigger. A frugal, hardworking man generally will accumulate more wealth than an indolent spendthrift. A brilliant scientist will command more respect than a skid row bum.

Nor are all of these differences of social and economic achievement the result of environment. Because people are individuals—genetically, biochemically, anatomically, and neurologically—differences in strength, intelligence, aggressiveness, and other traits will always exist. While environmental factors can and do exaggerate physical and mental differences between people, diversity and non-equality remain the natural biological order and hence are the natural social and economic order.

There is only one way to make all people even approximately economically or socially equal, and that is through the forcible redistribution of wealth and the legal prohibition of social distinction.

As Dr. Robert Nozick, of the Harvard Philosophy Department, has pointed out in *Anarchy, State, and Utopia*, economic equality requires a continuous and unending series of government interventions into private transactions. Even if people's incomes are made equal once, they will quickly become unequal if they have the liberty to spend their own money. For example, many more people will choose to pay $10 to hear Linda Ronstadt sing than will pay $10 to hear me sing, and Linda Ronstadt will very quickly become far wealthier than I am.

Economic equality can thus only be maintained by totalitarian control of people's lives, and the substitution of the decisions of a handful of state authorities for the free choices of millions of men and women.

Political equality is fundamentally inimical to economic and social equality. Free men are not economically equal, and economically equal men are not free. Because the achievement of social and economic equality inherently requires the forcible interference with voluntary choice, I will subsequently refer to the doctrine that social or economic equality should be imposed upon a society as *coercive egalitarianism*.

Equality as an Ethical Ideal

In reality people are unequal: Americans are—on average—far wealthier than Russians, doctors tend to earn more than garbage collectors, and so on. But *should* people be unequal?

At its root, egalitarianism is an ethical doctrine. It is often asserted that "ethics is just a matter of opinion" and that "one moral system is just as good as any other." But in fact any ethical code can be judged by at least three criteria: *(1) is it logical?*—have the basic concepts of the doctrine been meaningfully defined and are the arguments for it valid; *(2) is it realistic?*—is it a doctrine which human beings can live by, or does it require that people act in a way which is fundamentally contrary to their nature; and *(3) is it desirable?*—are the consequences of adopting the doctrine what are claimed, or would they be something entirely different; and if people adopt this doctrine will it lead to the creation of a society in which they are happy and fulfilled, or will it lead to a society of hopelessness, repression, and despair?

Let us now apply these criteria to the doctrine of coercive egalitarianism.

1. Is coercive egalitarianism logical? Egalitarianism states that all people should be equal, but few coercive egalitarians define "equality."

As stated previously, *complete* equality between people is an impossibility, so it can be rejected at once. But we are hardly better off when we speak of social or economic equality. Does "economic equality" mean equal income at a given age, for a given job, for a certain amount of work, or for a particular occupation? Does "equal wealth" mean identical possessions, possessions of identical value, or something entirely different? Does "social equality" mean equal status, equal popularity, equal opportunity, equal treatment, or what? All of these concepts of economic and social equality are distinctly different, and until they are defined, the doctrine of egalitarianism is illogical.

2. Is coercive egalitarianism realistic? People are different and have different values. To some happiness requires many material possessions, to others material possessions are relatively unimportant. To some people intelligence is a great value, to others strength or beauty are far more important. Because people differ both in their own characteristics and in the way in which they value traits in others, people will naturally discriminate in favor of some persons and against others.

Since variety and distinction are natural parts of the human condition, by demanding that people abandon such distinctions, coercive egalitarianism is contrary to human nature.

3. Is coercive egalitarianism desirable? Coercive egalitarianism, the doctrine of complete social and economic equality of human beings, logically implies a world of identical, faceless, interchangeable people. Such a world sounds much more like a nightmare than a dream, and indeed it is.

Perhaps no nation on earth has come closer to complete economic and social equality than Pol Pot's Cambodia. Under Pol Pot's regime entire populations were forcibly marched out of cities and everyone, regardless of age, sex, skills, or previous social status, was forced to labor with primitive agricultural implements on collective farms. In Pol Pot's Cambodia, everyone had to think, work, and believe the same; dissenters were killed on the spot.

In northern Cambodia stands the remains of one of Pol Pot's "model villages." The houses are neat, clean, and completely identical. Nearby sits a mass open grave with hundreds of human skeletons—the pitiful remains of those who displayed the slightest individuality. The village and mass grave are a fitting symbol of the fruits of coercive egalitarianism.

While coercive egalitarianism masquerades as an ethical doctrine, in fact it is the opposite. Ethics presumes that one can make a distinction between right and wrong for human beings. But coercive egalitarianism demands that we treat people equally, regardless of their differences, including differences in virtue. To demand that virtuous and villainous people—for example, Thomas Edison and Charles Manson—be treated equally, is to make ethical distinction impossible *in principle.*

In summary, coercive egalitarianism is illogical because it never defines precisely what "equality" consists of; it is unrealistic because it requires that we deny our values; and it is undesirable because it ultimately requires a society of human insects.

While coercive egalitarianism fails as an ethical doctrine, many contentions based upon coercive egalitarianism nevertheless remain emotionally compelling to many people. Let us now examine some of those contentions.

Myths of Egalitarianism

1. *Social and economic inequality are a result of coercion, an accident of birth, or unfair advantage.* Let us consider these contentions one at a time.

It is certainly true that *some* inequality is a result of coercion in such forms as conquest, theft, confiscatory taxes or political power. But it is hardly true that all inequality is a result of coercion. A person can, after all, become wealthy or popular because he or she is highly talented or extremely inventive, and talent and invention coerce no one.

Being born wealthy certainly constitutes an advantage, but hardly an insurmountable or unfair one. Sociological studies in the United States and Europe show tremendous mobility between lower, middle, and upper classes, despite advantages and disadvantages of birth. Except for all but the greatest fortunes, one's parents' wealth and success are no guarantee of one's own wealth or success. And there is nothing immoral about helping out one's own children as much as possible. Such aid takes away nothing to which anyone else is entitled.

Last, there is the argument that being born with below-average intelligence, or strength, or attractiveness constitutes an "unfair disadvantage." Here egalitarianism reveals itself to be (in the words of Dr. Murray Rothbard) "a revolt against nature." We can either act rationally and rejoice in our diversity and make the most of the abilities we do have, or we can damn nature and hate everyone who is in any way better than we are and attempt to drag them down to our level. I leave it to you which is the more rational and humane policy.

2. If people would only share the world's bounty equally, there would be enough for everyone, and no one need starve or be seriously deprived. This contention is based upon two false assumptions: (a) that wealth is a natural resource, so one person's gain is another's loss; and (b) that if the world's wealth were equally redistributed it would remain constant.

Wealth in fact is a product of human productivity and invention. Some people are poor *not* because others are wealthy, but because the poor are insufficiently productive (often because of authoritarian political systems).

Any attempt to redistribute the world's wealth by force would also greatly diminish the total wealth in existence for at least three reasons: (a) large-scale redistribution would disrupt the world's productive machinery, (b) confiscation of wealth would destroy the incentive to produce more (why bother producing if it's going to be taken from you anyway), and (c) the process of redistribution would require an enormously costly and essentially parasitic bureaucracy. (Not to mention losses from shooting people who resist, and starvation from bureaucratic inefficiency and mistakes.)

The cure for poverty is more productivity, less state economic intervention, and an end to barriers to trade. The cure is not redistribution of wealth.

3. It is better that everyone be poor than for some to have more than others. Better for whom? For the middle class and wealthy stripped of their property? For the poor robbed of the possibility of ever improving their lot?

The production and accumulation of wealth is the benchmark of human progress. Wealth in the form of better communications systems, environmental control, pest control, improved transportation, better medical care, more durable and attractive clothing, more comfortable housing, and so on, *ad infinitum,* improves the quality and increases the quantity of human life and makes possible leisure, science, and art. To attack wealth is to attack an essential condition for the achievement of virtually every human value from the fulfillment of physiological needs, to safety, to the pursuit of beauty and truth.

This argument reveals the ultimate and ugly motive of many egalitarians: A hatred of human ability per se. By that hatred they betray their human heritage and would condemn men to exist at the level of barbarians.

Free and Unequal vs. Coercive Egalitarianism

Equality of rights and equality under the law are preconditions for any just and humane society. But such political equality is the very antithesis of coercive egalitarianism.

Coercive egalitarianism asserts that people ought to be made equal *by force,* and that ability and virtue should be ignored or punished to bring all people down to the lowest common denominator.

The disabilities of others should evoke our compassion. But those disabilities do not justify the forced looting of the productive or the obliteration of liberty in the name of some undefined concept of equality.

The natural order of human society is diversity, variety, and inequality. The fruits of that natural order are progress, productivity, and invention. In the final analysis, virtue and compassion can only flourish in a world of men and women free and unequal.

Justice and Freedom

Leslie Snyder

The administration of a republic is supposed to be directed by certain fundamental principles of right and justice, from which there cannot, because there ought not to, be any deviation; and whenever any deviation appears, there is a kind of stepping out of the republican principle, and an approach toward the despotic one.

—THOMAS PAINE

* * *

Justice is the only foundation upon which a society of free and independent people can exist. Justice is a concrete, recognizable, and objective principle. It is not a matter of opinion.

In our day and age the word justice is rarely used in political and economic discussions. The entire reason for the existence of communities, laws, governments, and court systems has been forgotten. But if life and property are to be protected and secured, which is the purpose of society, then justice *must* be the rule. To quote Paine again, "A republic, properly understood, is a sovereignty of justice."

According to a 1931 Webster's dictionary, justice is the

This article, which appeared in the March 1980 issue of *The Freeman,* is excerpted from Ms. Snyder's book *Justice or Revolution* (1979).

"quality of being just; impartiality." Just is "conforming to right; normal; equitable." A 1961 Webster's dictionary says justice is "The principle of rectitude and just dealings of men with each other—one of the cardinal virtues. Administration of law. . ." A 1975 edition of a Grolier Webster dictionary says justice is "Equitableness; what is rightly due; lawfulness. . . ."

Since 1931 a new meaning of the word justice has been added, that of lawfulness, which is not only erroneous, but deceitful and misleading. Justice is not based on law; rather, law ought to be based on justice. It is only common sense, for men lived and worked together before laws were formed. Generally laws are passed to formalize what has preceded under common practice, what has stood the test of time as being just and equitable. Laws are common practice put down in black and white for all to see and know.

The ancient philosophers said that justice is speaking the truth and paying your debts, giving to each man what is proper to him, doing good to friends and evil to enemies. Therefore, there must be something more basic, more fundamental than laws on which to found justice. In fact, the French jurist Charles de Montesquieu (1689–1755) ably contended that "before laws were made, there were relations of possible justice. To say that there is nothing just or unjust but what is commanded or forbidden by positive laws, is the same as saying that before the describing of a circle all the radii were not equal."

Minding One's Own Business

The Greek philosophers had the simplest definition of justice. To Plato (c. 428–348 B.C.), in *The Republic*, Book IV, justice is simply "doing one's own business, and not being a busybody. . . . A man may neither take what is another's, nor be deprived of what is his own. . . . This is the ultimate cause and condition of the existence of all" other virtues in the state, "and while remaining in them is also their preservative."

In Book XII of Plato's *Laws,* the conclusion is drawn that "by the relaxation of that justice which is the uniting principle of all constitutions, every power in the state is rent asunder from every other." In other words, without justice the threads of society unravel and society disintegrates into barbarism.

Aristotle (384–322 B.C.) in *Nicomachean Ethics,* Book V, gives greater perception to what justice is. It "is found among men who share their life with a view to self-sufficiency, men who are free. . . . Therefore *justice is essentially something human.*" (Emphasis added.) In other words, free men may choose to be just or unjust. Justice, as an ethical term, is voluntary; ". . . a man acts unjustly or justly whenever he does such acts voluntarily." When wrong is done and done voluntarily, it then becomes an act of injustice. In short, "All virtue is summed up in dealing justly," said Aristotle.

More concretely, Aristotle claims, in *Rhetoric,* Book I, "Justice is the virtue through which everybody enjoys his own possessions in accordance with the law; its opposite is injustice, through which men enjoy the possessions of others in defiance of the law." There is the problem of using the law to legalize theft and to redistribute the property of one group to another group, but for the time being, we must assume Aristotle means the use of laws that are rightful and just. For when he says "justice has been acknowledged by us to be a social virtue, and it implies all others," he has laid the foundation of a just society.

Furthermore, Aristotle maintains that "legal justice is the discrimination of the just and the unjust." And, "Of political justice part is natural, part legal—natural, that which everywhere has the same force and does not exist by people's thinking this or that." Natural justice must precede law and form the basis of law thereon.

Michel de Montaigne (1533–1592), in his *Essays*, eloquently said: "The justice which in itself is natural and universal, is otherwise and more nobly ordered, than that other justice, which is special, national, and constrained to the ends of government." He continues, "There cannot a worse state of things be imagined, than where wickedness comes to be legitimate, and assumes with the magistrate's permission, the cloak of virtue. . . . The extremest sort of injustice, according to Plato, is where that which is unjust, should be reputed for just."

Hobbes on Natural Justice

In Thomas Hobbes' (1588–1679) Leviathan, further ground is laid on which to base natural justice. The names just and unjust, says Hobbes, when they are attributed to men's actions, signify conformity or nonconformity to reason. Therefore, "Justice . . . is a rule of reason by which we are forbidden to do anything destructive to our life, and consequently a law of nature."

Then Hobbes leads beautifully into the virtue of just actions: "That which gives to human actions the relish of justice is a certain nobleness or gallantness of courage, rarely found, by which a man scorns to be beholding for the contentment of his life to fraud, or breach of promise. This justice of the manners is that which is meant where justice is called a *virtue;* and injustice, a *vice."*

Earlier it was established that justice is the social virtue on which a just society is constructed. Hobbes adds to this not only by tying virtues to the laws of nature, but to moral philosophy as well. "Now the science of virtue and vice is moral philosophy; and therefore the true doctrine of the laws of nature is the true moral philosophy. . . . For moral philosophy is nothing else but the science of what is good and evil in the conversation and society of mankind." Thus, Hobbes establishes the fact that a *just society is a moral society.*

Saint Augustine (354–430) in *The City of God,* Book XIX, declares "Where, therefore, there is no true justice there can be no right. For that which is done right is justly done, and what is unjustly done cannot be done by right." Hence, justice precedes "rights."

Joseph Joubert eloquently phrased justice as truth in action.

Since practicing the virtue of justice is voluntary, man ought to have the courage to stand up and fight for what is right and against what is wrong. Cato the Younger said it this way: ". . . a man has it in his power to be just, if he have but the will to be so, and therefore injustice is thought the most dishonorable because it is least excusable."

Another way to consider what justice is, is to compare it with injustice. For example, in *Utilitarianism,* John Stuart Mill (1806–1873) states that " . . . it is just to respect, unjust to violate, the *legal rights* of any one." Second, ". . . injustice consists in taking or withholding from any person that to which he has a *moral right."* Third, "It is universally considered just that each person should obtain that (whether good or evil) which he *deserves.*" Fourth, "It is confessedly unjust to break faith with any one: to violate an engagement, either expressed or implied. . . ." Fifth, "It is, by universal admission, inconsistent with justice to be partial."

A Moral Issue

Mill, too, sees justice as a moral issue. He concludes: "Whether the injustice consists in depriving a person of a possession, or in breaking faith with him, or in treating him worse than he deserves, or worse than other people who have no greater claims, in each case the supposition implies two things—a wrong done, and some assignable person who is wronged. Injustice may also be done by treating a person better than others; but the wrong in this case is to his competitors, who are also assignable persons. . . . Justice implies something which it is not only right to do, and wrong not to do, but which some individual person can claim from us as his moral right."

Thomas Paine's *Dissertations* speak about justice where the public good is concerned. He maintains that, "The foundation-principle of public good is justice, and wherever justice is impartially administered, the public good is promoted; for as it is to the good of every man that no injustice be done to him, so likewise it is to his good that the principle which secures him should not be violated in the person of another, because such a violation weakens *his* security, and leaves to chance what ought to be to him a rock to stand on."

The great American constitutional lawyer of the nineteenth century, Lysander Spooner, wrote a pamphlet entitled: *Natural Law, or The Science of Justice,* which succinctly summarizes what justice is:

The science of mine and thine—the science of justice—is the science of all human rights; of all a man's rights of person and property; of all his rights to life, liberty, and the pursuit of happiness.

It is the science which alone can tell any man what he can, and cannot, do; what he can, and cannot, have; what he can, and cannot, say, without infringing the rights of any other person.

It is the science of peace; and the only science of peace; since it is the science which alone can tell us on what conditions mankind can live in peace, or ought to live in peace, with each other.

These conditions are simply these: viz., first, that each man shall do, towards every other, all that justice requires him to do; as, for example, that he shall pay his debts, that he shall return borrowed or stolen property to its owner, and that he shall make reparation for any injury he may have done to the person or property of another.

The second condition is, that each man shall abstain from doing to another, anything which justice forbids him to do; as, for example, that he shall abstain from committing theft, robbery, arson, murder, or any other crime against the person or property of another.

So long as these conditions are fulfilled men are at peace, and ought to remain at peace, with each other. But when either of these conditions is violated, men are at war. And they must necessarily remain at war until justice is re-established.

Through all time, so far as history informs us, wherever mankind have attempted to live in peace with each other, both the natural instincts, and the collective wisdom of the human race, have acknowledged and prescribed, as an indispensable condition, obedience to this one only universal obligation: viz., that each should live honestly towards every other.

The ancient maxim makes the sum of man's legal duty to his fellow men to be simply this: *"To live honestly, to hurt no one, to give to every one his due. . . ."*

Never has such a complex subject as justice been treated so clearly and simply. To summarize justice thus far: Justice means that each must be accountable for his own actions, entitled to the reward of his labor, and responsible for the consequences of his wrongdoings.

The love of justice should be instilled in every man, woman, and child—all should wish to see justice done. For without justice the rule of men (dictatorship), not of law, assumes power. Without justice, society disintegrates into barbarism, where courts of law are administered by favor and pull instead of objective law, and without objective laws, the individual is at the mercy of the ruling power and its agents. The ancient atrocities return, such as no trial by jury, confiscatory taxes on life and property, the purchasing of judges, legislators, and sheriffs; all previous forms of the prior administration of justice become part of the current machinery which administers not justice, but injustice or tyranny.

In short, all that is good rests on justice. Where there is no justice, there is no morality—no right or wrong—anything goes and usually does. Justice is a social virtue to be practiced by individuals. Justice demands that the individual reward or recognize good and condemn evil. To practice justice one should know a man for what he is and treat him accordingly, whether he be honest, dishonest, friend, or thief. The good should be rewarded, the bad punished.

The Highest Goal

Society cannot place before it a higher or nobler goal than the administration of justice. Thus, here is a bit of advice from *Conversations with Goethe,* March 22, 1825: "A great deal may be done by severity, more by love, but most by clear discernment and impartial justice."

Once the meaning of justice has been established, next comes the understanding of freedom and liberty, which are crucial because only under freedom can the individual achieve his highest potential and pursue his happiness.

To speak of liberty and freedom is to speak first of natural laws or the right of nature. Hobbes lays an excellent foundation of natural laws or rights. He affirms that the right of nature is the liberty each man has to use his own power for the preservation of his own life, and his own judgment and reason are the best means for achieving it.

The first law of nature, according to Jean Jacques Rousseau (1712–1778), results from man's nature. "His first law is to provide for his own preservation, his first cares are those which he owes to himself; and, as soon as he reaches years of discretion, he is the sole judge of the proper means of preserving himself. . . ."

Therefore, if man's first obligation is to provide for his own life, he must live under the proper conditions in which to sustain his life, namely, liberty. By liberty is understood the absence of external impediments, the absence of opposition.

Liberty Benefits All

In *The Constitution of Liberty*, Nobel-Prize winner Friedrich A. Hayek points out that liberty is a negative concept like peace. "It becomes positive only through what we make of it. It does not assure us of any particular opportunities, but leaves it to us to decide what use we shall make of the circumstances in which we find ourselves. . . ." He continues, "Liberty not only means that the individual has both the opportunity and the burden of choice; it also means that he must bear the consequences of his actions and will receive praise or blame for them. Liberty and responsibility are *inseparable*." (Emphasis added.)

To expound further, Mill explains that one cannot take away another's freedom no matter how sincerely one tries to protect another. Only by our own hands can any positive and lasting improvement in our lives be worked out. And through "the influence of these two principles all free communities have both been more exempt from social injustice and crime, and have attained more brilliant prosperity, than any others. . . ."

Further, ". . . any restriction on liberty reduces the number of things tried and so reduces the rate of progress. In such a society freedom of action is granted to the individual, not because it gives him greater satisfaction but because if allowed to go his own way he will on the average serve the rest of us better than any orders we know how to give."

In short, liberty is the only object which benefits all alike and should provoke no sincere opposition. Liberty "is not a means to a higher political end. It is itself the highest political end," says Lord Acton. It is required for security in the pursuit of the highest objects of private life and civil society.

Morality Requires Freedom

If liberty is to live upon one's own terms and slavery is to live at the mercy of another's, then it follows that to live under one's own terms means the individual has a choice of actions. He can be virtuous or not; he can be moral. Therefore, morality requires freedom. Thus, only free men can be just men!

In his *The Road to Serfdom,* Hayek ties liberty to morality. Since morals are of necessity a phenomenon of individual conduct, to be moral one must be free to make choices. Where man is forced to act by coercion, the ability to choose has been preempted. Only under liberty and freedom can man be moral. As a result, only "where we ourselves are responsible for our own interests . . . has our decision moral value. Freedom to order our own conduct in the sphere where material circumstances force a choice upon us, and responsibility for the arrangement of our own life according to our own conscience, is the air in which alone moral sense grows and in which moral values are daily recreated in the free decision of the individual. Responsibility, not to a superior, but to one's conscience, the awareness of a duty not exacted by compulsion . . . and to bear the consequences of one's own decision, are the very essence of any morals which deserve the name."

The facts have been established thus far that man must live under liberty to become as productive, as noble, and as just as he can, since liberty is the condition under which morality thrives. Also, only the individual knows what is best for himself. And finally, liberty does not provide opportunities, but leaves the individual free to choose those actions which he thinks will best suit him and to bear the consequences of those actions.

The Price of Freedom

There is one more thing to consider about freedom and liberty—the price. Tocqueville remarked, "Some abandon freedom thinking it dangerous, others thinking it impossible." But there is a third reason. Some abandon freedom thinking it too expensive. Freedom is not free. "Those who expect to reap the blessings of freedom, must, like men, undergo the fatigues of supporting it," noted Paine.

"Freedom is the most exacting form of civil government—it is, in fact, the most demanding state of all for man. That is because freedom demands—depends upon—self-discipline from both the governed and the governing. The foundation of freedom is self-government and the foundation of self-government is self-control," explains author Rus Walton, of *One Nation Under God*. Freedom requires more, however. It requires a strong and vigilant defense. "The greater the threat of evil, the stronger that defense must be. That which is right does not survive unattended; it, too, must have its defenders. . . ."

Is liberty worth the effort? According to Frederic Bastiat, all you have to do is look at the entire world to decide. That is, which "countries contain the most peaceful, the most moral, and the happiest people? Those people are found in the countries where the law least interferes with private affairs; where government is least felt; where the individual has the greatest scope, and free opinion the greatest influence; where administrative powers are fewest and simplest; where taxes are lightest and most nearly equal, and popular discontent the least excited and the least justifiable; where individuals and groups most actively assume their responsibilities, and, consequently, where the morals of . . . human beings are constantly improving; where trade, assemblies, and associations are the least restricted; . . . where mankind most nearly follow its own natural inclinations; . . . in short, the happiest, most moral, and most peaceful people are those who most nearly follow this principle: although mankind is not perfect, still, all hope rests upon the free and voluntary actions of persons within the limits of right; law or force is to be used for nothing except the administration of universal justice."

What this means to us today is that our society, so filled with government regulations and laws, has taken away many of our liberties. For example, we cannot go into some businesses without being licensed, taxed, and regulated. We are presumed guilty (of dishonesty) until proven innocent (which is impossible). Our reputations are continually under attack and, for the most part, stand for nothing. Honesty and integrity, once the backbone of our society, have been replaced by government regulations and promises. Under this system of injustice all of us are losing our liberties, wealth, and happiness.

What better way to summarize the spirit of liberty and freedom and justice than to quote Tocqueville, who said, "I should have loved freedom, I believe, at all times, but in the time in which we live I am ready to worship it."

On Liberty and Liberation

Bruce D. Porter

For at least half a century now the word liberty has been declining in popular usage and the word liberation has been advancing. Today in the United States the word liberty has all but disappeared from public discourse, while liberation has become a fashionable term, enthusiastically invoked in political oratory, in everyday conversation, and in respected works of scholarship.

This is not a mere case of linguistic drift. The decline of liberty and the rise of liberation reveal the extent to which doctrinal myths and political folly have come to dominate our age. Americans are forgetting the meaning of liberty in pursuit of a phantom liberation. Over two centuries ago at Buckinghamshire Edmund Burke observed that, "The people never give up their liberties but under some delusion." With mad abandon contemporary Americans are jettisoning many of their once-cherished freedoms and values as they seek an impossible form of liberation—from moral restraints, self-discipline, responsibility, work, necessity, competition, struggle, inequality, natural law, and the consequences of their own behavior. It is a senseless, tragic course which can lead only to subservience, dependency, and decadence. It is a delusion.

An imperative prerequisite to our survival as a free

This article appeared in the April 1980 issue of *The Freeman*. At the time he wrote it, Dr. Porter was a Research Fellow of Harvard University's Center for International Affairs.

nation is that we recapture—in our hearts and minds, as well as in our politics—an understanding of the true nature of liberty. A love of liberty and a clear comprehension of the foundations upon which it rests will quickly dispel every attraction of the false ideologies of liberation.

Liberty is a divine gift, one of the most priceless of God's bequests to man, and the natural, inalienable right of every person who enters the world. In simplest terms liberty may be defined as the freedom of the individual to shape his own destiny and to govern his own affairs. Of necessity this implies the freedom to choose one's associations, loyalties, beliefs, opportunities, and economic relationships, as well as the freedom to exercise control over the fruits of one's own labors.

Though liberty is God-given, mortal efforts are required to sustain and preserve it. Human institutions do not grant liberty, but they often usurp it. Individuals are born free, but they can willfully sell, abandon, or reject that birthright. For these reasons, liberty is never free. When not defended, it will not survive; when not exercised, it will atrophy.

Essentials of Liberty

Liberty can only endure when certain conditions are met. First, there must be *an absence of coercive actions* intended to impede the free exercise of will or to rob individuals of their labors and investments. Coercive force is justified only when it is imperative to the defense of liberty, i.e., when exerted to prevent a yet greater coercive act. Criminals and tyrants of every form stand ready to destroy human freedom, to rob the property of others, to impose their will upon whole societies. Their influence must be checked if liberty is to prosper.

A second necessary condition for the survival of liberty is that individuals possess and are free to acquire the *positive means needed to pursue rational ends*. These means include material resources, talent, initiative, knowledge, energy, discipline, and a love of progress and freedom. Liberty does not consist of undirected, impotent, and senseless expressions of the human will; rather, it thrives as the individual acquires power to act and to focus his efforts in meaningful directions. Liberty requires power—not power over others, but power to effect personal progress, to change one's circumstances for the better.

Thirdly, the preservation of liberty requires that individuals manifest *moral commitment and self-restraint* in the choice and pursuit of their goals. Liberty means the absence of coercive restraints, but it does not mean the absence of all restraints. We cannot escape the consequences of our own behavior. The unrestrained pursuit of power means enslavement to ambition, the unrestrained pursuit of wealth means enslavement to avarice, the unrestrained pursuit of pleasure means enslavement to passions.

Without moral limits liberty degenerates into license and license turns inevitably toward destructive ends. The moral authority which sets limits on the scope of an individual's actions must flow from within him, the product of conscience and reason; when imposed by a higher authority, however well-intentioned, moral laws are transformed into instruments of coercion and domination.

A Constitutional Structure

Keeping these conditions in mind, it is instructive to inquire into the kind of social structure which will foster liberty. In order to insure the first condition of liberty, a constitutional and legal framework must be erected and upheld, its principal end being to guard against all coercive challenges to personal liberty—whether from individuals, institutions, foreign armies, or from the state itself.

The threat to liberty of the state itself should be emphasized, for unless such a constitutional system is strictly self-limiting its administrative apparatus will grow in size and power until it comes to dominate the entire society according to its own vested interests. Consensus and consent are fundamental to the establishment and operation of a free government, but the goal sought is not so much "government of the people"—for this can imply that majorities deserve coercive power—as a *government of laws*, administered as impersonally and fairly as possible.

By itself alone a constitutionally limited government will never suffice to insure the survival of human liberty. This is because government cannot bring about the second and third conditions of liberty discussed above—the power and means necessary for positive action and the moral limits within which liberty operates. Government can be an arbiter, but it can never be a provider. It can enforce protective laws, but it cannot produce virtuous people or act as a higher moral authority.

A cycle of futility results whenever the state attempts to provide the resources and human energy necessary for progress. Every resource a government provides to the individuals in a society must first be taken from those individuals. Because the process of injecting them back into the society will always incur a net loss, the result over time will be economic stagnation, declining initiative in society as a whole, depletion of real resources, debasement of currency, decline in productive capital, and the disintegration of social cohesiveness. The end of this cycle of futility is the dependency of the people on the government and the death of liberty. Liberty is certain to perish in any society which relies solely on government to create the conditions of liberty.

No matter how carefully structured and well-defined are the legal rights, checks, and balances of a constitutional system, this cycle of futility will at some point ensue unless the citizens of the commonwealth possess a strong spirit of independence and self-reliance, and the moral sensibilities to recognize true liberty when they see it. When the moral will and independence of the majority of a population decline, the checks and balances of any system will erode. No constitutional system can long endure if its legislators are not devoted to higher principles, if its judiciary is corrupt, if its administrators do not place integrity above all other qualities.

Moral Foundations

The constitutional framework of liberty must rest upon a firm foundation: the love of independence in the hearts of a people, their moral commitment, and the vast human and material resources which they possess and independently control. The institutions which transmit this foundation from generation to generation are almost all private: families, churches, corporations, firms, associations, publishers, newspapers, and the like. (Schools can also play a key role if they are under the control of those who pay for them, rather than under the central government.) Standing independent from the state, these institutions are the foundations of a society's liberty. If the state encroaches upon their domain and subsumes their functions, liberty declines. But so long as a people cherish the moral and material resources which give them the power to be independent and so long as the state is a strictly limited constitutional government of laws, liberty will prosper.

The increasingly difficult and unfortunate circumstances in which America finds itself today may be traced in large part to a general decline in liberty. Genuine freedom continues to diminish even as large numbers of Americans are seduced by the muddle-headed mythology of liberation, believing that it will somehow make them freer. Quite the opposite consequence will result, for the doctrine and practice of liberation constitute a direct assault on the conditions and structure of liberty.

In order to discern the destructive potential underlying the multitude of contemporary theories and programs advocating liberation, it suffices simply to ask: liberation from what? We learn, to begin with, that we are to be liberated from "artificial" self-restraints and moral limits—from the third condition of liberty discussed above.

Proponents of liberation preach that freedom is an unrestrained, limitless, spontaneous expression of the human will, ignoring the reality that meaningful progress can only be made when disciplined efforts are rationally directed. Liberty is not a bundle of whims and passions. In order to promote this doctrine it is necessary to attack all the traditional and independent sources of morality: religion, family, private property, private schools, local control of education, corporate independence, and so forth. In this manner liberation seeks to undermine the very foundation of liberty.

"Effortless Abundance"

This is only the beginning. We are also to be liberated from work, want, necessity, and struggle. Thus, liberation ignores the second condition of liberty: that individuals must possess and acquire the positive instruments of action in order to be free. The assumption is that freedom—the power to act, choose, and progress—can somehow exist without effort and investment.

In the pursuit of this chimera goal of an effortless world of abundance for all, the advocates of liberation seek naturally to use the coercive power of the state in order to extract resources from others. In this manner liberation becomes a predatory doctrine which can only accomplish its ends by dismantling the constitutional checks of limited government and replacing it with an all-powerful bureaucracy devoted to central planning, income redistribution, economic dictatorship, and totalitarian control over individual lives. And thus perishes the first condition of liberty—the absence of coercive power.

Liberation is a delusion which cannot lead to real freedom because it is based on principles and values fundamentally contradictory to true liberty. The consequences of the decline of liberty and the rise of liberation in America have never been described more eloquently than by William Simon:

> There has never been such freedom before in America to speak freely . . . to publish anything and everything, including the most scurrilous gossip; to take drugs and to prate to children about their alleged pleasures; to propagandize for bizarre sexual practices: to watch bloody and obscene entertainment. Conversely, compulsion rules the world of work. There has never been so little freedom in America to plan, to save, to invest, to build, to produce, to invent, to hire, to fire, to resist coercive unionization,

to exchange goods and services, to risk, to profit, to grow.

. . . Americans are constitutionally free today to do almost everything that our cultural tradition has previously held to be immoral and obscene, while the police powers of the state are being invoked against almost every aspect of the productive process.[1]

It is not difficult to discern the logical end of this trend: America will be liberated of its liberty.

Prior to the American Revolution the world was imbued with the notion that liberty was dangerous and irresponsible, that its establishment could lead only to anarchy, indolence, and the breakdown of society. The birth of the American republic and the astonishing release of human energy and productivity which resulted shattered this myth forever. America was both free and stable; it possessed both liberty and order.

The liberty of America became the cherished ideal of oppressed peoples everywhere. Liberty suddenly acquired a respectable name. Never thereafter was it possible for the enemies of freedom to attack it frontally. The most bitter opponents of genuine liberty came to portray their policies, programs, and ideologies as pathways to freedom.

Instead of liberty, however, the favorite watchword became liberation. Under this banner march the tyrannies of our time, from Soviet Russia with its wars of national liberation to the kaleidoscope of coercive political programs in America which invoke the mirage of liberation. The twentieth century has been a century of liberation—of a war on freedom fought in the name of freedom.

The irony of America's present course is that in the

name of freedom from restraints, every source of independent power and morality is being undermined; in the name
of freedom from work, want, and scarcity, the constitutional framework of liberty is being dismantled, attacked,
and perverted past recognition. Beyond the irony stands
the very real tragedy that in the name of freedom we are
being led inexorably toward oppression and slavery.

---

1. William Simon, *A Time for Truth* (New York: Berkely Press edition, 1979), p. 251.

The Case for Economic Freedom

Benjamin A. Rogge

My economic philosophy is here offered with full knowledge that it is *not* generally accepted as the right one. On the contrary, my brand of economics has now become *Brand X*, the one that is never selected as the whitest by the housewife, the one that is said to be slow acting, the one that contains no miracle ingredient. It loses nine times out of ten in the popularity polls run on Election Day, and, in most elections, it doesn't even present a candidate.

I shall identify my brand of economics as that of economic freedom, and I shall define economic freedom as that set of economic arrangements that would exist in a society in which the government's only function would be to prevent one man from using force or fraud against another—including within this, of course, the task of national defense. So that there can be no misunderstanding here, let me say that this is pure, uncompromising *laissez-faire* economics. It is not the mixed economy; it is the unmixed economy.

I readily admit that I do not expect to see such an economy in my lifetime or in anyone's lifetime in the infinity of years ahead of us. I present it rather as the ideal we should strive for and should be disappointed in never fully attaining.

Dr. Rogge (1920–1980) was Dean and Professor of Economics at Wabash College in Indiana and a long-time trustee of FEE. This essay appeared in the February 1981 issue of *The Freeman*.

Where do we find the most powerful and persuasive case for economic freedom? I don't know; probably it hasn't been prepared as yet. Certainly it is unlikely that the case I present is the definitive one. However, it is the one that is persuasive with me, that leads me to my own deep commitment to the free market. I present it as grist for your own mill and not as the divinely inspired last word on the subject.

The Moral Case

You will note as I develop my case that I attach relatively little importance to the demonstrated efficiency of the free-market system in promoting economic growth, in raising levels of living. In fact, my central thesis is that *the most important part of the case for economic freedom is not its vaunted efficiency as a system for organizing resources, not its dramatic success in promoting economic growth, but rather its consistency with certain fundamental moral principles of life itself.*

I say, "the most important part of the case" for two reasons. First, the significance I attach to those moral principles would lead me to prefer the free enterprise system even if it were demonstrably less efficient than alternative systems, even if it were to produce a *slower* rate of economic growth than systems of central direction and control. Second, the great mass of the people of any country is never really going to understand the purely economic workings of *any* economic system, be it free enterprise or socialism. Hence, most people are going to judge an economic system by its consistency with their moral principles rather than by its purely scientific operating characteristics. If economic freedom survives in the years ahead, it will be only because a majority of the people accept its basic morality. The success of the system in bringing ever higher levels of living will be no more persuasive in the future than it has been in the past. Let me illustrate.

The doctrine of man held in general in nineteenth-century America argued that each man was ultimately responsible for what happened to him, for his own salvation, both in the here and now and in the hereafter. Thus, whether a man prospered or failed in economic life was each man's individual responsibility: each man had a right to the rewards for success and, in the same sense, deserved the punishment that came with failure. It followed as well that it is explicitly immoral to use the power of government to take from one man to give to another, to legalize Robin Hood. This doctrine of man found its economic counterpart in the system of free enterprise and, hence, the system of free enterprise was accepted and respected by many who had no real understanding of its subtleties as a technique for organizing resource use.

As this doctrine of man was replaced by one which made of man a helpless victim of his subconscious and his environment—responsible for neither his successes nor his failures—the free enterprise system came to be rejected by many who still had no real understanding of its actual operating characteristics.

Basic Values Considered

Inasmuch as my own value systems and my own assumptions about human beings are so important to the case, I want to sketch them for you.

To begin with, the central value in my choice system is individual freedom. By freedom I mean exactly and only freedom from coercion by others. I do not mean the four freedoms of President Roosevelt, which are not freedoms at all, but only rhetorical devices to persuade people to give up some of their true freedom. In the Rogge system, each man must be free to do what is his duty as he defines it, so long as he does not use force against another.

Next, I believe each man to be ultimately responsible for what happens to him. True, he is influenced by his heredity, his environment, his subconscious, and by pure chance. But I insist that precisely what makes man man is his ability to rise above these influences, to change and determine his own destiny. If this be true, then it follows that each of us is terribly and inevitably and forever responsible for everything he does. The answer to the question, "Who's to blame?" is always, "*Mea culpa,* I am."

I believe as well that man is imperfect, now and forever. He is imperfect in his knowledge of the ultimate purpose of his life, imperfect in his choice of means to serve those purposes he does select, imperfect in the integrity with which he deals with himself and those around him, imperfect in his capacity to love his fellow man. If man is imperfect, then all of his constructs must be imperfect, and the choice is always among degrees and kinds of imperfection. The New Jerusalem is never going to be realized here on earth, and the man who insists that it is, is always lost unto freedom.

Moreover, man's imperfections are intensified as he acquires the power to coerce others; "power tends to corrupt and absolute power corrupts absolutely."

This completes the listing of my assumptions, and it should be clear that the list does not constitute a total philosophy of life. Most importantly, it does not define what I believe the free man's *duty* to be, or more specifically, what I believe my own duty to be and the source of the charge to me. However important these questions, I do not consider them relevant to the choice of an economic system.

Here, then, are two sections of the case for economic freedom as I would construct it. The first section presents economic freedom as an ultimate end in itself and the second presents it as a means to the preservation of the noneconomic elements in total freedom.

Individual Freedom of Choice

The first section of the case is made in the stating of it, if one accepts the fundamental premise.

Major premise: Each man should be free to take whatever *action* he wishes, so long as he does not use force or fraud against another.

Minor premise: All economic behavior is "action" as identified above.

Conclusion: Each man should be free to take whatever action he wishes in his economic behavior, so long as he does not use force or fraud against another.

In other words, economic freedom is a part of total freedom; *if freedom is an end in itself, as our society has traditionally asserted it to be, then economic freedom is an end in itself, to be valued for itself alone and not just for its instrumental value in serving other goals.*

If this thesis is accepted, then there must always exist a tremendous presumption against each and every proposal for governmental limitation of economic freedom. What is wrong with a state system of compulsory social security? It denies to the individual his *freedom*, his right to choose what he will do with his own money resources. What is wrong with a governmentally enforced minimum wage? It denies to the employer and the employee their individual freedoms, their individual rights to enter into voluntary relationships not involving force or fraud. What is wrong with a tariff or an import quota? It denies to the individual consumer his right to buy what he wishes, wherever he wishes.

It is breathtaking to think what this simple approach would do to the apparatus of state control at all levels of government. Strike from the books all legislation that denies economic freedom to any individual, and three-fourths of all the activities now undertaken by government would be eliminated.

I am no dreamer of empty dreams, and I do not expect that the day will ever come when this principle of economic freedom as a part of total freedom will be fully accepted and applied. Yet I am convinced that unless this principle is given some standing, unless those who examine proposals for new regulation of the individual by government look on this loss of freedom as a "cost" of the proposed legislation, the chances of free enterprise surviving are small indeed. The would-be controller can always find reasons why it might seem expedient to control the individual; unless slowed down by some general feeling that it is immoral to do so, he will usually have his way.

Noneconomic Freedoms

So much for the first section of the case. Now for the second. The major premise here is the same, that is, the premise of the rightness of freedom. Here, though, the concern is with the noneconomic elements in total freedom—with freedom of speech, of religion, of the press, of personal behavior. My thesis is that these freedoms are not likely to be long preserved in a society that has denied economic freedom to its individual members.

Before developing this thesis, I wish to comment briefly on the importance of these noneconomic freedoms. I do so because we who are known as conservatives have often given too little attention to these freedoms or have even played a significant role in reducing them. The modern liberal is usually inconsistent in that he defends man's noneconomic freedoms, but is often quite indifferent to his economic freedom. The modern conservative is often inconsistent in that he defends man's economic freedom but is indifferent to his noneconomic freedoms. Why are there so few conservatives in the struggles over censorship, over denials of equality before the law for people of all races, over blue laws, and so on? Why do we let the modern liberals dominate an organization such as the American Civil Liberties Union? The general purposes of this organization are completely consistent with, even necessary to, the truly free society.

Particularly in times of stress such as these, we must fight against the general pressure to curb the rights of individual human beings, even those whose ideas and actions we detest. Now is the time to remember the example of men such as David Ricardo, the London banker and economist of the classical free-market school in the first part of the last century. Born a Jew, married to a Quaker, he devoted some part of his energy and his fortune to eliminating the legal discrimination against Catholics in the England of his day.

It is precisely because I believe these noneconomic freedoms to be so important that I believe economic freedom to be so important. The argument here could be drawn from the wisdom of the Bible and the statement that "where a man's treasure is, there will his heart be also." Give me control over a man's economic actions, and hence over his means of survival, and except for a few occasional heroes, I'll promise to deliver to you men who think and write and behave as I want them to.

Freedom of the Press

The case is not difficult to make for the fully controlled economy, the true socialistic state. Milton Friedman, in his book *Capitalism and Freedom,* takes the case of a socialist society that has a sincere desire to preserve the freedom of the press. The first problem would be that there would be no private capital, no private fortunes that could be used to subsidize an antisocialist, procapitalist press. Hence, the socialist state would have to do it. However, the men and women undertaking the task would have to be released from the socialist labor pool and would have to be assured that they would never be discriminated against in employment opportunities in the socialist apparatus if they were to wish to change occupations later. Then these procapitalist members of the socialist society would have to go to other functionaries of the state to secure the buildings, the presses, the paper, the skilled and unskilled workmen, and all the other components of a working newspaper. Then they would face the problem of finding distribution outlets, either creating their own (a frightening task) or using the same ones used by the official socialist propaganda organs. Finally, where would they find readers? How many men and women would risk showing up at their state-controlled jobs carrying copies of the *Daily Capitalist*?

There are so many unlikely steps in this process that the assumption that true freedom of the press could be maintained in a socialist society is so unrealistic as to be ludicrous.

Partly Socialized

Of course, we are not facing as yet a fully socialized America, but only one in which there is significant government intervention in a still predominantly private enterprise economy. Do these interventions pose any threat to the noneconomic freedoms? I believe they do.

First of all, the total of coercive devices now available to any administration of either party at the national level is so great that true freedom to work actively against the current administration (whatever it might be) is seriously reduced. For example, farmers have become captives of the government in such a way that they are forced into political alignments that seriously reduce their ability to protest actions they do not approve. The new trade bill, though right in the principle of free trade, gives to the President enormous power to reward his friends and punish his critics.

Second, the form of these interventions is such as to threaten seriously one of the real cornerstones of all freedoms—equality before the law. For example, farmers and trade union members are now encouraged and assisted in doing precisely that for which businessmen are sent to jail (i.e., acting collusively to manipulate prices). The blindfolded Goddess of Justice has been encouraged to peek and she now says, with the jurists of the ancient regime, "First tell me who you are and then I'll tell you what your rights are." A society in which such gross inequalities before the law are encouraged in economic life is not likely to be one which preserves the principle of equality before the law generally.

We could go on to many specific illustrations. For example, the government uses its legislated monopoly to carry the mails as a means for imposing a censorship on what people send to each other in a completely voluntary relationship. A man and a woman who exchange obscene letters may not be making productive use of their time, but their correspondence is certainly no business of the government. Or to take an example from another country, Winston Churchill, as a critic of the Chamberlain government, was not permitted one minute of radio time on the government-owned and monopolized broadcasting system in the period from 1936 to the outbreak in 1939 of the war he was predicting.

Each Step of Intervention Leads to Another

Every act of intervention in the economic life of its citizens gives to a government additional power to shape and control the attitudes, the writings, the behavior of those citizens. Every such act is another break in the dike protecting the integrity of the individual as a free man or woman.

The free market protects the integrity of the individual by providing him with a host of decentralized alternatives rather than with one centralized opportunity. As Friedman has reminded us, even the known communist can readily find employment in capitalist America. The free market is politics-blind, religion-blind, and, yes, race-blind. Do you ask about the politics or the religion of the farmer who grew the potatoes you buy at the store? Do you ask about the color of the hands that helped produce the steel you use in your office building?

South Africa provides an interesting example of this. The South Africans, of course, provide a shocking picture of racial bigotry, shocking even to a country that has its own tragic race problems. South African law clearly separates the whites from the nonwhites. Orientals have traditionally been classed as nonwhites, but South African trade with Japan has become so important in the postwar period that the government of South Africa has declared the Japanese visitors to South Africa to be officially and legally "white." The free market is one of the really great forces making for tolerance and understanding among human beings. The controlled market gives man rein to express all those blind prejudices and intolerant beliefs to which he is forever subject.

Impersonality of the Market

To look at this another way: The free market is often said to be impersonal, and indeed it is. Rather than a vice, this is one of its great virtues. Because the relations *are* substantially impersonal, they are not usually marked by bitter personal conflict. It is precisely because the labor union attempts to take the employment relationship *out* of the marketplace that bitter personal conflict so often marks union-management relationships. The intensely personal relationship is one that is civilized only by love, as between man and wife, and within the family. But man's capacity for love is severely limited by his imperfect nature. Far better, then, to economize on love, to reserve our dependence on it to those relationships where even our imperfect natures are capable of sustained action based on love. Far better, then, to build our economic system on largely impersonal relationships and on man's self-interest—a motive power with which he is generously supplied. One need only study the history of such utopian experiments as our Indiana's Harmony and New Harmony to realize that a social structure which ignores man's essential nature results in the dissension, conflict, disintegration, and dissolution of Robert Owen's New Harmony or the absolutism of Father Rapp's Harmony.

The "vulgar calculus of the marketplace," as its critics have described it, is still the most humane way man has yet found for solving those questions of economic allocation and division which are ubiquitous in human society. By what must seem fortunate coincidence, it is also the system most likely to produce the affluent society, to move mankind above an existence in which life is mean, nasty, brutish, and short. But, of course, this is *not* just coincidence. Under economic freedom, only man's destructive instincts are curbed by law. All of his creative instincts are released and freed to work those wonders of which free men are capable. In the controlled society only the creativity of the few at the top can be utilized, and much of this creativity must be expended in maintaining control and in fending off rivals. In the free society, the creativity of every man can be expressed—and surely by now we know that we cannot predict who will prove to be the most creative.

You may be puzzled, then, that I do not rest my case for economic freedom on its productive achievements; on its buildings, its houses, its automobiles, its bathtubs, its wonder drugs, its television sets, its sirloin steaks and green salads with Roquefort dressings. I neither feel within myself nor do I hear in the testimony of others any evidence that man's search for purpose, his longing for fulfillment, is in any significant way relieved by these accomplishments. I do not scorn these accomplishments nor do I worship them.

Nor do I find in the lives of those who do worship them any evidence that they find ultimate peace and justification in their idols.

I rest my case rather on the consistency of the free market with man's essential nature, on the basic morality of its system of rewards and punishments, on the protection it gives to the integrity of the individual.

The free market cannot produce the perfect world, but it can create an environment in which each imperfect man may conduct his lifelong search for purpose in his own way, in which each day he may order his life according to his own imperfect vision of his destiny, suffering both the agonies of his errors and the sweet pleasure of his successes. This freedom is what it means to be a man; this is the Godhead, if you wish.

I give you, then, the free market, the expression of man's economic freedom and the guarantor of all his other freedoms.

The Moral Premise and the Decline of the American Heritage

Paul L. Adams

Man in his very nature has need of a major premise— a philosophical starting point or Prime Mover, as it were, to give reason for his being, direction and order to his thinking, and initiative and impetus to his actions. With the Christian, this basic assumption stems from the belief that God, by Divine fiat, created man as a moral, rational being with freedom of choice, and that exercise of will and choice in both the moral and physical frames of reference is an awesome but unavoidable fact of existence.

Man's choice to partake of the "forbidden fruit" provided him with the promised knowledge of good and evil, but along with it came an incalculable complication of his circumstances. Nature became a challenge to his physical existence. Other people constituted to him a confused complex of variant relationships that ranged from love on one hand to virulent hatred on the other. God faded from his consciousness, and with that loss went also the meaning of man's struggle. Man was thus lost in the only sense in which he could be really lost, and the need was therefore critical for a major premise which promulgates for man a

The late Dr. Adams was president of Roberts Wesleyan University, North Chili, New York, and was a trustee of The Foundation for Economic Education. This article is reprinted from the March 1968 issue of *The Freeman*.

supreme purpose for life, a purpose which justifies the physical hardship, the social conflicts, the spiritual struggle, and the disappointments with which life is filled. Only such a premise delivers life from the insanity it sometimes appears to be—struggle without hope, achievement without happiness, victory without exaltation, death without resurrection.

Man, himself, throughout the concourse of his history has given ample evidence of his longing and need for an all-embracing purpose. He knows so little that is perfect, yet he always looks for perfection—a seminal response which derives from the moral image in which he was originally created and the perfection of the environment in which he found himself. Though corrupt by his own choice, he still yearns for the ideal, like some earthling wandering in a cosmic wasteland dreaming of the green hills of earth. Basically, he seeks a society which will fulfill his demands on nature, ameliorate his relationship with his fellow man, and provide the ultimate reason for existence. In the search, man's thinking has led him, inevitably, into metaphysical and ontological problems, to a consideration of the first principles of all existence.

It would be presumptuous, indeed, for me to attempt a definitive statement of the major premise with its detailed ramifications, and presumption is, among college professors, a sin of great magnitude. Perhaps, however, one might conclude that within such a premise are these parts: Man is a spiritual being, created by God and endowed with the freedom and responsibility of moral choice; his purpose in living is to glorify God by exercising his reason toward those ends that his highest moral nature urges, and his task is to refine his intelligence, develop his creativity, discipline his conscience, and clothe himself in robes of righteousness.

The Moral Premise—Like a Golden Thread

Man has never been without some first principle, some major premise, sometimes consciously, more frequently unconsciously, held up before him. It runs in some form like golden thread through man's history, and it may be noted in various efforts and forms that mark man's societal action. The Israelites had in Jehovah God the source of law in the observance of which was life. The Greeks promulgated *Natural Law* as an absolute reference point for man's excursions into lawmaking. The Romans embraced Stoicism and with it the Natural Law concept which, in the Western world, yielded place to the Divine law of Christianity. This is clearly seen in the Gelasian theory which placed absolute value on the sword of spiritual power.

All of these systems with their varied premises failed to produce the ideal society. The Hebrew system ended, oppressed by evil and corrupt kings. The Greek system, even in the Golden Age of Pericles, was marked by corruption, vice, weakness, and personal lust for power. The Roman could observe the cruelty and injustice of his state, and he suffered from tyrants who plundered the poor to lavish wealth on the idle, sensual, and effete nobility. The slight amelioration that feudalism supplied was due chiefly to the fact that there was less economic distance between master and serf—for goods were fewer, even in this paternalistic social order, and pillaged more frequently by incessant warring. Certainly, there was little understanding of nature, no mastery of production, and a very low level of social justice. Seemingly, man was destined to a perpetual slavery only thinly disguised in an embracing paternalism that left him without hope.

Christian Europe was not without hope, however, for

the sixteenth century saw a rebirth of the idea that man was free, must be free. Dramatically stated first in theological terms, the fuller implications in nontheological terms were soon asserted, and Europe began a long and costly march toward freedom. Costly, for human liberty has never been secured or maintained without sacrifice, and it was our own Jefferson who said, "Every so often the tree of liberty must be watered by the blood of patriots—and of tyrants."

The American Foundation

With all of the foregoing in mind, it can be assumed that those who raised a new nation on this continent had a wealth of history on which to draw. The responses of our forefathers were partly the product of a vicarious intellectual empiricism and partly the intuitive conclusions of liberty-loving men playing it by ear. What these men gave to America and the world was the moral premise embedded in a philosophy of moral absolutes. It was shaped and nurtured in the minds and hearts of people who recognized in it the last, best hope of man. These forebears of ours were of the breed of men who count not their own lives dear unto themselves; they were prepared to die for America and for freedom. Need I remind you that it was a young man not yet twenty-two who said in a last magnificent moment of life, "I only regret that I have but one life to give to my country"?

These great men espoused a moral absolute which accepted God as creator, as ultimate Truth, and they believed man to be a moral creature, responsible to God, and capable of discharging that responsibility only through freedom of choice. It logically follows, then, that freedom is more than just another attribute. It is so essential that life without it loses significance. These Founding Fathers saw in freedom and liberty the only perfection a human society can know, for in freedom's house the individual can shape his own perfections and follow his noblest aspirations. The exercise of freedom, then, is for man the perfecting of his humanity—not that the exercise will ever be perfect, but the continuing exercise represents a constant affirmation of the eternal principle that man can find himself only in God.

Limited Government

These men of great vision clearly understood that the only real threat to liberty and freedom is government, for men assign a sanctity to government not accorded to individuals and groups. But government is a faceless thing and can hide the predators who lurk behind its façade and exercise its function; and governments assume, quite naturally it seems, government's right to a monopoly of physical force. Fearing government, and the natural tendency of power to beget power, these men established a constitution which attempted to assure man's freedom by limiting the sphere of government to a workable minimum. The clear intent was to magnify the responsibility of the individual and subordinate government to its primary function of serving freedom's cause.

Even among its most ardent devotees, there was never any suggestion that this Constitution was a panacea for all the social ills to which man is heir. There was no guarantee of identical status for individuals or groups. There was no promise of material rewards. There was only the implicit assumption that freedom and liberty were their own rewards and worth any sacrifice. The Constitution promised only the system itself, but under it liberty and freedom were to be nurtured. It was Benjamin Franklin who saw the only flaw, and he stated it in simple terms when he suggested that perhaps the people might not keep what they had acquired. It was George Washington who stated in eloquent prose that liberty is guaranteed only by the eternal vigilance of those who share its vision.

These architects of nation were men of great faith—faith in the substance of things hoped for, the evidence of things not seen—faith in their vision of a vast land and great people—faith in the triumph of truth over error, of justice over injustice, of right over tyranny, of knowledge over ignorance, of reason over prejudice, and the ultimate triumph of eternal values over the temporal. Faith in such a vision together with commitment to the program for its fulfillment constituted in their thinking an irresistible force that would shake the world—and it did. In addition, it gave rise to a compelling spirit of national mission.

Eternal Vigilance

It is a truism that tragedy lurks close to the surface of all enterprises of great pith and moment. George Bernard Shaw suggested that there are two great tragedies in life. One is to not get your heart's desire; the other is to get it. The observation is so applicable to the American scene that it arouses almost a response of sharp physical pain. America had her great dream, her grand design. History provided her with the opportunity to realize it. So she avoided the first of the tragedies that Mr. Shaw suggested. The alternate tragedy was left to be realized, for tragedy must follow the failure to understand the tremendous demand such a society places on the individual. It calls for enormous self-discipline in behalf of freedom's preeminent claim; it requires a conscious articulate sensitivity to freedom's climate; and it mandates a firm dedication to freedom's methods and goals along with a determination to live with the results.

It is not debatable that we have had an imperfect and uneven performance in this regard. The student of American history recalls the demarché of the Federalist party into unconstitutionalism to retain power. It can hardly go unnoticed that there were those who were blind to the implications of education for a substantial segment of our society, including women. Even more compelling shortly after the centennial year of Appomattox Court House is the thought that there were those who insisted on the immediate attainment of their ends and refused to recognize longer that the Constitution provided a certain, if slow, mechanic for resolving great inequities and injustice. This impatience sent men to graves like beds and finally resulted in the slaughter of more Americans than World War I and World War II combined.

Unhappy though these examples be, we note with satisfaction that the Federalist returned to make the great right decision in 1800, and that educational opportunity has approached universality in this nation. We could even say that although the larger lessons of the so-called *irrepressible conflict* were lost on us, we have at times demonstrated our belief that the nature of our system cannot be defined in terms of any appeal to the doctrine that might and right are inseparable.

With liberty and freedom identified in the Constitution and accepted as the norm for human action, we demonstrated a vitality and creativity that produced achievement which first caught the attention of the world and then beckoned her disinherited millions to the "lifted lamp beside the golden door." We enlarged individual opportunity, secured religious toleration, and established the basis for political diversity and cultural pluralism. We educated the masses, refurbished the concept of individual justice and charity, and we took over leadership of the revolution in communication, transportation, and production. Our free market led the world in the production and distribution of goods for the benefit of all classes. Somewhere along the line, too, we began to develop a distinct literature of merit and other artistic forms. Finally, and without great fanfare, we assumed world leadership in moral idealism as a natural concomitant of our commitment to principles based in the eternal verity of the moral law.

Obstacles to Be Overcome

Such have been the fruits of the American system, and such a nation or system, meeting as it did man's age-old search for an ideal society, should fear no challenge. Nature had been transformed into an ally; a beginning had been made toward a solution of the omnipresent problem of human relationships; and man's right and need to know and experience God had been left unrestricted. We who received such a heritage should fear no challenge, yet we are alarmed by a challenge of so great a magnitude that we seem unable to plot its dimensions. Wisdom and intelligence, however, as well as the instinct for survival dictate that the problem must be stated, understood, and attacked.

There are those, undoubtedly, whose disquiet is solely in terms of the problem posed by nuclear physics. These people might think beyond it, but the possibility of a nuclear war produces in them a trauma that makes further rational thought on their part impossible. Those of whom this is descriptive tend to view the great ultimate catastrophe as physical death, forgetting that the great moral premise assigns little significance to the fact of mere physical existence. They would establish a new commandment which may be simply stated, "And now abideth the mind, the spirit, the body, these three, but the greatest of these is the body." It is not to be expected that those who hold such a belief could or would give rise to any inspired resolution, for that which they treasure most is most easily subject to threats and force.

Then there are those who react to the problem in materialistic terms. These have altered the supreme moral principle to read, "Man shall live by bread alone." The member of this group is quite likely to attach himself to any of the several simplifications which this group has institutionalized in policy: the answer to any domestic problem is governmental spending to raise everyone's material standard of living; neutralists such as Tito will be won to our side if our gifts are large and continuous; the communist will soften his attitude toward the United States and the noncommunist world if we allow them the trade advantages of our productive system.

Again, there is a class we could call passivists, and, like some of their medieval forebears who went into monastic seclusion, they seek to escape the world of decision and action. A tendency of the members of this class is to rely on discussion, fruitless though it may be, and on a complete negation of decisive action. Discussion becomes for them not a means but an end, and failure is not failure, for nonproductive discussion guarantees the need of still further discussion. No international conference is a failure, in this light, as long as it ends without definitive commitment. There is some truth in the assertion that protracted discussion on a point at issue often results in a blurring of the thought of both parties, but it logically follows that in such a situation, the party with commitment to a principle and a concomitant course of action stands in the least danger.

Detoured by Relativism

None of those in the classes just mentioned sees the challenge to the American heritage in its true dimensions, and obviously they have little understanding of the resources necessary to meet the challenge. The basic problem is the failure of Americans to dedicate and rededicate themselves to the great moral premise—*freedom under God*. As dedication to that premise built the American heritage, decline from it has given rise to the problems that appear in the guise of insecurity — the fear of physical extinction, the compensation of materialism, and indecision.

The decline was initiated by the introduction of a philosophy of relativism with its inherent negation of moral absolutes. This philosophy relieves man of all responsibility; it erodes his moral standards, for morals, it says, are a product of man's own thinking and are therefore subject to change. Further, it has no fixed reference point; rather it has a multitude of reference points, discoverable only by a process of expediency which itself becomes the criterion for judgment. Such thought canonizes Niccolò Machiavelli, who baldly and boldly asserted that the end justifies the means. In such a philosophy, man is not free; he is rather a pawn of history, and he has significance only as he participates in great mass movements. In action, the philosophy is expressed in positivism which denies any supernatural standard and acclaims any law as valid if there is sufficient force in the lawgiver to enforce it. Such a philosophy does not produce Nathan Hales. It is more apt to produce those who seek the undisciplined refuge of mass anonymity and mass conformity. The end of such a system is pictured in Orwell's *1984,* in which he describes a society where *Big Brother* decides what is truth for the unresisting masses. Orwell doesn't say it, but the tragedy is that under such a system, life doesn't really matter.

Improper Methods

The increasing acceptance of such a philosophy has spawned an incredible number of value standards and courses of action not consistent with our original premise and the institutionalizing of liberty. Time forbids a discussion of them, but some of the more dangerous may be listed. There are those who change or pervert the Constitution to gain the ends they desire, and the ends are presented as good ends to justify the action. It was for good reasons that the Gracchi started the process of violating the Roman constitution. The end of the process was the destruction of liberty in Rome, for each succeeding constitutional violation takes less explanation and less and less justification. Eventually the constitutional image is lost, and the term itself becomes a shibboleth.

Then, there are those who forget that material wealth is a happy by-product of our pursuit of a morally legitimate goal, and they relentlessly pursue the materialistic largess of nature as an end in itself. It is again the old story of selling the birthright for a mess of pottage. The goal of this philosophy is ever greater materialism with less and less effort. This idea seems to offer a built-in contradiction, but still the belief persists that we have invented a slot machine which pays off for everybody.

Again, there are those who pervert the definition of freedom to mean an absence of fear, of individual responsibility, of self-discipline, and they include within its context the strong presumption of egalitarian doctrines. These find the answer to all of our problems in the increase of central, bureaucratic government. Washington is their Mecca. They do not, perhaps, make a pilgrimage to Washington, but well they might, for not only is their money there, it is fast becoming a repository of the American soul. In international relations, these people have a naive faith in the United Nations, assign to it a supernatural aura, and claim for it a practical success not demonstrable in logic or actuality.

A Time for Rededication

Finally, there are those who are totally oblivious to the fact that the American forefathers, like the early Christians, were men whose vision and faith were such that they intended to turn the world upside down—and did so. We have lived in the golden heritage of their dedication to a great moral principle and the abundant life it provided. That we have grown insensitive to such a principle presages failure where they succeeded. We cannot escape the fact that the virility of communism stems from the fact that the communist is committed totally to the belief that it is necessary to change the world—and as an individual he is prepared to give himself to realize such an end. We cannot change the form or substance of the communist movement or threat. We can, however, reclaim, revive, and renew the American heritage as the eternal answer to those who would, under any guise, enslave the free spirit of man.

The innumerable paths of history are thick with the dust

of decayed nations that knew the passing radiance of a glorious moment. Khrushchev and communism promised to bury the American heritage because it no longer serves history's purposes. For me, I fear no physical threat communism can offer. I do fear the retreat from our heritage. I do not fear Khrushchev's judgment. I fear the inexorable judgment of God's law which has ordained man's freedom. Should this nation so blessed by God forget His ordinance, then we have no valid claim to existence. We will have failed those who lived and died that we might be free as well as the serf of the future who will not long remember our moment of history. As Americans we can, as one has said, "spend ourselves into immortality" in freedom's battle or we can make our way carelessly to nameless graves and be part of the dust of history's passing parade.

IV. THE CRISIS OF OUR AGE

Moral Criticisms of the Market

Ken S. Ewert

According to an author writing in a recent issue of *The Nation* magazine, "The religious Left is the only Left we've got." An overstatement? Perhaps. However, it points to an interesting fact, namely that while the opposition to free markets and less government control has declined in recent years among the "secular left," the political-economic views of the "Christian left" seem to remain stubbornly unchanged.

Why is this so? Why are the secular critics of the market mellowing while the Christian critics are not?

Perhaps one major reason is the different criteria by which these two ideological allies measure economic systems. The secular left, after more than half a century of failed experiments in anti-free-market policies, has begrudgingly softened its hostility towards the market for predominantly pragmatic reasons. Within their camp the attitude seems to be that since it hasn't worked, let's get on with finding something that will. While this may be less than a heartfelt conversion to a philosophy of economic freedom, at least (for many) this recognition has meant taking a more sympathetic view of free markets.

However, within the Christian camp the leftist intellec-

Mr. Ewert is the editor of *U-Turn,* a quarterly publication addressing theological, political, economic, and social issues from a biblical perspective. This essay appeared in the March 1989 issue of *The Freeman.*

tuals seem to be much less influenced by the demonstrated failure of state-directed economic policies. They remain unimpressed with arguments pointing out the efficiency and productivity of the free market, or statistics and examples showing the non-workability of traditional interventionist economic policies. Why? One likely reason is that the criteria by which these thinkers choose to measure capitalism are fundamentally moral in nature, so much so that socialism, despite its obvious shortcomings, is still preferred because of its perceived moral superiority. In their eyes, the justness and morality of an economic system are vastly more important than its efficiency.

If indeed the Christian critics of the market are insisting that an economic system must be ultimately judged by moral standards, we should agree and applaud them for their principled position. They are asking a crucially important question: is the free market a moral economic system?

Unfortunately, these thinkers have answered the question with a resounding "No!" They have examined the free market and found it morally wanting. Some of the most common reasons given for this indictment are that the market is based on an ethic of selfishness and it fosters materialism; it atomizes and dehumanizes society by placing too much emphasis on the individual; and it gives rise to tyrannical economic powers which subsequently are used to oppress the weaker and more defenseless members of society.

If these accusations are correct, the market is justly condemned. But have these critics correctly judged the morality of the free market? Let's re-examine their charges.

I. Selfishness

The market, it is suggested, is based on and encourages an ethic of selfishness. According to critics of the market, mere survival in this competitive economic system requires that we each "look after Number One." Individuals are encouraged to focus on the profit motive to the exclusion of higher goals and as a result selfishness becomes almost a virtue. And this, it is noted, is in stark contrast with the self-sacrificial love taught by the Scriptures. Instead of rewarding love, compassion, and kindness towards others, the free market seems to reward self-orientation and self-indulgence. Instead of encouraging us to be concerned about our neighbor, the free market seems to encourage us to be concerned about ourselves. Individuals who might otherwise be benevolent, according to this view, are corrupted by the demands of an economic system that forces them to put themselves first. In the thinking of these critics, the market is the logical precursor to the "me generation."

However, this charge is superficial and misleading in several respects. It is important to remember that while the free market does allow "self-directed" economic actions, it does not require "selfish" economic actions. There is an important distinction here. It should be obvious that all human action is self-directed. Each of us has been created with a mind, allowing us to set priorities and goals, and a will, which enables us to take steps to realize these goals. This is equally true for those who live in a market economy and those who live under a politically directed economy. The difference between the two systems is not between self-directed action versus non-self-directed action, but rather between a peaceful pursuit of goals (through voluntary exchange in a free economy) versus a coercive pursuit of goals (through wealth transferred via the state in a "planned" economy). In other words, the only question is how will self-directed action manifest itself: will it take place through mutually beneficial economic exchanges, or through predatory political actions?

Clearly the free market cannot be singled out and condemned for allowing self-directed actions to take place, since self-directed actions are an inescapable part of human life. But can it be condemned for giving rise to selfishness? In other words, does the free market engender an attitude of selfishness in individuals? If we define selfishness as a devotion to one's own advantage or welfare without regard for the welfare of others, it is incontestable that selfishness does exist in the free economy; many individuals act with only themselves ultimately in mind. And it is true, that according to the clear teaching of Scripture, selfishness is wrong.

But we must bear in mind that although selfishness does exist in the free market, it also exists under other economic systems. Is the Soviet factory manager less selfish than the American capitalist? Is greed any less prevalent in the politically directed system which operates via perpetual bribes, theft from state enterprises, and political purges? There is no reason to think so. The reason for this is clear: selfishness is not an environmentally induced condition, i.e., a moral disease caused by the economic system, but rather a result of man's fallen nature. It is out of the heart, as Christ said, that a man is defiled. Moral failure is not spawned by the environment.

It is clear that not all self-directed action is necessarily selfish action. For example, when I enter the marketplace in order to earn wealth to feed, clothe, house, and provide education or medical care for my children, I am not acting selfishly. Likewise, if you or I want to extend charity to a needy neighbor or friend, we must first take "self-directed" action to create the wealth necessary to do so. Such action is hardly selfish.

The point is this: the free market allows individuals to peacefully pursue their chosen goals and priorities, but it doesn't dictate or determine those priorities. It does not force an individual to focus on his own needs and desires, but leaves him or her at liberty to be self-centered or benevolent. My ultimate goal may be self-indulgence, or I may make a high priority of looking after others—the choice is mine. As to which I should do, the market is silent. As an economic system, the market simply does not speak in favor of selfish or unselfish priorities.

However, the free market, while not touching the heart of a man or eliminating selfishness, does in fact restrain selfishness. It channels self-centered desires into actions that are beneficial to others. This is so because in order to "get ahead" in the free economy, we must first please other people by producing something which is of use and value to them. In other words, the market disciplines each of us to look outwards and serve others. Only by doing so can we persuade them to give us what we want in exchange.

We will return to this theme later, but for now the point is that in a very practical sense, the workings of the market persuade even the most self-indulgent among us to serve others and to be concerned about the needs and wants of his neighbor. True, the motivation for doing so is not necessarily pure or unselfish, but as the Bible so clearly teaches, it is only God who can change the hearts of men.

Furthermore, the free market, because of the incredible

wealth it allows to be created, makes living beyond our-selves practicable. In order to show tangible love toward our neighbor (minister to his or her physical needs) we must first have the wealth to do so.

We sometimes need to be reminded that wealth is not the natural state of affairs. Throughout most of history the majority of people lived under some sort of centrally con-trolled economic system and were forced to devote most of their energies to mere survival. Often all but the wealthiest individuals lacked the economic means to look much beyond themselves and to aid others who were in need.

But the productivity spawned by economic freedom has radically changed this. In a free market, we are not only able to choose unselfish values and priorities, but we are also able to create the wealth necessary to fulfill them prac-tically.

II. Materialism

Another moral indictment of the market, closely related to the charge of selfishness, is the belief that the market fosters materialism. The example most often used to demonstrate the market's guilt in this area is the per-ceived evil effect of advertising. It is contended that advertising creates a sort of "lust" in the hearts of con-sumers by persuading them that mere material posses-sions will bring joy and fulfillment. In this sense, the mar-ket is condemned for creating a spirit of materialism and fostering an ethic of acquisitiveness. The market in gen-eral, and advertising specifically, is a persistent temptress encouraging each of us to concentrate on the lowest level of life, mere material goods.

This charge can be answered in much the same manner as the charge of selfishness. Just as allowing free exchange doesn't require selfishness, neither does it require material-ism. It is true that when people are economically free, mate-rialism is possible, and certainly there are materialistic peo-ple in market economies. But this hardly warrants a condemnation of the market. Materialism, like selfishness, can and will occur under any economic system. It is obvi-ous that a desire for material goods is far from being unique to capitalism. Witness, for example, the response of shop-pers as a store puts out a new rack of genuine cotton shirts in Moscow or a shipment of fresh meat arrives in a Krakow shop.

Although the role of advertising has been much maligned, it in fact provides a vital service to consumers. Advertising conveys information. It tells consumers what products are available, how these products can meet their needs, and what important differences exist among com-peting products. The fact that this is a valuable function becomes apparent if you imagine trying to buy a used car in a world without advertising. Either your choice of cars would be severely limited (to those cars you happen to stumble upon, i.e., gain knowledge of) or you would have to pay more (in the form of time and resources used in seek-ing out and comparing cars). In either case, without the "free" knowledge provided by advertising, you would be much worse off.

But the economic role of advertising aside, does adver-tising actually "create" a desire for goods? If it does, why do businesses in market-oriented economies spend billions of dollars each year on consumer research to find out what customers want? Why do some advertised products not sell (for example, the Edsel) or cease to sell well (for example, the hula hoop)? In the market economy consumers are the ultimate sovereigns of production. Their wants and pri-orities dictate what is produced; what is produced doesn't determine their wants and priorities. Many bankrupt businessmen, left with unsalable (at a profitable price) products wistfully wish that the reverse were true.

Moreover, the Bible consistently rejects any attempt by man to ascribe his sinful tendencies to his environment. If I am filled with avarice when I see an advertisement for a new Mercedes, I cannot place the blame on the advertisement. Rather I must recognize that I am responsible for my thoughts and desires, and that the problem lies within myself. After all, I could feel equally acquisitive if I just saw the Mercedes on the street rather than in an advertisement. Is it wrong for the owner of the Mercedes to incite my desires by driving his car where I might see it? Hardly.

Just as God did not allow Adam to blame Satan (the advertiser—and a blatantly false advertiser at that) or the fruit (the appealing material good) for his sin in the Garden, we cannot lay the blame for materialism on the free market or on advertising. The materialist's problem is the sin within his heart, not his environment.

If we follow the environmental explanation of materialism to its logical conclusion, the only solution would appear to be doing away with all wealth (i.e., eliminate all possible temptation). If this were the appropriate solution to the moral problem of materialism, perhaps the moral high ground must be conceded to the state-run economies of the world after all. They have been overwhelmingly successful at destroying wealth and wealth-creating capital!

III. Impersonalism and Individualism

Another common criticism of the market economy is its supposed impersonal nature and what some have called "individualistic anarchy." According to many Christian critics, the market encourages self-centered behavior and discourages relational ties in society. The non-personal market allocation of goods and services is seen to be antithetical to the seemingly higher and more noble goal of a loving and interdependent community. Because of the economic independence that the market affords, the individual is cut off from meaningful relationships with his fellow human beings and divorced from any purpose beyond his own interests. In short, the free market is accused of breeding a pathetic and inhumane isolation.

But does the market encourage impersonal behavior? Certainly not. It is important to understand that the presence of economic freedom does not require that all transactions and relationships take place on an impersonal level. For example, many people have good friendships with their customers, suppliers, employees, or employers. While these relationships are economic, they are not merely economic and they are not impersonal.

Furthermore, while the market leaves us free to deal with other people solely on the basis of economic motives, we are not required nor even necessarily encouraged to do so. We are completely free to deal on a non-economic basis. Suppose that I am in the business of selling food, and I find that someone is so poor that he has nothing to trade for the food that I am offering for sale. In the free market I am completely free to act apart from economic motives and make a charitable gift of the food. I have in no way lost my ability to act in a personal and non-economic way.

Community Relationships

So the market is not an inherently impersonal economic system. Nor is it hostile to the formation of community relationships.

An excellent example of a community which exists

within the market system is the family. Obviously I deal with my wife and children in a non-market manner. I give them food, shelter, clothing, and so on, and I certainly don't expect any economic gain in return. I do so joyfully, because I love my family and I value my relationship with them far above the economic benefits I forgo. Another example is the church. I have a non-economic and very personal relationship with people in my church. And there are countless teams, clubs, organizations, and associations which I can join, if I choose. If I want, I can even become part of a commune. The market economy doesn't stand in the way of, or discourage, any of these expressions of community.

But now we come to the heart of this objection against the market: what if people will not voluntarily choose to relate to each other in personal or community-type relationships? What if they choose not to look beyond their own interests and work for some purpose larger than themselves? The answer to this is the rather obvious question: Who should decide what is the appropriate degree of relationship and community?

True community, I submit, is something which must be consensual, meaning it must be voluntarily established. Think of a marriage or a church. If people do not choose to enter into these relationships when they are free to do so, we may judge their action to be a mistake, but by what standard can we try to coerce them into such relationships? Even if there were some objective standard of "optimum community," it is not at all clear that we would create it by robbing people of their economic freedom. There is no reason to believe that individuals living under a system of economic "planning" are less isolated or have more community by virtue of their system. The fact that individuals are forced into a collective group hardly means that a loving and caring community will result. Love and care are things which cannot be coercively extracted, but must be freely given.

Moreover, the free market actually encourages the formation and maintenance of the most basic human community—the family. As the utopian socialists of past centuries—including Marx and Engels—recognized, there is a vital connection between private property and the integrity of the family. Destroy the one, they reasoned, and the other will soon disintegrate.

Their motives were suspect but their analysis was correct. When the state fails to protect private property and instead takes over the functions traditionally provided by the family (such as education, day care, health care, sickness and old-age support), the family unit is inevitably weakened. Family bonds are undermined as the economic resources which formerly allowed the family to "care for its own" are transferred to the state. There is little doubt that the disintegration of the family in our country is in large part due to state intervention. Instead of turning toward and receiving personal care from within the family, individuals have been encouraged to turn toward the impersonal state. The result has been the disintegration of family bonds. It is state economic intervention—not the free-market system—which is inherently impersonal and antithetical to true human community.

IV. Economic Power

The objection to the market on the grounds of impersonalism is based on the same fallacy as were the previously discussed charges of selfishness and materialism. Each of these claims indicts the market for ills which in fact are common to all mankind—faults that would exist under any economic system. Impersonalism, selfishness, and materialism are the consequence of the fall of man, not the fruit of an economic system which allows freedom. If these sinful tendencies are an inescapable reality, the question that must be asked is: "What economic system best restrains sin?"

This brings us to a fourth moral objection to the market which is often espoused by the Christians of the left: that the market, which is often pictured as a "dog-eat-dog" or "survival of the fittest" system, leaves men free to oppress each other. It allows the economically powerful to arbitrarily oppress the economically weak, the wealthy to tread upon and exploit the poor. According to this view, wealth is power, and those with wealth will not necessarily use their power wisely and justly. Because the nature of man is what it is, this "economic power" must be checked by the state and restrained for the public good.

But does the market in fact allow individuals to exploit others? To begin with, there is a great deal of misunderstanding about this thing called "economic power." The term is in fact somewhat of a misnomer. When we speak of power, we normally refer to the ability to force or coerce something or someone to do what we desire. The motor in your car has the power to move the car down the road; this is mechanical power. The police officer has the power to arrest and jail a lawbreaker; this is civil power. But what of economic power? If I possess a great deal of wealth, what unique ability does this wealth confer?

In reality what the critics of the market call economic power is only the ability to please others, and thus "economic power" is not power in the true sense of the word. Regardless of a person's wealth, in the free market he can get what he wants only by pleasing another person through offering to exchange something which the other deems more valuable. Wealth (assuming it is not used to buy political power) doesn't bestow the ability to apply force to or dominate another individual.

Take for example the employer of labor, an individual who is often considered to be the embodiment of economic power and an exploiter of those less powerful than himself. It is often forgotten that an employer can get what he wants—employees for his business—only by offering something which pleases them, namely a wage which they consider better than not working, or better than working for someone else. He has no power to force them to come and work for him, but only the power to offer them a better alternative.

What ensures that he will want to make them a pleasing offer? The fact that doing so is the only way to get what he is interested in, namely their labor, provides a very strong incentive. But suppose the prospective employee is in very desperate straits and almost any wage, even one which seems pitifully low, will please him enough to work for the employer. In this situation, it seems as if the employer can get away with paying "slave wages" and exploiting the economically weaker employee.

This scenario, however, ignores the effects of the competition among employers for employees. In the market economy, employers are in constant competition with other employers for the services of employees. They are "disciplined" by this competition to offer top wages to attract workers. Because of competition, wages are "bid up" to the level at which the last employee hired will be paid a wage which is very nearly equivalent to the value of what he produces. As long as wages are less than this level, it pays an employer to hire another employee, since doing so will add to his profits. Economists call this the marginal productivity theory of wages.

But what if there were no competing employers? For example, what about a "one-company town"? Without competition, wouldn't the employer be able to exploit the employees and pay "unfair" wages?

First of all, it is important to remember that in the free market, an economic exchange occurs only because the two trading parties believe that they will be better off after the exchange. In other words, all exchanges are "positive sum" in that both parties benefit. Thus if an employee in this one-company town is willing to work for low wages, it is only because he or she places a higher value on remaining in the town and working for a lower wage than moving to another place and finding a higher paying job. The "power" that the employer wields is still only the ability to offer a superior alternative to the employee. In choosing to remain and work for a lower wage, the employee is likely considering other costs such as those of relocating, finding another job, and retraining, as well as non-monetary costs, such as the sacrifice of local friendships or the sacrifice of leaving a beautiful and pleasant town.

Moreover, this situation cannot last for long. If the employer can pay wages that are significantly lower than elsewhere, he will reap above-average profits and this in turn will attract other employers to move in and take advantage of the "cheap labor." In so doing, these new employers become competitors for employees. They must offer higher wages in order to persuade employees to come and work for them, and as a result wages eventually will be bid up to the level prevailing elsewhere.

Economic Ability to Please

What is true for the employer in relation to the employee is true for all economic relationships in the free market. Each individual, though he may be a tyrant at heart, can succeed only by first benefiting others—by providing them with an economic service. Regardless of the amount of wealth he possesses, he is never freed from this requirement. Economic "power" is only the economic ability to please, and as such it is not something to be feared. Far from allowing men to oppress each other, the free market takes this sinful drive for power and channels it into tangible service for others.

It is also important to consider that the only alternative to the free market is the political direction of economic exchanges. As the Public Choice theorists have so convincingly pointed out in recent years, there is no good reason to suppose that people become less self-interested when they enter the political sphere. In other words, to paraphrase Paul Craig Roberts, there is not necessarily a "Saul to Paul conversion" when an individual enters government. If he was power-hungry while he was a private-market participant, he likely will be power-hungry after he becomes a "public servant."

But there is an important difference. In contrast with economic power, political power is truly something to be feared because of its coercive aspect. The power-seeking individual in government has power in the true sense of the word. While in the market he has to please those he deals with in order to be economically successful, the same is not true, or is true to a far lesser degree, in the political sphere. In the political sphere he can actually abuse one group of people but still succeed by gaining the favor of other groups of people.

A classic example is a tariff. This economic intervention benefits a small group of producers (and those who work for or sell to the producers) at the expense of consumers who have to pay higher prices for the good in question. The politician gains in power (and perhaps wealth) because of the significant support he can receive from the small but well-organized group of producers. Other examples of the use of political power that clearly benefit some individuals at the expense of others are government bail-outs, subsidies, price supports, and licensing monopolies. The fact that these types of legislation continue despite the fact that they harm people (usually the least wealthy and most poorly organized) demonstrates the tendency of mankind to abuse political power.

In fact, virtually every state intervention into the economy is for the purpose of benefiting one party at the expense of another. In each of the cases mentioned above, some are exploited by others via the medium of the state. Therefore, if we are concerned about the powerful oppressing the weak, we should focus our attention on the abuse of political power. It, and not the so-called "economic power" of individuals acting within the free market, is the true source of tyranny and oppression. Our concern for the downtrodden should not lead us to denigrate economic freedom but rather to restrain the sphere of civil authority.

V. Conclusion

The free market is innocent of the charges leveled at it by its Christian critics. Its alleged moral shortcomings turn out to be things which are common to mankind under both free and command economic systems. While it is true that the free market restrains human sin, it makes no pretense of purging people of their selfishness, materialism, individualism, and drive for power. And this, perhaps, is the true sin in the eyes of the market's critics.

The market is explicitly non-utopian. It doesn't promise to recreate man in a new and more perfect state, but rather it acknowledges the moral reality of man and works to restrain the outward manifestations of sin. In this sense the free market is in complete accord with Biblical teachings. According to Scripture, man cannot be morally changed through any human system, be it religious, political, or economic, but moral regeneration comes solely through the grace of God.

If the Christian critics of the market expect an economic system to change the moral character of people, they are sadly mistaken. Such a task is clearly beyond the ability of any human institution or authority. We must be content to restrain the outward expression of sin, and this is something which the free market does admirably.

The Psychology of Cultism

Ben Barker

Cults are not a new phenomenon: they may be as old as man—or even animal herds. Cults may form around an individual, an object, an animal, or a concept. Invariably, the members of the cult ascribe magical powers to their object of worship—powers to manipulate the environment to protect the cult members against evil spirits, the devil, natural disasters, bankruptcy, illness, or whatever.

The core concept in cultism is a followership dependent upon someone or something *outside itself* to assist it in coping with a threatening external environment. The more inadequate and inferior the follower feels himself to be, the more magical and mystical the omnipotence projected onto the leader. However, it is a mistake to focus on the leader or object of veneration. The leader is usually merely a resourceful individual perceptive enough to recognize the varied types of helplessness in those about him who offers to take away those feelings. That his offer is frequently overstated and illusory is beside the point. The point is that the followers willingly take the bait—hook, line, and sinker.

Many were shocked by the submissive, dependent, compliant followers of Charles Manson who carved x's in their foreheads and chanted on the Los Angeles County

Ben Barker, M.D., a physician specializing in psychiatry and emergency medicine, originally presented these ideas in a speech for medical staff personnel. It was published in the April 1980 issue of *The Freeman*.

Courthouse steps. They were even more shocked to learn that some men and women had brutally annihilated other human beings on Manson's satanic command. Then there were the ill-fated followers of Jim Jones whose beliefs led them to a rotting death in the steamy jungles of Guyana. Numerous other examples could be cited. Where do they all come from? We shake our heads and wonder, while physicians and other societal leaders continue to reinforce exactly the type of behavior that will produce more cultists.

The Roots of Dependency

What are the roots of dependency in human behavior? The answer should be obvious. Each of us began life as a totally dependent parasite encased in a constant-temperature liquid environment with our nutritional needs satisfied effortlessly.

Through some miracle, the maternal host does not set up an appropriate foreign body rejection reaction and the fetus enjoys this total dependency state for some 40-odd weeks before expulsion.[1]

It is presumptuous to assume that this experience precedes awareness. Single-cell living forms demonstrate avoidance behavior to noxious stimuli. Are they aware? If they are, then is it not reasonable to suppose the fetus to be at least as aware? For me, though, the strongest evidence that the intrauterine life is experienced as pleasurable is the sustained effort adults make to recreate a similar experience through environmental manipulation. "To be waited on hand and foot" by spouse, servant, child, and others has long been associated with "all the things money can buy."

Once expelled from the uterus, the infant must struggle to meet some of his own needs. The struggle is multifaceted, beginning with an immature autonomic nervous system which must stabilize his internal environment in the face of a shifting external environment. Mother assists in this process by attempting through appropriate nurturing techniques to minimize the fluctuations of heat, cold, air circulation, and the like upon the infant. He remains extremely dependent upon her even though the biological umbilical cord has been ruptured. A more profound attachment persists which defies logical analysis.

In a slow, incomprehensible, years-long process, mother gradually weans the infant from his dependence on her. One of her tools is to promote his interaction with other adults, siblings, and peers. Obviously, no two parents accomplish this task in exactly the same way nor do any two individuals react identically to the same stimulus. However, there *are* cultural similarities in the process which conspire to create more than surface similarities in the same generation of offspring.

Herein rests the central point of my thesis: the cultural factors which have produced so many dependent, submissive followers among our youth are also behind the decline and fall of the United States as a force of geopolitical significance. Excessive dependency is endemic in our society and those who are in positions of power and prestige—including many in my profession—encourage and perpetuate this dependency.

An Age of Specialization

We live in an age of specialization so extreme that most of us are truly helpless outside our specialties. Our "system" thus has become an incredibly complex web of interacting specialties which provides great comfort when all is going well but reduces us to extreme helplessness in times of crisis. Examples abound: Supermarkets are very convenient unless trucks stop delivering. Automobiles are a nice way to get around unless there is no gasoline. Washing machines are dandy unless yours breaks down and the repairman has a two-week waiting list.

The trade-off in our age of technological marvels is this: We gain convenience and security but may sacrifice self-reliance and independence. For example, antibiotics are available over the counter in many countries and individuals are free to take the responsibility for the management of their own illnesses. But here in the United States, we do not have that freedom. In fact, patients here have been so programmed to depend upon physicians that we must take responsibility for *all* their bumps, bruises, and sniffles—hardly leaving us with adequate time to care for those who truly require our skilled services.

Our cult of dependency medicine has been so successful that disenchanted followers are literally suing us out of business. They are impatient and demanding that all diseases be cured—and cured now! In turning over the responsibility for their health to us, they gave us an illusory omnipotence. Our fallibility crushes this illusion and their response is vindictive anger. Discredited cult leaders are adjudged harshly by their disappointed followers.

The Drug Cult

Perhaps the largest cult of all that our profession has had a hand in is the drug cult. By that, I don't mean the "Superfly" white El Dorado Cadillac jockey who drives his exotic automobile through Harlem or Watts nor do I refer to the Mafia Godfather, the French Connection mystery men, or the Colombian cocaine millionaires. I'm talking about the "drugstore cult"—the widespread dependence of American citizens on the soothing syrups and pills available on the shelves of drugstores, supermarkets, newsstands, and elsewhere. It is the cult that has pushed Valium into the number one all-time best-seller spot.

Our undergraduate, professional, and postgraduate medical education is drug-oriented and drug-saturated, hence our primary weapon against illness is, of course, pharmacological. Was it not fitting and symbolic that so many at Jonestown were put out of their misery by an injection from a doctor? They trusted him to do the *right* thing.

Not only medicine but many other careers and skills have enthroned science and the scientific technique. Our educational systems perpetuate the myths of science *ad nauseam*. How much of the science and math shoved down your throats in high school, college, and medical school were really useful to you either in specialty training or in practice? Admit that much of your schooling is pure ritual and you will see that "education" itself has become a cult. College graduates enter the real world with magical expectations, waving their hard-earned degrees in the wind. When their skills are not snapped up, they are disillusioned and angry.

Schooling as Religion

In attempting to achieve power over the environment, students have literally endowed the schooling process with the status of religious veneration and plugged themselves into it. The teachers and professors are the high priests and the process is supposed to mystically and mysteriously protect the follower from risk or harm if the prescribed rituals are followed. Believe it or not, many who educate themselves into overcrowded fields simply return to school for another degree. Others of the educated cultists simply change cults.

Basically, then, we see that the psychology of cultism is simply the persistence of the parent/child relationship beyond an appropriate time. Followers or members feel helpless or overwhelmed by an environment they perceive as threatening and respond to this feeling by embracing a concept or leader to whom they ascribe magical power.

This is a sign of excessive dependency; and excessive dependency in a society can come either from inadequate parental directing toward self-reliance, individual rejection of such directing, or programming from external sources which directs towards dependency. Additionally, the environment may become truly so threatening that dependency upon an authority or higher power source may be appropriate, in war, say, or in specific subcultures as depicted in the film, "The Godfather." Modern technology also shares the guilt, for it has contrived to capture a formerly active and mobile social order and transformed it into a sedentary spectator society.

The principal villain in this transformation process is television. By and large, it is a dehumanization process which tends to dull the senses and produce emotional zombies who respond primarily to subliminal and repetitive advertisement slogans. What then occurs is much akin to disuse atrophy: the spirit within dwindles like melting wax and the mind dulls. The products of this process suffer endemic obesity and emotional indifference to their actual environment.

What Jim Jones and his ilk have offered to these unfortunates is an antidote to the poisonous, dehumanizing processes induced by the age of technology. Few who leap for the bait really care that the antidote itself is toxic, for what they have been experiencing is a living death and any escape hatch is acceptable, even if it leads into an endless maze. The visible result is the phenomena of cults so alive in the land today.

In a society of people programmed almost from birth to follow-the-leader, it is inevitable that some will fall into the clutches of mad leaders. That is but one of the many consequences of the loss of self-reliance and of independent judgment in American citizens. Before joining in an emotional condemnation of "cults," perhaps it would be best to understand that a cult is but a system of worship or ritual. It is a system of belief gone pathological, to be distinguished from religious beliefs which inculcate independence.

Freedom of Worship

The freedom to worship God after your own manner of belief is as valuable to the spirit of independence as is freedom of speech. These freedoms, guaranteed by the First Amendment to the Constitution, are about all we have left of the dream of the Founding Fathers and should not be carelessly dismissed.

Genuine religious beliefs have the special quality of satisfying intellectual and emotional needs simultaneously. They account for unequal life fates, promise release from illness and suffering, and offer hope for a better life. They are, indeed, a special, poorly understood, potentially adaptive set of ego defense mechanisms. Do we psychiatrists have a socially sanctioned right to intervene in religious beliefs, particularly when we know so little about the influence of religion on psychopathology?

If we deprive someone of his religion, what substitute do we have for him? And ought we to impose such a substitute? Physicians for years have ignored nutrition, exercise, and relaxation as techniques for combating or preventing illnesses. Indeed, we have ignored preventive medicine itself. We are, for the most part, disease-oriented high priests in a cult of science and technology which is leading us all into a fate which appears particularly unattractive. Chronic stress-related diseases plague both us and our patients (hypertension, strokes, heart attacks, colitis, ulcers, asthma, and so forth), yet we persist in disregarding the spiritual element in man and rely solely upon chemical potions and invasive techniques to combat diseases.

Perhaps God *does* exist. Perhaps He was around before Plato and Aristotle. Perhaps He spoke to Moses and Paul and many others. Perhaps His Holy Spirit *is* within each human being and resists the sadness of a mechanized, depersonalized, technological social order. Media manipulators who sensationalize the fates of unfortunate cultists cannot destroy the source of all life which beats within each of our breasts and breathes freely of the air that His plants provide.

The psychology of cultism is but one indication of an intrinsic desire in each of us to offer veneration to the Creator. This process becomes pathological only if the surrogate leader is mad, as with Jim Jones, or when the path followed leads into a blind maze, as with scientific technology. Almost every day another "accepted" scientific fact is discredited in yet another laboratory experiment. It appears, then, that science offers no final solutions or ultimate explanations. Is our own worship of the microscope and the wonders of microbiology, neurochemistry, and physiology as misplaced as the blind faith that Jones's followers had in him?

Blind Departures from Basic Principles of Freedom

This nation was founded upon principles taken from the Judeo-Christian ethic and as long as these prevailed, we grew and prospered. Now, there is no prayer in the schools and unionized, socialist teachers insidiously program our youth. Mindless violence and senseless trivia beam at us from the television, our newspapers are full of lies and scantily clad females posing for underwear ads. Heroin is the opiate of the ghetto, alcohol of the middle-class community, and cocaine of the wealthy. Valium, which we supply, is abused by all social classes.

We correctly perceive the sea as a dangerous, hostile environment for man and few would attempt to navigate it for any significant distance without the benefits of a buoyant and protective superstructure. What many fail to realize is that man's journey on dry land is at least as hazardous. In neglecting the spiritual aspects of our own existences, and of our patients' as well, we are up a creek without either boat or paddles.

Cults, worthless dollars, gasoline shortages, and dependent patients are the long-term consequences of too many of us learning to rely on Big Brother. The processed foods we eat and drink are as suspect as the poisoned potion was in Guyana—it simply takes longer for them to kill us.

Erich Fromm tells us that all human beings are religious in one way or another, religion being "any system of thought and action which . . . gives the individual the frame of orientation and object of devotion he needs."[2] The psychology of cultism is all around us, as men elect to place their faith and trust in other men, their machines or their technological products.

As long as we pass on shallow values to our youth and let them see us worshipping at the altar of science, or the government, or the dollar, or gold—they will do likewise.

As long as we promote dependency in our patients, we are reinforcing the psychology of cultism. The white coat and the stethoscope are counterproductive when used as talismans in a cult of science. We should learn and teach self-reliance and preventive medicine principles, for when these attitudes and values are mixed with genuine faith in the Creator, we may return to being a nation of healthy and sane individuals rather than a society of drugged, dependent sheep and we may finally reverse the decline of the United States as a force of geopolitical significance.

---

1. Cf. S. Ferenczi, "Stages in the Development of the Sense of Reality," *Outline of Psychoanalysis,* by J. S. Van Tesslar, p. 112.

2. Ashok Rao, M. D., and Jennifer A. Katze, M. D., "The Role of Religious Belief in a Depressed Patient's Illness," *Psychiatric Opinion,* June 1979, pp. 39–43.

The Disease from Which Civilizations Die

John K. Williams

Saint Augustine once lamented that he knew precisely what he meant by the word "time" until asked to state what he meant. I sympathize with the saint. I know full well what I mean by the noun "civilization," but pinning down the word is a singularly frustrating exercise. *Webster's New World Dictionary of the American Language*—a work somewhat inordinately given to using the term *et cetera*—tells me that "civilization" is related to "social organization of a high order, marked by the development and use of a written language and by advances in the arts and sciences, government, etc." and thus indicates "the total culture of a particular people, nation, period, etc." and "countries and peoples considered to have reached a high stage of social and cultural development." This helps—particularly the reference to the "development and use of a written language" and "advances in the arts and sciences, government, etc."—but I am still dissatisfied: I know not a few men and women deeply involved in government, and not completely ignorant of the arts and sciences, whom I hesitate to describe as "civilized." It is, as the King of Siam remarked to Anna, "a puzzlement."

The Reverend Dr. John K. Williams, popular author, lecturer, and philosopher, served FEE as a resident scholar. He continues to carry the banner for liberty in his native Australia. This essay appeared in the September 1985 edition of *The Freeman*.

Non-dictionary definitions of and comments about "civilization" and the "civilizing process" compound confusion. Martin Crombie asserts that "the alchemy of civilization transforms vicious animals ruled by instinct into human beings governed by reason," but Eric Berne tells us that "we are born princes and the civilizing process turns us into frogs." José Ortega y Gasset insists that "civilization is nothing else but the attempt to reduce force to being the last resort," but Will Rogers wryly observes that no one can "say that civilization doesn't advance, for in every war they kill you in a new way." On the one hand, Winston Churchill affirms that "to fight for the preservation of civilization is to fight for the survival of the human race," but on the other hand Ralph Waldo Emerson insists that "the end of the human race will be that it will eventually die of civilization." When these conflicting utterances are blended, and are spiced by the suggestion of Calvin Coolidge that "civilization and profits go hand in hand" and the observation of Alan Coult that "the flush toilet is the basis of Western civilization," the search for a definition of civilization begins to look like an exercise in futility.

Civilizations Die But a Continuity Remains

For all this, while no one of us may be able precisely to say what he or she means by "civilization," all of us understand, even if we do not agree with, the assertion that civilizations seem to die. Civilization itself may continue, and much that past civilizations have achieved may be absorbed by new civilizations and thus conserved, but particular civilizations, like individual men and women, are seemingly destined to be born, to grow, to flourish, to fade, and to die.

While it is easy to concede that such a process has characterized civilizations of yesteryear, it is not so easy to believe that this is also true of our own civilization. And yet, the cosmos of which we are a part, and thus human history itself, are vital and dynamic, not lifeless and static. Change is thus inevitable. Since change is of the very essence of reality, no particular state of affairs, and hence no particular form of civilization, are forever. And that is not terrible: rather, it is ground for hope. Tomorrow is not predestined to be a rerun of today. A world more prosperous, more peaceful, more committed to liberty than is our world, is a real and exciting possibility.

I have been unable, alas, to identify the reference, but an observation I noted in a desk calendar and wrote down says it all. "Civilization is a stream with banks. The stream is sometimes filled with blood from people killing, stealing, shouting, and doing things historians usually record, while on the banks, unnoticed, people build homes, make love, raise children, sing songs, write poetry, and even whittle statues. The story of civilization is the story of what happened on the banks. Historians are pessimists because they ignore the banks for the river." The words are those of Will and Ariel Durant, but where in their writings they are found I do not know.

What happens on the banks is marked by *continuity*. One generation inherits and builds upon what previous generations have achieved. In this sense, the insights and discoveries of particular civilizations last. And in this sense, what is great and glorious about our civilization can last. Hence my willingness to affirm that "the American Way" can last and will last. In so speaking I am not, incidentally, seeking to flatter you. The "American Way" has a long history. Insights and ideals for which innumerable people over millennia fought and died came, perhaps by an accident of history, the defining characteristics of "the American Way." Your nation, after all, is unique in that it was "conceived in liberty."

What *can* last and what, I believe, *will* last, are the principles so many for so long sought to establish, and which in this new nation "became flesh." What can and will last is, so to speak, the ringing affirmation that "all men are created equal, that they are endowed by their Creator with certain unalienable rights, that among these are Life, Liberty, and the pursuit of Happiness."

While we cannot pretend that our civilization as it is shall endure until the end of human history, the way to preserve and pass on to those who follow us what is magnificent and awesome about the American Way is to defend all that is excellent in our civilization as it is. Being human—being material creatures living in a spatio-temporal, physical world—we *cannot* defend an abstraction called "civilization itself." Just as the only way to serve an abstraction called "humanity" is to serve particular flesh-and-blood human beings, so the only way to further the cause of civilization as such is to cherish and conserve a particular civilization.

We serve civilization as such, and can *only* serve civilization as such, by serving the best in our own civilization. And one way to do this is to ask what it is that we can do to combat the forces that weaken, that undermine, that erode a particular civilization. Hence the title of my address and the question I wish to explore: *What is the disease from which civilizations die?*

Thucydides

In using the word "disease" I am borrowing a meta-phor, an image used some two-and-a-half millennia ago by a Greek historian named Thucydides.

Thucydides loved the city-state of Athens. His devotion was not to the buildings and environment one could point to, but to a way of life which Athens in the fifth century B.C. embodied. In words Thucydides ascribes to a great Athenian leader named Pericles, that way of life is thus described:

> Our constitution is called a democracy because power is in the hands not of a minority but of the entire people. When it is a question of settling private disputes, everyone is equal before the law. . . . And, just as our political life is free and open, so is our day-to-day life in relation to each other. We do not get into a state with our next-door neighbor if he enjoys himself in his own way, nor do we give him the kind of black looks which, though they do no real harm, still do hurt people's feelings. We are free and tolerant in our private lives; but in public affairs we keep to the law. This is because [the law] commands our deep respect . . . especially . . . those unwritten laws which it is an acknowledged shame to break. It seems just as natural to us to enjoy foreign goods as our own local products . . . and our city is open to the world. . . . We regard wealth as something to be properly used, rather than something to boast about, and as for poverty, no one need be ashamed to admit it. The real shame is not in being poor, but in not taking practical measures to escape from poverty. Here each individual is inter-

ested not only in his own affairs, but in the affairs of [Athens] as well.[1]

Now it must be confessed that this description of the Athenian way is not a little idealized. The institution of slavery was a reality in Athens, just as it was in all Greek city-states of the fifth century B.C. Again, power in Athens could be said to be "in the hands . . . of the entire people," if and only if women did not count as people. Yet for all this, Thucydides' description accurately captures something of what was so magnificent about his beloved Athens, a civilization that gave birth to thinkers, writers, and artists whose insights and works still live, having become part of "civilization itself." Yet the civilization that was Athens did *not* live. It died.

Early in the work from which I have quoted, Thucydides describes a mysterious plague which swept through Athens, elaborating in detail the symptoms those suffering from the disease displayed. At one level this section of his history *is* simply history, a painstaking record of a significant event which most certainly did occur. Yet more than a simple description of what happened is intended. Thucydides *uses* this description as a controlling symbol for his entire work. Athenian civilization itself suffered, he asserts, from a "disease," a disease characterized by particular symptoms. This disease, which in the case of Athens proved fatal, is the disease all men and women of good will must fear. For it is the disease from which civilizations die.

Human Beings and Human Nature

Thucydides frequently uses the phrase, "human nature being what it is" and similar phrases. By so speaking, he is indicating at least two realities, two constants about men and women. First, *human beings are rational.* Men and women are capable of *thought.* They can formulate goals and rationally seek out ways to realize these goals. They can recall, consider, and learn from the past and thereby plan for the future. They can envisage not simply an immediate and given present, but a distant and possible future. *Human nature is rational.*

Now rationality dictates, insists Thucydides, the rule of law. Long-term objectives can be realized by an individual if and only if he or she can count upon other people behaving in an essentially predictable way. By this is meant *not* that the individual cannot or should not be spontaneous and creative, and thus unpredictable, but that *some rules and conventions governing the way people relate to each other must exist and must be respected.* Rule by a tyrant's whim or a mob's caprice is undesirable, apart from anything else, precisely because such rule is erratic and unpredictable, precluding cooperative, long-term endeavors. What is permitted today might be forbidden tomorrow; undertakings made in the present might not be fulfilled in the future. Social coordination and cooperation demands, insists Thucydides, the rule of law. And as rational beings, men and women can perceive that this is so.

The Rules of Law

Like many of his contemporaries, Thucydides divides "laws" broadly defined into four groups or sets. First, and perhaps weakest, are the rules signified by the word *manners.* People breaking these rules tend to be regarded as somewhat uncivilized and uncouth, but that is all. Ill-mannered people may not be invited to dinner parties, but they are not perceived as *"bad"* people.

Then come the rules signified by the word *morals*. These rules are significantly stronger than the rules we call "manners." People breaking *these* rules are perceived not simply as irksome, antisocial irritants but as *evil* people.

Third come the rules making up the *written laws* of a community. These rules, stronger than both manners and morals, are the rules which, if broken, incur a penalty imposed by a court. While some "immoral" actions may also be "illegal" actions, not all are. Thus the sexual license so uproariously depicted in the plays of the Athenian comedian, Aristophanes, while certainly not *illegal,* was no less certainly regarded as *immoral.* The sphere of morality, and the sphere of legality, were not perceived by the Greeks as identical.

Manners. Morals. The written laws. And a fourth set of rules: the *"unwritten laws which it is an acknowledged shame to break."* These laws were perceived *as so* basic, *so* fundamental, *so* important, that they did not need to be written down. For the Greeks, these laws were two: honor the dead, and honor the gods, including the gods of others. In a sense, these two laws reduce to a single imperative: respect other people as people, possessing a worth in and of themselves, and respect the values other people hold, even if those values are other than one's own. In more contemporary language, we might define the "unwritten laws" as what some philosophers call *reciprocal respect for autonomy,* a respect for the personhood of other people and their capacity to formulate and strive to realize their own peaceful, noncoercive visions of the "good life." The "unwritten laws."

Rationality, then, dictates obedience to these laws. It is

in one's own interest that one is part of a community where certain expectations can be held and long-term goals can be pursued. To be sure, one cannot, given these rules, do exactly what one might wish at a given moment, but neither can anyone else. There is thus an incalculably valuable payoff, a payoff more than compensating for the irksome restraint of not always being able to behave with impunity. So affirms reason. So asserts the rationality that is part of human nature.

Alongside rationality is found a second characteristic of "human nature": *a drive to seek immediate, here-and-now pleasure.* Men and women resent whatever curbs their freedom to seek such pleasure. Regardless of the dictates of sweet reason, they chafe at the bit. Thus if a person can acquire the power to defy the rules social cooperation and coordination demand, that person will defy them. If a person can acquire the power to defy the rules and get away with it, that person will, asserts Thucydides, tend to do precisely that.

The first rules to go are usually manners. Then morals bite the dust. Then the written laws are defied. Finally, the "unwritten laws" are forgotten. Resentment and envy are fostered, the powerless detesting the powerful. Factions proliferate. Barbarism reigns.

A Tyrant Is Born

And then, asserts Thucydides, comes the end, in one of two forms. A social order without coordination is powerless to defend itself against the disciplined onslaughts of an external power. Or—and more frequently—a people sinking into the chaos of barbarism panic. They cry out for someone—anyone—who will restore some semblance of cohesion and order. And invariably that someone emerges. He promises to give the people what, in desperation, they are grasping for. He promises to restore social order and the rule of law. *But at a price.* In exchange, men and women must surrender their liberty. In this way, the tyrant is born.

Thucydides describes in great detail the symptoms observable as this disease—the disease from which civilizations die—inexorably works its way toward its terrible end, progressively eroding the structures and practices that are, so to speak, the central nervous system of a civilized community. I quote him at some length.

"Revolutions broke out in city after city, and in places where the revolutions occurred late, the knowledge of what had happened previously in other places caused still new extravagances . . . in the methods of seizing power and . . . unheard-of atrocities in revenge. To fit in with the change of events, words, too, had to change their usual meanings. What used to be described as a thoughtless act of aggression was now regarded as the courage one would expect to find in a party member; to think of the future and wait was merely another way of saying that one was a coward. . . . Fanatical enthusiasm was the mark of a real man . . . ; [any-one] who held violent opinions could always be trusted; anyone who objected to [such opinions] became a suspect. . . . Family relations were a weaker tie than party member-ship, since party members were . . . ready to go to any extreme for any reason whatever. These parties were not formed to enjoy the benefits of the established laws, but simply to acquire power. . . ."

Continues Thucydides: "Love of power . . . was the cause of all these evils. . . . Leaders of parties in the cities had programs which appeared admirable—on the one side equality for the masses, on the other side safe and sound government by an aristocracy. Yet by professing to serve the public interest, party leaders and members in truth sought to win . . . prizes for themselves. . . . [With] the conventions of civilized life thrown into confusion, human nature, always ready to offend even where laws exist, showed itself in its true colors . . . , repealing general laws of humanity which . . . give a hope of salvation to all."[2]

Thus the symptoms. Then the end. Whether externally imposed or internally generated, tyranny and despotism triumph. Liberty dies, and with it a civilization. The joyous songs of a free and civilized people are silenced. The disease from which civilizations die has worked its way to its end.

Here endeth a brief and sketchy lesson from a volume penned by a genius whose name is never heard by many students. They prefer, you see, "relevant" books and contemporary names. And those of us who should know better capitulate, fearful of incurring our children's wrath. We proffer amusing mini-courses about ephemeral interests instead—then wonder why it is our young know little about the heritage that is rightly theirs.

Moral Decline

As a preacher, I might be expected to point to the breakdown in Western societies of moral rules. Clearly, all is not well. In his monumental volume, *Modern Times: The World from the Twenties to the Eighties*,[3] Paul Johnson documents the rise in the West of moral relativism and moral subjectivism. More and more, moral rules are perceived *either* as arbitrary prescriptions and proscriptions relative to a particular society, having no rootage or grounding in the nature of things, *or* as expressions of personal taste, a difference over the merits of cruelty for its own sake being akin to a difference over the merits of a particular flavor of ice cream.

Yet in spite of this, I suggest that anyone tempted to assert that our civilization has sunk to hitherto depths of moral depravity, read some history. The eighteenth-century writer, Tobias Smollett—author of that ever-delightful work, *The Expedition of Humphrey Clinker*—describes the highways of his day as being "infested with violence and assassination" and the cities of his age as "teem(ing) with the brutal votaries of intemperance and lewdness." London in 1839 boasted 933 brothels and 844 houses of ill-fame to serve a population of some two million people. Hooliganism is no more rampant in New York City today than it was in *nineteenth*-century London, where gangs such as the "Bucks" and "Corinthians" perfected traditions of sheer terrorism elaborated by their eighteenth-century predecessors, the notorious "Mohocks." Consider this description of the Mohocks: "Nobody who was alone was safe from their cowardly assaults. They attacked at random any unarmed person who was out after dark. They assaulted unprotected women; they drove their swords through sedan-chairs; they pulled people from coaches, slit their noses with razors, stabbed them with knives, ripped the coach to pieces, and then . . . killed."[4]

The barbaric behavior of English soccer fans which recently shocked a disbelieving world has its parallels in the eighteenth century, the major difference being not the mindlessness of the behavior but the fact that, today, we at least *are* shocked.

The situation is complex. There *is* something depraved about an age witnessing self-styled world leaders applauding a speech delivered by Idi Amin on October 1, 1975, at that cabal of tyrannies laughingly described as the United Nations. There *is* something profoundly disturbing about a generation of adults that seemingly has lost its moral nerve, leaving the young to improvise their manners and morals as best they can. Yet to assert that we are experiencing an unprecedented moral decline is to go beyond the evidence. Suffice to suggest that, if we take seriously Thucydides' claim that a disregard of the rules we call manners and morals is indeed symptomatic of the disease from which civilizations die, we cannot be complacent with impunity.

The Rule of Law

What *is* beyond dispute is that we today have largely departed from the rule of law. "When it is a question of settling private disputes, *everyone is equal before the law,*" asserts Thucydides. Citizens of Western nations not so long ago could echo this assertion. Today they cannot.

The Founding Fathers of this nation meant by "equality" precisely what Greeks such as Thucydides meant by the term *isonomia*—namely, *equality before the law.* There are to be no special laws for special classes or castes or elites, laws privileging some but disadvantaging others. Indeed rules which *do* single out particular individuals or particular sets of individuals were not, for the Greeks, properly called laws at all, but "edicts" or "decrees." Even when such rules are backed by the majority, they remain other than laws proper, "the decrees of the *demos*—the people—correspond(ing)," as Aristotle puts it, "to the edicts of the tyrant."

This truth was clearly and unambiguously perceived by those who in the seventeenth and eighteenth centuries defended the political philosophy of classical—*classical*—

liberalism, and was no less clearly perceived by your Founding Fathers. They established a republic, not an unrestricted democracy; they advocated not the absolute rule of any majority but the constitutionally defended liberties of minorities, even minorities of one; they defended not rule by any principles securing majority approval, but by principles of conduct equally applicable to all. Justice was portrayed as a blindfolded figure. She did not see *who* stood before her. That did not matter, for whoever you were— rich or poor; Catholic, Protestant, Jew, or "Infidel"; educated or unlettered—your "rights" were the *same.*

This understanding of the "rule of law" is utterly vital for a free and civilized community. Rules which single out special classes, castes, or elites breed the factionalism and scheming Thucydides laments, foster the envy Thucydides deplores, and precipitate the civil strife and dissension Thucydides fears. No matter what impressively high-minded terms are appealed to as justification for any departure from the rule of law properly understood—"social justice" or whatever—the outcome remains the same. And that outcome is disaster for a free and civilized society.

And let us not delude ourselves. In recent decades Western civilization *has* witnessed a departure from the rule of law, classically defined. Justice is no longer blindfolded, supremely indifferent as to who it is standing accused before her. She peeks! "Tell me who you are," she asserts, "and *then* I shall tell you your rights." The notion that all enjoy absolutely equal "rights"—essentially the "right" to formulate and strive to realize *any* vision of the "good life," given only that such striving and such visions are peaceful, and that all are to be protected by government from violence, theft, and fraud—has been unspeakably attenuated. "Equality of rights" and "equality before the law" have succumbed to a different vision of "equality"—an egalitarian sameness secured by edicts and decrees which advantage some but disadvantage others.

The very nature of government thus changes. No longer is government given the vital but limited task of enforcing a single set of rules, protecting all from actual or threatened violence, theft, and fraud, and thereby ensuring that all *are* equally free to formulate and strive to realize their own visions—their *diverse but noncoercive* visions—of the "good life." Rather, government becomes the means whereby one group of people seeks favors and advantages at the expense of rival groupings of people. A massive redistributive apparatus proliferates zero-sum games whereby some gain and others lose. Factionalism is encouraged, envy is increased, and government becomes not the protector of all but what Frederic Bastiat, the great French classical liberal thinker, called "the fictitious entity by which everyone seeks to live at the expense of everyone else."[5] And according to Thucydides, this eroding of the rule of law signifies the presence of the disease from which civilizations die.

The Family

I make no apologies for drawing your attention to Thucydides' specific reference to *the weakening of family ties* as a further symptom of the disease from which civilizations die. Indeed I would urge you to read a singularly scholarly volume penned by the courageous Russian dissident, Igor Shafarevich, entitled *The Socialist Phenomenon*.[6] While a mathematician by training—indeed until recently Shafarevich was a professor of mathematics at Moscow University—he displays in this volume an utterly awesome historical knowledge, and he uses that knowledge to document with compelling thoroughness the hatred statists and collectivists invariably have had for the family unit. It would seem to be the case that opposition to individual liberty inevitably leads to opposition to the family.

Because I am committed to the rule of law, I cannot and do not advocate laws specifying the family unit and deliberately seeking to foster and favor the family unit. I must, in the name of the rule of law, oppose all rules the objective of which is the realization of some particular vision of the "good life"—save, of course, visions involving the actual or threatened coercion of people not sharing those visions.

What I oppose in the name of the rule of law is the perhaps unintentional weakening of the traditional family by welfare schemes which in practice encourage a breakdown of the family unit. It would be impertinent for me to refer to the situation in your nation. But I can refer you to Charles Murray's devastating critique of American social welfare policy, *Losing Ground.*[7]

All I ask is that governments mind their own business and get out of the way as individuals organize their social relationships. The traditional family is, in my judgment, so grounded in biological and emotional reality that it can look after itself. The only further suggestion I make is that individuals caring about strengthening the traditional family, involve themselves in voluntary organizations assisting families in trouble—financial assistance, counseling, and so on.

Be that as it may, the undermining of the family is, as Thucydides perceived so long ago, a symptom of the disease from which civilizations die.

Individual Integrity

Finally, according to Thucydides, the disease from which civilizations die afflicts the "best" members of a society, not simply the "worst." Given immoral social institu-

tions, the "best" are tempted to compromise their principles. By so yielding, however, those who should know better become infected cells carrying the disease, rather than
healthy antibodies fighting the invader.

Some lines of George Meredith say it all:

In tragic life, God wot,
No villain need be. Passions spin the plot:
We are betrayed by *what is false within.*

I know the alibis, being extremely gifted in the less than
noble art of rationalization. I am robbed, say, by a pickpocket. At some future date, I acquire some clout over the
pickpocket. Is it not proper that I retrieve all or some of
what rightly is mine? Similarly, is it not right that I join in
the scramble to the government trough, retrieving what has
been taken from me, at least in part? *But the analogy is
flawed.* We are not retrieving from the pickpocket what is
ours; we are rather sending him out to pick other pockets—
including those of our children and our children's children—and sharing in the loot. We are partners in crime, not
victims enjoying a measure of restitution.

I am not referring to forms of involvement in a less than
ideal system that cannot be avoided. In my nation, the only
way I can opt out of a socialized medical system is to seek
out some ex-doctor, struck off the lists, and negotiate an
undisclosed cash payment; and frankly I'm not prepared to
entrust my physical well-being to some probably incompetent rogue. I go to the ballet, even though I know that
money coercively extracted from football fans and movie
buffs (for the most part less affluent than am I), is subsidiz-
ing my extravagant tastes. Total disengagement with a less
than ideal system is acquired only by opting out, and, with

like-minded souls, seeking a deserted island on which to set up a utopia—but such islands are few and the pioneering spirit is not, alas, mine.

I am, however, referring to an involvement we could avoid *if we were willing to pay the price.* Many of those who state that they value liberty, and a politico-economic system informed by liberty, tolerate in themselves a measure of involvement with statist structures that is not necessary, and which makes their professed values ring hollow. In this sense we are, in Meredith's words, betrayed by "what is false within," becoming carriers of the disease from which civilizations die.

Conclusion

No person with eyes to see, and certainly no person with eyes alert to the symptoms detailed by Thucydides of the disease from which civilizations die, can entertain the fantasy that all is well with our civilization. Yet I am utterly convinced that our situation is far from hopeless, and that the "disease" can be curbed and conquered.

I believe the American inheritance is the greatest inheritance ever given to any nation: "A *new* nation, *conceived* in liberty, and *dedicated* to the proposition that all men are created equal." In this land the dream of the ages was earthed, and became the very foundation upon which a people began to build. The revolution that gave you birth was unique. Other revolutions ended in terror or Napoleonic empire. *Your* revolution challenged at its beginning, and has challenged ever since, all dominations and tyrannies, all prejudices and bigotries, all predatory institutions enslaving and debasing the free spirit of humanity. Your revolution enshrined and still enshrines the cry that people are not chattels, not pawns on a planner's chessboard, not divided by "nature" into lords and serfs. It is therefore sacrilege to enslave them, infamous to engineer them, criminal to degrade them and seek to smother the liberty that burns in their being.

And that is your strength. For the liberty upon which this nation was and is built is not merely a value created by or equal to a taste some of us happen to have acquired. It is grounded in the very nature of human reality. In the absence of private property rights, the absence of changing relative money prices in a market economy—in the absence, to put it bluntly, of economic and individual liberty—a community literally *cannot* use what it has to acquire what it wants, and the hungry will not be fed, the naked will not be clothed, the destitute will not be sheltered.

More, there is in the human spirit a yearning that can never utterly be silenced, a yearning for freedom to formulate one's own vision of the "good life" and seek to realize that vision. I know that there is another voice and another yearning—a voice that whispers fearfully of the risks and responsibilities freedom involves, and a yearning to be carried through life. Yet the voice that says, "Stand on thy feet, take up thy bed and walk," has the last word, for it is stronger than the voice which, in the name of an illusory security, lures us toward the collective grave of statism.

You and I are on the side of life. Yes, we must act as though everything depended upon the labors of our hands, the intensity of our thinking, the devotion of our hearts. Yet if liberty *is* written into the very structure of our individual and social being, victory in the end is sure. If only we stop compromising; if only we as educationalists and adults do what A. N. Whitehead said we *must* do, and expose our children to the "habitual vision of greatness" by telling them the story of humanity's struggle toward freedom; if only we stop apologizing or indulging in neurotic guilt, *and* stand tall at mention of the "American Way" as I have defined and as your forefathers defined it and not as foolish rabble-rousers define it. If only we do this the victory shall be ours. Of course there will be setbacks. Of course there will be disappointments. Since when has the long, slow journey from the slavery of Egypt to the promised land of freedom been other than through a wilderness? Yet that "wilderness and the solitary place *shall* be made glad, and the desert *shall* rejoice; it *shall* blossom abundantly and rejoice even with joy and singing."

---

1. Thucydides, *The Peloponnesian War*, trans. Rex Warner (Harmondsworth: Penguin Books, 1954), pp. 145–146.

2. *Ibid.*, pp. 242–245.

3. Paul Johnson, *Modern Times: The World from the Twenties to the Eighties* (New York: Harper and Row, 1983).

4. Cited by J. Hemming, *Individual Morality* (London: Nelson, 1969), p. 6.

5. Frederic Bastiat, "The State," trans. S. Cain, in *Selected Essays on Political Economy*, George B. de Huszar, ed. (Irvington-on-Hudson, N.Y.: Foundation for Economic Education, 1968), p. 144.

6. Igor R. Shafarevich, *The Socialist Phenomenon* (New York: Harper and Row, 1980).

7. Charles Murray, *Losing Ground: American Social Policy, 1950–1980* (New York: Basic Books, 1984).

A Moral Order

Edmund A. Opitz

The Pilgrims and Puritans who settled along the northeast coast of this country during the seventeenth and eighteenth centuries had sailed across the rugged Atlantic seeking a piece of land where they might put their deepest religious convictions into practice. They were called Dissenters or Separatists; they were estranged from the doctrines and practices of the government church of the nation from which they fled. For their faith they had suffered various hardships and some persecution. Alexis de Tocqueville, writing of the men and women who established Plymouth Colony observed: " . . . it was a purely intellectual craving that exiled them from the comforts of their former homes; and in facing the inevitable sufferings of exile their object was the triumph of an idea." That idea was conveyed by a motto that Thomas Jefferson used on his personal seal: "Rebellion to tyrants is obedience to God."

These early settlers were not peasants or serfs; they were clergymen and teachers, farmers and men of business. Many had degrees from Cambridge University. The late Samuel Eliot Morison, a Harvard professor specializing in early Massachusetts history, declared that there was a

The Reverend Mr. Opitz served on the senior staff of The Foundation for Economic Education for 37 years. This essay appeared as a Foreword to a 1996 FEE publication, *A Moral Basis for Liberty*, by Robert A. Sirico.

higher percentage of Ph.D.'s in the Puritan population in the 1640s than in any time since, in this country!

The "idea" referred to by Tocqueville had been spreading in England even before the Reformation; it bears directly upon the English people having, for the first time, the Bible in their own tongue. The idea of a new commonwealth, fired by reading in the Old Testament of "the people of the covenant," launched in America what Tocqueville described as "a democracy more perfect than antiquity had dared dream of." John Cotton, who has been rightly called the patriarch of New England, served as minister of The First Church of Boston from 1633 until his death in 1653. Cotton Mather wrote that John Cotton "propounded to them an endeavor after a theocracy, as near as might be, to that which was the glory of Israel, the 'peculiar people.'"

The Puritan regime, taken by itself, might seem to us a pretty rigorous affair. But these people were in what might be termed a fortress-under-siege situation. The first order of business was survival under conditions more primitive than they had experienced in England. Most survived, more people arrived from abroad. They had an educated ministry in every town; they were readers; they had regular news sheets and engaged in vigorous pamphleteering. All towns had a large measure of self-government; they learned about self-government by practicing it in local town meetings. And there were, in the pulpits of the time, vigorous and articulate spokesmen for liberty. Here, for instance, is Reverend Daniel Shute of the Second Parish in Hingham, in 1759: "Life, Liberty, and Property are the gifts of the Creator." And again: "Mankind has no right voluntarily to give up to others those natural privileges, essential to their happiness, with which they are invested by the

Lord of all; for the improvement of these they are account-able to Him." (I had the privilege of serving in Dr. Shute's pulpit two centuries later.)

The difficulties and dangers of travel in early New England forced each village to generate its own resources. The colonists hunted and fished, grew their own food, and traded with the Indians. Early on the Pilgrims practiced communal farming, putting all crops into a common warehouse from which all shared. But if every member of a community gets an equal share from unequal productivity it is inevitable that production will slow down. This happened in Plymouth, and the rules were changed. Under the new order each family worked its own plot of land and worked harder knowing that what they produced belonged to them, and would not be turned over to nonproducers or inefficient workers. As a result the general level of prosperity rose.

The local churches in New England shared the same creed and were perforce independent of one another; there was no ecclesiastical body to supervise them. A small group of ministers met in Cambridge, Massachusetts, in 1648 and drew up a document that came to be labeled The Cambridge Platform, affirming that the exigencies of the New England situation at the time dictated that each local church must take charge of its own affairs. This polity was called "congregational," and the churches which practiced it were Congregational Churches. This denomination played an important role in American history, not only in New England but in other parts of the continent as the West was settled.

The early settlers on these shores, whom we've discussed briefly, did not improvise or invent the ideas they brought with them. These people were the heirs of sixteen

centuries of cultural, intellectual, and spiritual development of one of the world's great civilizations: the culture
called European Civilization, or Christendom. There are
several other great civilizations, of course, and it is not to
disparage them to say that we are the heirs of Western Civilization, which is in some ways unique. It is, in the first
place, *our* civilization, and American Civilization was
launched from it as a base.

By the fourth quarter of the eighteenth century there
were thirteen colonies. The population was approximately
3,000,000. They were a literate people, knowledgeable in
history and apt to quote from Cicero and other Romans; not
fond of Plato with his utopia and its "guardians." They
were industrious: farmers, merchants, craftsmen, teachers,
writers. Paraphrasing Sir Francis Bacon, they acted on the
premise that we work for two reasons: for the glory of God,
and for the improvement of Man's estate. A job was a calling. Adam Smith's *Wealth of Nations* came out in two volumes in 1776 and hundreds of copies were sold in the
colonies. And no wonder; Smith gave his readers a rationale for what they were already doing. And he was a free
trader, which the British were not; the British interfered
with trade and treated the colonists as if their main purpose
was to give King George some extra income.

The nations of Europe had national churches operating
under government funding and control. The colonists had
been working toward the idea that churches should be free
and independent, and eventually—with the Constitution—
the idea became fact. Their way of life demonstrated that
the town did not need a government to tell the people what
to do; the Bible told them what to do, and what not to do.
The Commandments forbade murder, theft, false witness,
adultery: The Law is needed to deter those who might wan-

tonly kill a human being, and to punish the culprit who has taken another's life. Private property is a sacred trust; the thief who steals what belongs to another, or the arsonist who burns his home, deserves punishment. False witness may be slander or libel; more importantly it is breach of contract, which is to go back on one's word. "Life, Liberty, and Property" was the popular slogan.

These rules and others come to us in our Bible as the Ten Commandments. And they are also graven into the very nature of things in terms of the way this universe works; general obedience to these Commandments is necessary if we are to have a society, and some society is our natural environment. Only within some society is the full potential of our nature realized.

Imagine a town with a population of 10,000. Two of its inhabitants are dimwitted and spaced out from time to time. They find life pretty dull. They watch lurid videos and read weird magazines and decide to become satanists, just the two of them. The town soon learns that it has a couple of "serial killers" in its midst. The town panics after three bodies are found on three successive days. The police are pressured to get tough; gun shops are sold out; houses are double-bolted, alarm systems installed; armed vigilante groups form spontaneously. Suspicions are rife. The town has ceased being a civic organization and turns into an armed camp—all because a tiny fraction of one percent of its population has turned to murder. We have here a cause-and-effect sequence as convincing as a lab test: this universe has a moral order as an integral part of its natural order, simply awaiting discovery by wise men and seers, and its practice by the rest of us.

The moral order is the Natural Law, an important concept rooted in Greek and Roman thought, and part of the intellectual equipment of European thinkers until recent times. It was a central element in the legal philosophy of our Founding Fathers. It was also referred to as the Higher Law, and as such is part of the title of Edwin Corwin's important little book of some sixty years ago, *The "Higher Law" Background of American Constitutional Theory.* Positive Law, in contrast to the Natural Law, is the kind of law enacted by legislators, or decreed by commissions. The Natural Law is discovered; a positive law is good law if it accords with the Natural Law; bad law if it runs counter to the Natural Law.

The Founding Fathers appealed to Natural Law argument in their attacks on restrictive legislation that impaired their rightful liberties. Jefferson declared that God had made the mind of man free, implying that any interference with men's peaceable actions, or any subordination of one man to another is bad law; it violates the fundamental intent of Nature and Nature's God.

Thus they conceived the idea of a separation of powers in government—Executive, Legislative, and Judicial—plus a retention of certain prerogatives in the several states. This was the purpose of the remarkable group of men who met to forge an instrumentality of government in conformity with the Natural Law, based on the widely held conviction that God is the Author of Liberty. In short, our political liberties were not born in a vacuum; they emerged among a people who believed in their unique destiny under God— the God whose nature, works, and demands they gleaned from the Old and New Testaments. The eighteenth-century New England clergymen were learned men and often spoke along these lines. Many sermons made their way into print and Liberty Press has favored us with a mammoth one-volume collection of them. Such messages contributed much to the mental climate of the time, which Jefferson and his committee drew upon to compose the immortal words that give our Declaration of Independence its enduring influence.

The Declaration is the first of the documents upon which this nation was founded, the others being the Articles of Confederation, the Constitution, and the Northwest Ordinance.

Let's examine the opening words of the Declaration: "*We* hold these truths to be self-evident. . . ." The Declaration did not say that "these truths *are* self-evident," or that *all men* hold them to be such. This is not true. Were it possible for us to cross-examine the "We" who offered the Declaration, they might explain that "We" are speaking, first, for those of us here gathered; and second, for the generality of our fellows whom we judge to share our view as determined by the clergy they admire, the pamphlets they write and circulate, the Committees of Correspondence, and the documents emanating from the legislators of the thirteen colonies. "We" are the end result of long exposure to the Bible, which teaches us that we are created beings and not the accidental end result of a chance encounter of atoms; and that we belong on this planet, earth, which was created to teach us what we need to know in order to grow, train our characters, and become the mature men and women we have it in us to be. God has given us reason and free will, which we often misuse so as to cause a breach between God and ourselves, and for our sins Christ died on the cross— not just for some of us but for all of us. It is in this sense that "all men are created equal," male and female, master and bondsman. They are unequal and different in other respects, as common observation convinces us. Richard Rumbold, convicted in England because of his beliefs, ascended the scaffold in 1685 and uttered these immortal words: "none comes into the world with a saddle on his back; neither does one come booted and spurred to ride him." Jefferson quoted these words in one of his letters; it's a fair surmise that they had an effect on his own thinking and writing.

A group of extraordinary men assembled in Philadelphia and gave us a Constitution. In 1789, after much debate, it was accepted by the required number of states and the United States of America took its place among the nations of the world.

While the Constitution was being debated and argued out, 1787–1789, three very able public men who were also philosophers—James Madison, John Jay, and Alexander Hamilton—presented the case for adoption in the public press, 85 essays in all. The essays were gathered in book form as *The Federalist* (or sometimes *The Federalist Papers*), which has long assumed its place as a major work of political philosophy, certainly the finest exposition of the nature and requirements of a republican form of government. It is an indispensable treatise and rationale for the governmental structures essential to equal freedom in a civilized social order, as envisioned by the men we refer to as the Founding Fathers. My suspicion is that in today's colleges few political science majors are exposed to it.

The Declaration opens with a theological statement, asserting that our rights are Creator-endowed. This plants the idea of a political order rooted in the Transcendent, designed to maximize individual liberty in society, and incorporating the great "Thou Shalt Nots" of the Ten Commandments. The citizens were already earning their daily bread by working along free-market economy lines even before they discovered *The Wealth of Nations*. Thus our threefold society: religious-moral; legal-political; and economic-commercial. These three sectors interact and mutually implicate one another, supporting one another as well.

People tend to act out their beliefs, and our characters are shaped by our deepest and most firmly held convictions. As we believe, so will we become; and as *we* are so will our societies be. The religious, moral, and political convictions of our late eighteenth-century forebears were not improvised on the spot; they were supported by eighteen centuries of Western experience in religious, ethical, and political matters. History has its ups and downs, its gigantic swings, and some historians find major changes about every five hundred years from the beginning of the Christian era. The modern age might find its pivotal point at the time of the Renaissance, Reformation, and Counter Reformation. Christendom was sharply divided; minor sects proliferated. It was a time of exploration; the West came to realize that there were other civilizations, far more ancient than Christendom, with religions of their own, including sacred scriptures. A few Western philosophers began to realize that there is no reason why the God they believed in, the God of the Bible, should limit his attention to one narrow part of the world, and a relative newcomer at that, on the world scene. Well, we do have something to learn from Islam, Buddhism, and Hinduism, as well as from Taoism and Confucianism. And they have a lot to learn from us. But that's another story.

Most of us do not create the ideas and assumptions which guide our everyday actions; we borrow from thinkers of the past whose names we may not know. Joseph Wood Krutch taught at Columbia University and was a well-known drama critic with the mind of a philosopher. Here's his thumbnail description of how the modern mind was formed, the assumptions we habitually act upon: "The fundamental answers which we have on the whole made, and which we continue to accept, were first given in the seventeenth century by Francis Bacon, Thomas Hobbes, and René Descartes, and were later elaborated by Marx and the Darwinians." He lists these items in chronological order:

1. The most important task to which the human mind may devote itself is the "control of nature" through technology. Knowledge is power. (Bacon, 1561–1626)

2. Man may be completely understood if he is considered to be an animal, making predictable reactions to that desire for pleasure and power to which all his other desires may, by analysis, be reduced. (Hobbes, 1588–1679)

3. All animals, man excepted, are pure machines. (Descartes, 1596–1650)

4. Man, Descartes notwithstanding, is also an animal and therefore also a machine. (Darwin, 1809–1882)

5. The human condition is not determined by philosophy, religion, or moral ideas because all of these are actually only by-products of social and technological developments which take place independent of man's will and uninfluenced by the "ideologies" they generate. (Marx, 1818–1883)

These observations are tendentious, of course. But there does seem to be a warped streak in the philosophies of the past four or five centuries as they wander away from common sense. An observation from University of Glasgow professor C. A. Campbell seems pertinent: "As history amply testifies, it is from powerful, original and ingenious thinkers that the queerest aberrations of philosophic theory often emanate. Indeed it may be said to require a thinker exceptionally endowed in these respects if the more paradoxical type of theory is to be expounded in a way which will make it seem tenable even to its authors—let alone to the general public."

Some modern philosophers seem to have given up on man, and even distrust their own reason. Here is the brilliant Bertrand Russell, for example, from his celebrated essay entitled *Free Man's Worship*. "Man," he writes, "is the product of causes which had no prevision of the end they were achieving; his origin, his growth, his hopes and fears, his loves and his beliefs, are but the outcome of accidental collocations of atoms." Russell has just stated one of his beliefs which, on his own showing, is the result of an accidental coming together of some atoms, to which the categories true and false do not apply. He continues: "Brief and powerless is man's life; on him and all his race the slow, sure doom falls pitiless and dark. Blind to good and evil, reckless of destruction, omnipotent matter rolls on its relentless way." Matter is simply inert, until the mind of some human decides to use it to further some human purpose. Omnipotent, indeed! To Russell's credit he does admit that "good" is real and so is "evil." Obviously we cannot be blind to that which is not there!

Russell has done brilliant work in mathematics, and also in the philosophy of science. But if Man is in such a sorry state as Russell thinks, then ordinary humans need a keeper. Enter the humanitarian with a guillotine! Actually, the record shows that human beings play a variety of roles, both good and evil. We know the horrors of twentieth-century totalitarianism and collectivism, but also the glories of Periclean Athens, Florence at its peak, Elizabethan England, the late eighteenth-century colonists who laid down the political structures of a free society. Nearly every person has untapped skills and strengths, drawn upon only when urgently needed. We needed them in the 1780s and 1790s, and they gave us the legal framework for a market economy. The market operated here more freely than ever before—or since. There were government interventions all the way along, of course, increasing after the Civil War. But even then the market was so open and free that, of the thirty million immigrants who came to these shores during the last three decades of the nineteenth century, nearly every one got a job. Looking back we would be shocked by some of the working conditions; but the workers compared their present employment to the much worse situations back in the old country. Here, at least, they could work their way up the ladder and they were confident that their children would fare better than they.

In aristocratic England rural poverty did not attract much attention, but when these poor folk flocked into the cities, poverty became a concern of many well-intentioned folk. We know something of the slum scene in mid-eighteenth-century London as depicted in William Hogarth's drawings. Things were not much better a hundred and fifty years later, according to Jack London, who spent some time exploring slum life in London and wrote up his findings in his *People of the Abyss*. There's something of a novelist's embellishments in the book but there's no doubt that many men, women, and children lived miserably. What is the cause of poverty, and the remedy?

A poor society is one saddled with low productivity, and low productivity means a low ratio of capital to labor, i.e., few tools and little machinery. Poverty has been the fate of most people who've ever lived on this globe. We began to move in the direction of prosperity when people in our section of the planet began to till their own plots of land and then enjoy the full fruits of their labor. Human ingenuity was turned loose, resulting in more and better tools provided by increasingly skilled workers in various crafts. The concept of private property was redefined and people began to trade more freely.

A few men had speculated about economics before Adam Smith, but he made of it a new science, inspiring scholars for the next two centuries. We now know how to create the conditions for optimum economic well-being. It is now possible to have a free and prosperous commonwealth. First, operate within the political order envisioned by the Declaration of Independence and the Constitution; this gives us the Rule of Law—one law for all persons alike because we are one in our essential humanness. Secondly, put into practice the truths of economics gleaned from the classic treatises from Adam Smith to Ludwig von Mises, and other scholars of today. Third, there is the moral factor. We have in our time suffered from loss of touch with the transcendent aspect of human experience, although we are intimately involved with it, in the case of our own minds. The mind transcends the body, but they interact with one another. The mind-body problem is as ancient as philosophy. We know that they interact although how they interact is something of a puzzle. The body is an object in space and time, compounded of the common chemicals found in the earth's crust. The body can be weighed and measured; it can be looked at and touched. But the mind has no such characteristics. It is immaterial but it can affect the material body, guide its actions, generate certain illnesses, or enhance its wellness.

Your mind transcends your body, and yet is also acting in it and with it. Analogously, it might be suggested that God, conceived as Spirit, transcends this universe and yet is immanent within it. This is a mystery, of course, but hardly more of a mystery than how your mind interacts with your body. From this perspective the idea of the Natural Law or the moral order as a real part of this mysterious universe falls into place.

But a new religion emerged in the West during the nineteenth century to challenge Christianity: socialism. This is a pseudo-religion, really, but during the first several decades of the nineteenth century it aroused a moral fervor comparable to that of the early Christians. In 1848 a movement was launched by two Church of England clergymen, Charles Kingsley and F. D. Maurice, called Christian socialism. Their aim was to vindicate for "the Kingdom of Christ" its "true authority over the realms of industry and trade," and "for socialism its true character as the great Christian revolution of the 19th century."

The year 1848 also saw publication of *The Communist Manifesto,* which referred to its socialist rival in derisive terms: "Christian Socialism is but the holy water with which the priest consecrates the heartburnings of the aristocrat."

The movement spread in England, and into the United States where its common name was the Social Gospel. A popular slogan was: "Christianity is the religion of which Socialism is the practice." Well-known theologians contended that, "To be a Christian and not a Socialist, is to be guilty of heresy!"

Socialists of all stripes have, from the beginning, spoken as if they had a monopoly of all the virtues; only socialists strive for justice in society, peace between nations, and help for the poor. As a matter of fact, all men and women of good will want to see other people better off; better fed, clothed, and housed; better educated; healthier and benefiting from skilled medical care; peace among the nations and just relations within the nation.

Socialists would endorse these goals, to which they would add a utopian vision. But the means the socialist employs is at odds with his goals. The socialist would structure his society along the lines of a chain of command all the way to the masses at the bottom. The operational imperatives of a socialistic society cancels out the socialist dream. No society organized socialistically has been able to provide sufficient goods and services to raise its masses above the poverty level; and the citizenry are not free men and women. For a century and a half it was a religion that dominated the lives of millions; it is now revealed as a "religion" whose god has failed. The failure of this false deity offers us a clue: turn in the opposite direction to find the true God and His moral order.

Not all proponents of the free-market economy, private property order are theists, and they do have a concern for an ethic compatible with capitalism, referring to "enlightened self-interest" as the guide to right conduct. This is not a sound theory, in my view, nor is it an accurate reading of the ethic appropriate to a capitalist economy.

Enlightened self-interest as a moral principle has its advocates, but it exhibits some logical difficulties. The term has no referent, or else it has as many referents as there are selves. And each self's interest may differ from day to day. Continuity is lacking because no enduring principle can be deduced from any multiple of private inclinations. Furthermore, if a person is urged to pursue his own interest he cannot be denied the right to decide what that interest is. For, if A is allowed to decide for B what B's self-interest is then B will be acting out A's interest and not his own! There's no norm or standard transcending both A and B by which we might be able to determine who might be right and who wrong.

So, "Do your own thing" is the rule, and the weak doing their thing are at the mercy of the strong doing theirs. The clever and unscrupulous doing their thing have the rest of us at a disadvantage. If every individual merely pursues his own interest or pursues his private advantage, it is impossible from this starting point to arrive at any sort of a general rule, or principle or ethical norm. Mr. B might *call* something a norm or principle, but only because his self-interest dictates that he do so. And if there are no moral rules, why should Mr. B., having been told to pursue self-interest, refrain from fraud or theft or aggression when his self-interested calculation of costs and benefits determines that the benefits accruing to him outweigh the costs. When all is said and done, there is no substitute for the time-tested code built into the nature of things, whose mandates form the necessary foundation of a good society: Don't murder; Don't steal; Don't assault; Keep your word; Fulfill your contracts.

Furthermore, the self-interest ethic does not represent an accurate rendering of the capitalist ethos, although most defenders of capitalism have adopted it. In the market economy the consumer's needs, wants, and desires are sovereign; entrepreneurs wishing to maximize profits obediently accept the dictates of the market. No one is forced to become an entrepreneur, but if he does assume that role he must subordinate his own desires to the demands of his customers.

Let Ludwig von Mises show just how much self-abnegation the entrepreneur must practice. "In the market society," he writes, "the proprietors of capital and land can enjoy their property only by employing it for the satisfaction of other people's wants. They must serve the consumers in order to have any advantage from what is their own. The very fact that they own means of production forces them to submit to the wishes of the public. Ownership is an asset only for those who know how to employ it in the best possible way for the benefit of the consumers. It is a social function" *(Human Action,* p. 684).

Mises also said: "For in an unhampered market society the consumers daily decide anew who should own and how much he should own. The consumers allot control of the means of production to those who know how to use them best for the satisfaction of the most urgent wants of the consumers. . . . [The owners]. . . . are mandataries of the consumers, bound by the operation of the market to serve the consumers best" (p. 683).

Such is the free-market extension of the Good Samaritan Ethic; to which one can only say Amen!

Freedom and Majority Rule

Edmund A. Opitz

The publisher of the London *Times* came to this country a few years after the First World War. A banquet in his honor was held in New York City, and at the appropriate time Lord Northcliffe rose to his feet to propose a toast. Prohibition was in effect, you will recall, and the beverage customarily drunk by Northcliffe in his homeland was not available here. So Northcliffe raised his glass of water and said: "Here's to America, where you do as you please. And if you don't, they make you!"

Here, in this land of the free, "we" as voters had amended the Constitution to punish conduct which "we"—as consumers—had been enjoying. If you point out that the Eighteenth Amendment had been inserted into the Constitution by majority vote, and that therefore "we" had done it to "ourselves," you need to be reminded that the "we" who did it were not the same people as the "ourselves" to whom it was done!

The Eighteenth Amendment was annulled in 1933. Shortly thereafter another prohibition law was passed, this one a prohibition against owning gold. Under the earlier dispensation you could walk down the street with a pocketful of gold coins without breaking the law; but if you were caught carrying a bottle of whiskey you might be arrested. Then the rules were changed, and you could carry

This essay appeared in the January 1977 issue of *The Freeman*.

all the whiskey you wanted, but if you had any gold in your pocket you could be thrown in jail!

Our scientists are exploring outer space looking for intelligent life on other planets. I hope they find some, because there's none to spare on planet earth! With how little wisdom do we organize our lives, especially in the areas of government and the economy!

The fundamental issue in political philosophy is the limitation of governmental power; it is to determine the role of law, the functions appropriate to the political agency. The basic question may be phrased in a variety of ways: What things belong in the public domain? What things are private? What tasks should be assigned to Washington or some lesser governmental agency, and in what sectors of life should people be free to pursue their own goals? When should legal coercion be used to force a person to do something against his will? In view of government's nature, what is its competence? What are the criteria which enable us to distinguish a just law from an unjust law?

These are questions we cannot avoid. It is true that we don't have to debate them, or even think about them; but we cannot help acting on them. Some theory about government is the hidden premise of all political action, and we'll improve our action only as we refine our theory.

What Functions Are Appropriate?

In the light of government's nature, what functions may we appropriately assign to it? This is the question, and there are two ways to approach it. The approach favored today is to count noses—find out what a majority of the people want from government, and then elect politicians who will give it to them! And believe me, they've been giving it to us! The party that wins an election is "swept into office on a ground swell of public opinion," as popular mythology has it; and of course the winners have "a mandate from the people." That's spelled *Peepul*.

I do not accept this approach to political philosophy, and will offer some reasons for rejecting it. Neither did our forebears accept this approach. Every political thinker in the West from Plato down to modern times has taken a different tack. Now the mere fact that something is enshrined by tradition is no reason for accepting it; we accept something because we believe it to be true. But anything which is both tried and true has a lot going for it. Let me try to sketch briefly the way our forebears went about the intellectual and moral problem of trying to figure out what government should do, and how we determine whether or not a law is just.

The backbone of any legal system is a set of prohibitions. The law forbids certain actions and punishes those who do them anyway. The solid core of any legal system therefore, is the moral code, which, in our culture is conveyed to us by the Mosaic Law. The Sixth Commandment of The Decalogue says: "Thou shalt not commit murder" and this moral imperative is built into every statute which prescribes punishment for homicide. The Eighth Commandment forbids stealing, and this moral norm gives rise to laws punishing theft.

There is a moral law against murder because each human life is precious; and there is a moral law against theft because rightful property is an extension of the person. "A possession," Aristotle writes, "is an instrument for maintaining life." Deprive a person of the right to own property and he becomes something less than a person; he becomes someone else's man. A man to whom we deny the rights of ownership must be owned by someone else; he becomes another man's creature—a slave. The master-slave relation is a violation of the rightful order of things, that is, a violation of individual liberty and voluntary association.

The Gift of Life

Each human being has the gift of life and is charged with the responsibility of bringing his life to completion. He is also a steward of the earth's scarce resources, which he must use wisely and economically. Man is a responsible being, but no person can be held responsible for the way he lives his life and conserves his property unless he is free. Liberty, therefore, is a necessary corollary to life and property. Our forebears regarded life, liberty, and property as natural rights, and the importance of these basic rights was stressed again and again in the oratory, the preaching, and the writings of the eighteenth century. "Life, Liberty and Property are the gifts of the Creator," declared the Reverend Daniel Shute in 1767 from the pulpit which I occupied some 200 years later. Life, liberty, and property are the ideas of more than antiquarian interest; they are potent ideas because they transcribe into words an important aspect of the way things are.

Our ancestors intended to ground their legal and moral codes on the nature of things, just as students of the natural sciences intend their laws to be a transcription of the way things behave. For example: physical bodies throughout the universe attract each other, increasing with the mass of the attracting body and diminishing with the square of the distance. Sir Isaac Newton made some observations along these lines and gave us the law of gravity. How come gravitational attraction varies as the inverse-square of the distance, and not as the inverse-cube? One is as thinkable as the other, but it just happens that the universe is prejudiced in favor of the inverse-square in this instance; just as the universe is prejudiced against murder, has a strong bias in favor of property, and wills men to be free.

Immanuel Kant echoed an ancient sentiment when he declared that two things filled him with awe: the starry heavens without, and the moral law within. The precision and order in nature manifest the Author of nature. The Creator is also the Author of *our* being and requires certain duties of us, his creatures. There is, thus, an outer reality joined to the reality within, and this twofold reality has an intelligible pattern, a coherent structure.

This dual arrangement is not made by human hands; it's unchangeable, it's not affected by our wishes, and it can't be tampered with. It can, however, be misinterpreted, and it can be disobeyed. We consult certain portions of this pattern and draw up blueprints for building a bridge. If we misinterpret, the bridge collapses. And a society disintegrates if its members disobey the configuration laid down in the nature of things for our guidance. This configuration is the moral order, as interpreted by reason and tradition.

We're in fairly deep water here, and this is as far into theology as I shall venture. The point, simply put, is that our forebears, when they wanted to get some clues for the regulating of their private and public lives, sought for answers in a reality beyond society. They believed in a sacred order which transcends the world, an order of creation, and believed that our duties within society reflect the mandates of this divine order.

Take a Poll

This view of one's duty is quite in contrast to the method currently popular for determining what we should do; which is to conduct an opinion poll. Find out what the crowd wants, and then say "Me too!" This is what the advice of certain political scientists boils down to. Here is Professor James MacGregor Burns, a certified liberal and the author of several highly touted books, such as *The Deadlock of Democracy* and a biography of John F. Kennedy. Liberals play what Burns calls "the numbers game." "As a liberal I believe in majority rule," he writes. "I believe that the great decisions should be made by numbers." In other words, don't think; count! "What does a majority have a right to do?" he asks. And he answers his own question. "A majority has the right to do anything in the economic and social arena that is relevant to our national problems and national purposes." And then, realizing the enormity of what he has just said, he backs off: ". . . except to change the basic rules of the game."

Burns' final disclaimer sounds much like an afterthought, for some of his liberal cohorts support the idea of unqualified majority rule. The late Herman Finer, in his anti-Hayek book entitled *Road to Reaction*, declares "For in a democracy, right is what the majority makes it to be" (p. 60). What we have here is an updating of the ancient "might makes right" doctrine. The majority does have more muscle than the minority, it has the power to carry out its will, and thus it is entitled to have its own way. If right is whatever the majority says it is, then whatever the majority does is O.K., by definition. Farewell, then, to individual rights, and farewell to the rights of the minorities; the majority is the group that has made it to the top, and the name of the game is winner take all.

The dictionary definition of a majority is 50 percent plus 1. But if you were to draw up an equation to diagram modern majoritarianism it would read:

50 percent + 1 = 100 percent;
50 percent - 1 = ZERO!

Amusing confirmation comes from a professor at Rutgers University, writing a letter to the *Times*. Several years ago considerable criticism was generated by the appointment of a certain man to a position in the national government. Such criticism is unwarranted, writes our political scientist, because the critics comprise "a public which, by virtue of having lost the last election, has no business approving or disapproving appointments by those who won." This is a modern version of the old adage, "To the victor belong the spoils." This Rutgers professor goes on to say, "Contrary to President Lincoln's famous but misleading phrase, ours is not a government by the people, but government by government." So there!

The Nature of Government

What functions may we appropriately assign to the political agency? What should government do? Today's answer is that government should do whatever a majority wants a government to do; find out what the Peepul want from government, and then give it to them. The older and truer answer is based upon the belief that the rules for living together in society may be discovered if we think hard and clearly about the matter, and the corollary that we can conform our lives to these rules if we resolve to do so. But I have said nothing so far about the nature or essence of government.

Americans are justly proud of our nation, but this pride sometimes blinds us to reality. How often have you heard someone declare, "In America, 'We' are the government." This assertion is demonstrably untrue; "We" are the society, all 215 million of us; but society and government are not at all the same entity. Society is all-of-us, whereas government is only some-of-us. The some-of-us who comprise government would begin with the president, vice president, and cabinet; it would include Congress and the bureaucracy; it would descend through governors, mayors and lesser officials, down to sheriffs and the cop on the beat.

A Unique Institution

Government is unique among the institutions of society, in that society has bestowed upon this one agency exclusive legal control over the weaponry, from clubs to hydrogen bombs. Governments do use persuasion, and they do rely on authority, legitimacy, and tradition—but so do other institutions like the church and the school. But only one agency has the power to tax, the authority to operate the system of courts and jails, and a warrant for mobilizing the machinery for making war; that is government, the power structure. Governmental action is what it is, no matter what sanction might be offered to justify what it *does*. Government always acts with power; in the last resort government uses force to back up its decrees.

Society's Power Structure

When I remind you that the government of a society is that society's power structure, I am not offering you a novel theory, nor a fanciful political notion of my own. It is a truism that government is society's legal agency of compulsion. Virtually every statesman and every political scientist—whether Left or Right—takes this for granted and does his theorizing from this as a base. "Government is not reason, it is not eloquence;" wrote George Washington, "it is force." Bertrand Russell, in a 1916 book, said, "The essence of the State is that it is the repository of the collective force of its citizens." Ten years later, the Columbia University professor, R. M. MacIver spoke of the state as "the authority which alone has compulsive power." The English writer, Alfred Cobban, says that "the essence of the state, and of all political organizations, is power."

But why labor the obvious except for the fact that so many of our contemporaries—those who say "we are the government"—overlook it? What we are talking about is the power of man over man; government is the legal authorization which permits some men to use force on others. When we advocate a law to accomplish a certain goal, we advertise our inability to persuade people to act in the manner we recommend; so we're going to force them to conform! As Sargent Shriver once put it, "In a democracy you don't compel people to do something unless you are sure they won't do it."

In the liberal mythology of this century, government is all things to all men. Liberals think that government assumes whatever characteristics people wish upon it—

like Proteus in Greek mythology who took on one shape after another, depending on the circumstances. But government is not an all-purpose tool; it has a specific nature, and its nature determines what government can accomplish. When properly limited, government serves a social end no other agency can achieve; its use of force is constructive. The alternatives here are law and tyranny—as the Greeks put it. This is how the playwright Aeschylus, saw it in *The Eumenides:* "Let no man live uncurbed by law, nor curbed by tyranny."

The Moral Code

If government is to serve a moral end it must not violate the moral code. The moral code tells us that human life is sacred, that liberty is precious, and that ownership of property is good. And by the same token, this moral code supplies a definition of criminal action; murder is a crime, theft is a crime, and it is criminal to abridge any person's lawful freedom. It becomes a function of the law, then, in harmony with the moral code, to use force against criminal actions in order that peaceful citizens may go about their business. The use of legal force against criminals for the protection of the innocent is the earmark of a properly limited government.

This is an utterly different kind of procedure than the use of government force on peaceful citizens—whatever the excuse or rationalization. People should not be forced into conformity with any social blueprint; their private plans should not be overridden in the interests of some national plan or social goal. Government—the public power—should not be used for private advantage; it should not be used to protect people from themselves.

Well, what *should* the law do to peaceful, innocent citizens? It should let them alone! When government lets John Doe alone, and punishes anyone who refuses to let him alone, then John Doe is a free man.

In this country we have a republican form of government. The word "republic" is from the Latin words, *res* and *publica,* meaning the things or affairs which are common to all of us, the affairs which are in the public domain, in sharp contrast to matters which are private. Government, then, is "the public thing," and this strong emphasis on public serves to delimit and set boundaries to governmental power, in the interest of preserving the integrity of the private domain.

What's in a name?, you might be thinking. Well, in this case, in the case of *republic,* a lot. The word "republic" encapsulates a political philosophy; it connotes the philosophy of government which would limit government to the defense of life, liberty, and property in order to serve the ends of justice. There's no such connotation in the word "monarchy," for example; or in aristocracy or oligarchy.

A monarch is the sole, supreme ruler of a country, and there is theoretically no area in the life of his citizens over which he may not hold sway. The king owns the country and his people belong to him. Monarchical practice pretty well coincided with theory in what is called "Oriental Despotism," but in Christendom the power of the kings was limited by the nobility on the one hand, and the Emperor on the other; and all secular rulers had to take account of the power of the Papacy. Power was played off against power, to the advantage of the populace.

Individual Liberty

The most important social value in Western civilization is individual liberty. The human person is looked upon as God's creature, gifted with free will which endows him with the capacity to choose what he will make of his life. Our inner, spiritual freedom must be matched by an outer and social liberty if man is to fulfill his duty toward his Maker. Creatures of the state cannot achieve their destiny as human beings; therefore, government must be limited to securing and preserving freedom of personal action, within the rules for maximizing liberty and opportunity for everyone.

Unless we are persuaded of the importance of freedom to the individual, it is obvious that we will not structure government around him to protect his private domain and secure his rights. The idea of individual liberty is old, but it was given a tremendous boost in the sixteenth century by the Reformation and the Renaissance.

The earliest manifestation of this renewed idea of liberty was in the area of religion, issuing in the conviction that a person should be allowed to worship God in his own way. This religious ferment in England gave us Puritanism, and early in the seventeenth century Puritanism projected a political movement whose members were contemptuously called Whiggamores—later shortened to Whigs—a word roughly equivalent to "cattle thieves." The king's men were called Tories—"highway robbers." The Whigs worked for individual liberty and progress; the Tories defended the old order of the king, the landed aristocracy, and the established church.

One of the great writers and thinkers in the Puritan and Whig tradition was John Milton, who wrote his celebrated plea for the abolition of Parliamentary censorship of printed material in 1644, *Areopagitica*. Many skirmishes had to be fought before freedom of the press was finally accepted as one of the earmarks of a free society. Free speech is a corollary of press freedom, and I remind you of the statement attributed to Voltaire: "I disagree with everything you say, but I will defend with my life your right to say it."

Adam Smith extended freedom to the economic order, with *The Wealth of Nations*, published in 1776 and warmly received in the thirteen colonies. Our population numbered about 3 million at this time; roughly one-third of these were Loyalists, that is, Tory in outlook, and besides, there was a war on. Despite these circumstances 2,500 sets of *The Wealth of Nations* were sold in the colonies within five years of its publication. The colonists had been practicing economic liberty for a long time, simply because their governments were too busy with other things to interfere—or too inefficient—and Adam Smith gave them a rationale.

The Bill of Rights

Ten amendments to the Constitution were adopted in 1791. Article the First reads: "Congress shall make no law respecting the establishment of religion, or prohibiting the free exercise thereof . . ." The separation of church and state enunciated here was a momentous first step in world history. Religious liberty, freedom of the press, free speech and the free economy are four departments of the same liberating trend—the Whig movement.

The men we refer to as the Founding Fathers would have called themselves Whigs. Edmund Burke was the chief spokesman for a group in Parliament known as The Rockingham Whigs. In 1832 the Whig Party in England changed its name to one which more aptly described its emphasis on liberty. It became the Liberal Party, standing for free trade, religious liberty, the abolition of slavery, extension of the franchise, and other reforms.

Classical Liberalism is not to be confused with the thing called "liberalism" in our time! Today's "liberalism" is the exact opposite of historical Liberalism—which came out of the eighteenth-century Whiggism—which came out of the seventeenth-century Puritanism. The labels are the same; the realities are utterly different. Present-day liberals have trouble with ideas, as ideas, so they try to dispose of uncomfortable thoughts by pigeonholing them in a time slot. The ideas of individual liberty, inherent rights, limited government and the free economy are, they say, eighteenth-century ideas. What a dumb comment! The proper test of an idea is not the test of time but the test of truth!

You may be wondering why I have not yet used the word "democracy," although I've spoken of monarchy, oligarchy, and liberalism. Well, I'll tell you. Our discussion has focused on the nature of government, and we have discovered that the essence of government is power, legal force. Once this truth sinks in we take the next step, which is to figure out what functions may appropriately be assigned to the one social agency authorized to use force. This brings us back to the moral code and the primary values of life, liberty, and property. It is the function of the law to protect the life, liberty, and property of all persons alike in order that the human person may achieve his proper destiny.

Voting Is Appropriate for Choosing Officeholders

There's another question to resolve, tied in with the basic one, but much less important: How do you choose personnel for public office? After you have employed the relevant intellectual and moral criteria and confined public things to the public sector, leaving the major concerns of life in the private sector . . . once you've done this there's still the matter of choosing people for office.

One method is choice by bloodline. If your father is king, and if you are the eldest son, why you'll be king when the old man dies. Limited monarchy still has its advocates, and kingship will work if a people embrace the monarchical ideology. Monarchy hasn't always worked smoothly, however, else what would Shakespeare have done for his plays? Sometimes your mother's lover will bump off the old man, or your kid brother might try to poison you.

There's a better way to choose personnel for public office; let the people vote. Confine government within the limits dictated by reason and morals, lay down appropriate requirements, and then let voters go to the polls. The candidate who gets the majority of votes gets the job. This is democracy, and this is the right place for majority action. As Pericles put it 2,500 years ago, democracy is where the many participate in rule.

Voting is little more than a popularity contest, and the most popular man is not necessarily the best man, just as the most popular idea is not always the soundest idea. It is obvious, then, that balloting—or counting noses or taking a sampling of public opinion—is not the way to get at the fundamental question of the proper role of government within a society. We have to think hard about this one, which means we have to assemble the evidence; weigh, sift, and criticize it; compare notes with colleagues, and so on. In other words, this is an educational endeavor, a matter for the classroom, the study, the podium, the pulpit, the forum, the press. To count noses at this point is a cop-out; there's no place here for a Gallup Poll.

To summarize: The fundamental question has to do with the scope and functions of the political agency, and only hard thinking—education in the broad sense—can resolve this question. The lesser question has to do with the choice of personnel; and majority action—democratic decision—is the way to deal with it. But if we approach the first question with the mechanics appropriate to the second, we have confused the categories and we're in for trouble.

"Democratic Despotism"

We began to confuse the categories more than 140 years ago, as Alexis de Tocqueville observed. His book *Democracy in America*, warned us about the emergence here of what he called "democratic despotism," which would "degrade men without tormenting them." We were warned again in 1859 by a professor at Columbia University, Francis Lieber, in his book *On Civil Liberty and Self-Government:* "Woe to the country in which political hypocrisy first calls the people almighty, then teaches that the voice of the people is divine, then pretends to take a mere clamor for the true voice of the people, and lastly gets up the desired clamor." Getting up the desired clamor is what we call "social engineering," or "the engineering of consent."

What is called "a majority" in contemporary politics is almost invariably a numerical minority, whipped up by an even smaller minority of determined and sometimes unscrupulous men. There's not a single plank in the platform of the welfare state that was put there because of a genuine demand by a genuine majority. A welfarist government is always up for grabs, and various factions, pressure groups, special interests, causes, ideologies seize the levers of government in order to impose their programs on the rest of the nation.

Let's assume that we don't like what's going on today in this and other countries; we don't like it because people are being violated, as well as principles. We know the government is off the track, and we want to get it back on; but we know in our bones that Edmund Burke was right when he said, "There never was, for any long time . . . a mean, sluggish, careless people that ever had a good government of any form." Politics, in other words, reflects the character of a people, and you cannot improve the tone of politics except as you elevate the character of a significant number of persons. The improvement of character is the hard task of religion, ethics, art, and education. When we do our work properly in these areas, our public life will automatically respond.

Large numbers are not required. A small number of men and women whose convictions are sound and clearly thought out, who can present their philosophy persuasively, and who manifest their ideas by the quality of their lives, can inspire the multitude whose ideas are too vague to generate convictions of any sort. A little leaven raises the entire lump of dough; a tiny flame starts a mighty conflagration; a small rudder turns a huge ship. And a handful of people possessed of ideas and a dream can change a nation—especially when that nation is searching for new answers and a new direction.

You Can't Sell Freedom to a Starving Man

Ridgway K. Foley, Jr.

Of all the clichés denigrating liberty, the most pernicious consists of the comment, designed in any of its varying forms to terminate the conversation entirely, that "your ideals and ideas may be laudable, but you can't talk liberty to a man with an empty belly or whose children want for food and clothing." This essay proposes to investigate the validity of that response.

* * *

Freedom consists of the absence of organized, coercive restraint against individual human action.[1] It is indivisible in two respects: (1) restraint in one aspect of life affects creative action in other categories; (2) restraint of one member of society adversely affects all other men.

Consider the first postulate. One cannot enjoy meaningful liberty of association or freedom of speech while suffering under economic or political bondage. Freedom of speech or press offers an illusory value if the potential speaker or writer cannot purchase air time on radio or television, or a soap box, or newsprint from the governmentally controlled factory, or a sound truck, either because of restrictive regulatory laws preventing free entry into the market, or by virtue of discriminatory norms against pro-

---

This essay appeared in the December 1976 issue of *The Freeman*.

ducers by means of economic controls, or because of debasement by means of state monopoly of the medium of exchange. The right to vote means little if the government apparatus counts results for but a single candidate, or if the state limits the access to the polling booth or ballot box by enactment and enforcement of civil and criminal penalties.

Recur to the second proposition. Simply put, *my freedom depends on yours.* Deprivation of the rights of the slave affects the master in several discrete ways.

• First, the predator must expend a portion of his creative energy in the destructive pursuit of constraining his fief. Absent coercion, he could devote his entire energy resources to creative endeavors. Wars provide an apt example of squandered creativity: Witness the millions of barrels of oil (which could have heated homes and propelled automobiles) wasted in recent violence.

• Second, looters lose the chance to thrive upon the created value which the slave, if free, would produce and trade for other goods, services, and ideas. The material well-being of any society depends upon the aggregate of creative output from each member, the proficiency of each individual producer, and the velocity of exchange (a factor of the voluntary channels of communication). Slaves produce only the amount necessary to maintain life in a barely acceptable station and to avoid or reduce pain.

• Third, masters lose qualitatively, since the *quality* of output diminishes with the introduction of compulsion. A coercive society enjoys fewer goods, begrudging services and less exciting ideas and culture than a free society.

• Fourth, and perhaps most saliently, a slave state loses *moral* force as well as material largess, a subject discussed hereafter.

We may define liberty, then, in Leonard Read's felicitous phrase, as the absence of man-concocted restraints upon creative human action.[2] At the ideal, each man should be entitled to manage his own life and to seek his own destiny as he sees fit, so long as he observes the equal and reciprocal freedom deserved by every other man. Such a concept limits the role of the state—the official restraining force imposed upon society—to prevention of aggression and coercive settlement of disputes by rules of common justice.

The Morality of Theft

Observation of the passing scene reveals many instances of looting and theft. One unschooled in the philosophy of freedom might immediately conclude that such a statement refers to the rapid increase in violent or deceitful crimes such as forgery, robbery, burglary, obtaining money by false pretenses, and shoplifting penalized by the several state or national governments. In fact, I refer to the unpenalized, officially sanctioned, state-favored instances of theft which appear in guises too numerous to mention. Every occasion when the state takes property from an unwilling donor and gives it to some other individual affords an example of legalized plunder. Food stamps, subsidies to Penn Central and Lockheed Aircraft, social security, inflation, mandatory automobile insurance, civil tort rules which "diffuse" risks by imposing liability without fault—the list is truly endless, limited only by the ingenuity of men abusing power conferred upon them by the political system. Appellations of "transfer payments," "negative income taxation," "redistributive liability," and the like cannot cloak the true nature of the act: *Theft.*

Why decry the concept of theft, if performed by the pure of heart for a commendable purpose? After all, most proponents of these many and varied legislative or judicial enactments seek grand and deserving goals of preventing hunger, illness, and alienation or providing "necessary" goods and services. Few of them, despite their arrogance and predilection to power, really exemplify consummate evil.

The answer to the moral question lies in contemplation of ends and means. Few men of virtue and good will dispute the ideal of dispelling poverty, illness, and loneliness, or of providing everyone with food for thought and body. Most observers agree upon goals—they diverge upon the means to the end. Those imbued with the freedom philosophy recognize that the end pre-exists in the means,[3] that filthy means will defile innocent and praiseworthy ends.

Theft deserves disdain because it conflicts with fundamental morality, with the right to life, and with the precept of justice. A seminal moral rule commands treatment of individual human beings as ends, not as means—as persons of worth, not as objects to be molded. The thief treats the victim as a means to his own ends. The legally protected thief performs a greater iniquity, for he refuses to acknowledge the moral opprobrium necessarily attached to his crime; he treats the victim as unworthy to manage his own affairs.

Again, theft contradicts the concept of a human being's right to live his life in accordance with the dictates of his conscience. Property consists of the value which man creates by the application of his being and his talents to natural resources; it can only be viewed rationally as an extension of a life. One lives by creating; one dies by stagnating. Thus, deprivation of property amounts to a partial taking of human life. Moreover, the act of thievery devastates the fundamental precept of justice: Respect for free individual choice.[4] Approval of the power to forcibly or deceitfully deprive another of a part of his life *necessarily contradicts* a respect for the human right to choose between alternatives.

In essence, comprehension of the moral questions associated with theft devolves to an inquiry: Why doesn't might make right? Theft, after all, can only be accomplished by the application of stealth and trickery or by employment of personal or political force. The fact and the scale of legally sanctioned plunder renders this inquiry no mere philosopher's debating point. It is all too real and affects each of us in striking and personal fashion.

Immanuel Kant[5] provided some insight into the moral question of whether "might makes right" when he suggested the "silver rule" as a measuring rod: Individuals should shun actions which they would not will as universal rules of conduct. Few rational beings would voluntarily choose to live in a world governed by force, without moral constraint of any kind. Chaos necessarily reigns; personal planning becomes impossible; life terminates early and after an unpleasant duration. Such conditions would forestall even rudimentary exchange or growth of capital, relegating mankind to the cave and the forests from which it so recently and hesitatingly emerged. Merely imagining a world where theft, or rape, or murder occurred on a daily basis without official reprisal registers shock on the minds of most human beings. Such conduct would invite retaliation in the form of blood feuds, vigilante justice or civil war.

One could refute the contention that "might makes right" on three bases,[6] any one of which would serve as sufficient justification for a contrary rule.

• First, experience dispels any necessary correlation between force and propriety. Recorded history imparts example after example of the use of violence to accomplish improper goals—propriety measured by the subjective values of those deprived of life, liberty, or property. The neighborhood bully may be stronger than you, but that doesn't mean he possesses any greater native intelligence, charm, wit, cultural accomplishments or other attributes more or less universally desirable. Indeed, the contrary is more often true: The bully, be he individual, corporate, or national in scope, often possesses a low, mean, and not particularly endearing character.

• Second, a related pragmatic reason flows from the Kantian silver rule: Force and power tend to breed more aggression, and man cannot exist as well (or at all) spiritually or materially in a chaotic world regularly visited by coercion. Might-makes-right just plain fails to work as well as the alternative. A better material and spiritual life with happier men and more abundant goods and services flows from cooperation, not coercion.

• Third, common morality, denoted as natural law, the theory of natural rights, Christianity, rationality, or some other similar phrase suggests that men should not treat other men inhumanely. All three reasons interrelate, but the third or moral concept differs from its siblings in one important respect: It constitutes an appeal to faith rather than provable, empirical fact. However, this feature does not deprive the tenet of validity. History manifests a growing recognition that each individual human being possesses inalienable natural rights merely because of his humanity, and that no other individual should trespass upon such rights in the absence of prior personal aggression. If this precept be relegated to the status of a mere value judgment, it certainly has gained ascendency in recent years although it still falls far short of universal acceptance. Since theft of private property involves the

344 / Ridgway K. Foley, Jr.

deprivation of an extension of one's life—our essential humanity derives in part from the value we create—theft violates the principle of common morality or natural rights.

Therefore, one can say with the confidence undergirded by logic and natural law that theft in general constitutes an immoral act because might does not make right and power tends to deprive men of a portion of their life. It remains to consider whether theft can ever be justified under any circumstances. The admonition, "you can't sell freedom to a starving man," possesses two root assumptions denying the universality of the normative rule that theft constitutes immorality. If freedom varies, directly or inversely, with the visceral satisfactions of the human being, it follows that (1) hungry people need not abide by rules of common morality while productive people must follow such rules and, (2) freedom cannot provide the precondition necessary to prevent want and poverty. Neither assumption can withstand rigorous analysis.

The Universality of Moral Conduct

No accepted ethical or religious code exempts starving men from adherence to established or accepted standards *except* if that code be based upon the doctrine of might-makes-right. The Marxian tenet "from each according to his ability, to each according to his need" presupposes a social agency which will forcibly compel transfer from "producers" to "needy," as well as perform the concomitant function of determining "ability" and "requirement." Every other system dependent upon transfer payments or social redistribution of income relies upon *force*. Only these systems justify the use of violence by hungry, ill-clothed, or other "needy" folk in order to satisfy their wants. Contrast the known axiological precepts handed down through history: Do the Judeo-Christian heritage, the Islamic tradition, Hindu teachings, or the like differentiate between producers and consumers insofar as their normative conduct is concerned? Merely to state the question elicits a negative response.

One should not confuse the assertion that the poor as well as the producer should obey the same rules with the question of whether the creator of goods, services, and ideas should share his abundance with others less fortunate on an individual and voluntary basis. The two concepts, while related, state two entirely different principles: (1) all men regardless of status should respect the lives, liberties, properties, choices, and subjective values of all other individuals who do not commit aggression; (2) one blessed with a surfeit of material or spiritual goods should share with less fortunate individuals on a mutually satisfying voluntary basis. A violation of the first axiom deserves human reprisal to revenge the breach, protect others similarly situated, and deter like conduct. No human sanction should attend a violation of the second axiom because no human being possesses the right, the insight, or the ability to enforce their ethical norm since the norm itself depends upon subjective views of the Eternal Truth of the Universe.

Unjustifiable Intervention

In essence, the suggestion that hungry men cannot appreciate liberty results from a confusion of these two separate postulates. Similarly, most justification of government intervention into private lives stems from a perversion of these two distinct rules, each touching a specific aspect of human action. The canard that an ill-fed individual cannot comprehend freedom springs from a belief that it is proper to invade or destroy the human rights of others in order to secure a "good" end, such as the prevention of poverty or ill health.

In simple words, one should not destroy another's right to choose except where that actor would not willingly select the course of action which would lead to sharing with others whom the party possessing power perceives as appropriate beneficiaries. This commingling of the two moral precepts renders each of them nugatory. The first axiom suffers because the exception guts the entire meaning. The second axiom falls because voluntarism becomes coercion and thus obviates the entire concept. A sense of wrongdoing clouds the whole transaction, leaving producer-victim, the transferring power, and poor recipient-beneficiary each with a pervasive recognition of evil inherent in their affair which does not accord with moral law.

In like manner, the belief that moral rules need not be universally applied partakes of the corruption of the two separate axioms: You can't sell freedom to a starving man because he is first justified in invading the rights of others in order to satisfy his wants because they ethically should assist him.

Several reasons, each sufficient alone, support the proposition that moral conduct applies universally.

• First, separate treatment betrays the egalitarian ideal, the subject of so much current prattle. Yet it is in this precise context that equality deserves meaning, for true juristic equality means equality before the law—equal rights, equal responsibilities.

• Second, relative morality, on whatever basis, necessarily results in disillusionment, bitterness, hatred, envy, and other unlovely human attributes: In short, such a dichotomy will bring the sinister side of human nature to the fore. The taker will take even when the justification disappears, coming to believe that taking constitutes a personal right; the victim will resent this invasion of his life and fight back in many and myriad ways including the use of force and cunning, the production of shoddy goods, or a transfer to the taker class. Power and violence naturally tend to breed similar offspring.

• Third, definition of terms renders application of the distinction impractical if not impossible. Who shall define "production" and "need" (or who "starves"), and how shall these terms be defined? Starvation and need vary by the minute; they represent highly subjective decisions, for almost every individual "needs" something he does not possess, given a world full of insatiable subjective wants and blessed with limited resources. Acceptance of a dual standard dependent upon hunger pangs would reduce morality to an ephemeral and transitory discipline subject to endless debate and a chaotic result: Victims who honestly believe that they fall within the taker class will take umbrage; they may even fight back, leading to unending aggression.

Thus, common sense makes manifest that moral rules must apply in an evenhanded manner. Starving men possess no right to invade the persons or property of others, nor are they justified or exempt from ethical rules precluding such action. Freedom attaches equally to all men: It includes the freedom to fail as well as succeed. Life's losers cannot vent their spleen on those who are more successful, and thereby receive moral approval.

Freedom Dispels Want

One who claims that "you can't sell freedom to a starving man" really means "freedom is all right in its place, but these people are starving and they will receive sustenance only if I coerce you into giving them food." This proposition fails on two counts.

• First, the near-universal acceptance of the second axiom (the obligation to share) and mankind's natural empathy for fellow human beings in trouble virtually guarantees that no one shall starve in a free society. Strangely enough, the acceptance of the second axiom and man's sympathetic response become heightened the more open society becomes; statism and compulsion cultivate ugliness, alienation, and a lack of camaraderie. The guarantee against starvation does not insure against want of material things; mankind will always experience unfulfilled desires, given his nature of a being possessing insatiable wants in a world of limited resources.

• Second, the statement seems to contend that a free society cannot produce and distribute those goods, services, and ideas required to alleviate starvation. The converse is true. A free market, operating without restraints upon human creative output, produces a greater abundance of material value than any other method known to mankind because the free market or voluntary exchange system accords with the basic nature of man. The market reflects the competing subjective values of each member of society and thus more nearly approximates the sum of all those desires.

This assertion of the material productiveness of the market does not rest merely upon unproved theory; it gains support from empirical and historical fact. The freer the culture, the better clothed, fed, and housed its citizens. The rapid improvements in the standard of living of all Americans during the nation's first century derived from the relative freedom of the citizenry. Compare the average life span in medieval England (5 years) with that of the present-day United States (70 years) and one immediately perceives that we heard relatively little about the "starving man" in history because he died so young. Few of the wealthy in merrie olde England lived as well as the average high school dropout today.

Stripped to its essence, the cliché "you can't sell freedom to a starving man" exemplifies a brazen demand by the one uttering the response that he be accorded the power to impose his will upon unwilling human beings—all in the good name of the elimination of poverty. Logic, common sense, empirical fact, and history demonstrate that just the contrary effect will take place, that coercion results in fewer individuals enjoying fewer goals which they subjectively value.

The Curse of Gradualism

One can interpret the phrase under discussion in yet another manner. It could mean that a hungry man will not listen to, or understand, the esoteric discussion of liberty and will voluntarily choose an aggressive society to alleviate his suffering. Thus, runs the argument, someone in power must appease the voracious masses before educating them to the virtues of liberty.

Insofar as the question depicts a communication problem, believers in liberty must hone their tools of expression to fit every need. Relative freedom helped restore conflict-ravaged West Germany after the Second World War; the

Germans, hungry as they were, accepted the ideas and responsibilities of freedom from Mr. Erhard. The concept of freedom and its relation to prosperity bear retelling because all of us need constant reminders, but conveyance of the idea to everyone, hungry or not, does not present difficult, let alone insolvable, problems.

Insofar as the inquiry poses a question of consistency, libertarians must remain steadfast against the importunings of gradualism which would betray the ideal by imposing coercive tactics as a means of filling stomachs "temporarily."[7] The "temporary" in this situation tends to become ingrained and immutable, misleading the unknowing into the assumption that coercion (1) has always been there and (2) is necessary to accomplish the end. The result: an inefficient and uneconomic United States Postal Service which has never been able to compete with private enterprise save for its monopolistic protections, which constantly raises rates and reduces the quality of service, and which has incurred budget deficits almost every year for the past two centuries. It requires little imagination to appreciate the results if "feeding starving men" were left to the tender mercies of compulsive bureaucracy: The nation would perish within five years!

---

1. For a detailed discussion see Ridgway K. Foley, Jr., "Individual Liberty and the Rule of Law," *The Freeman*, June 1971, pp. 357–358; and Ridgway K. Foley, Jr., "A Rationale For Liberty," *The Freeman*, April 1973, pp. 222–229.

2. Leonard E. Read, "Justice versus Social Justice," in *Who's Listening?* (Irvington-on-Hudson, N.Y.: The Foundation for Economic Education, Inc., 1973), p. 93 *et seq.*

3. See Leonard E. Read, "The Bloom Pre-Exists in the Seed," in *Let Freedom Reign* (Irvington-on-Hudson, N. Y.: The Foundation for Economic Education, Inc., 1969), pp. 78–86.

4. Ridgway K. Foley, Jr., "In Quest of Justice," *The Freeman*, May 1974, pp. 301–310.

5. Immanuel Kant, *Fundamental Principles of the Metaphysic of Morals* (New York: The Liberal Arts Press, 1949), p. 21.

6. Obviously, this essay does not purport to deal with the questions of why might does not make right or with the nature and scope of an alternative postulate for mankind in great detail. Such an undertaking requires more extensive development than is requisite for the topic under discussion.

7. Leonard E. Read, "Right Now!", *Notes from FEE* (Irvington-on-Hudson, N.Y.: The Foundation for Economic Education, Inc., May 1975), discusses the problems inherent in gradualism.

The Roots of "Anticapitalism"

Erik von Kuehnelt-Leddihn

In many minds, "capitalism" has come to be a bad word, nor does "free enterprise" sound much better. I remember seeing posters in Russia in the early 1930s depicting capitalists as Frankenstein monsters, as men with yellow-green faces, crocodile teeth, dressed in cutaways and adorned by top hats. What is the reason for this widespread hatred for capitalists and capitalism despite the overwhelming evidence that the system has truly "delivered the goods"? In its mature stage it indeed is providing, not just for a select few but for the masses, a standard of living cordially envied by those bound under other politico-economic arrangements. There are historic, psychological, and moral reasons for this state of affairs. Once we recognize them, we might come to better understanding the largely irrational resentment and desire to kill the goose that lays the golden eggs.

In Europe there still survives a considerable *conservative* opposition against capitalism. The leaders of conservative thought and action, more often than not, came from the nobility which believed in an agrarian-patriarchal order. They thought workers should be treated by manufacturers as noblemen treated their agricultural employees and household servants, providing them with total security for

Dr. Kuehnelt-Leddihn is a philosopher, linguist, world traveler, and lecturer whose home is in Austria. This essay appeared in the November 1972 issue of *The Freeman*.

their old age, care in the case of illness, and so forth. They also disliked the new business leaders who emerged from the middle classes: the *grand bourgeois* was their social competitor, the banker their disagreeable creditor, not their friend. The big cities with their smoking chimneys were viewed as calamities and destroyers of the good old life.

We know that Marx and Engels in the *Communist Manifesto* furiously attacked the aristocratic social movement as a potential threat to their own program. Actually, most of the leading minds of Christian anticapitalist thought (equally opposed to socialism) were aristocrats: Villeneuve-Bargemont, de Mun, Liechtenstein, Vogelsang, Ketteler.

Bias Against Capitalism Not of Worker Origin

Armin Mohler, the brilliant Swiss-German neo-conservative, has recently explained that one of the weakest points of contemporary conservative thought, still wrapped in the threads of its own obsolete agrarian romanticism, is its hostility against modern technology. How right he is! The exception might have been Italy with its tradition of urban nobility and of patricians who, even before the Reformation, engaged in trade and manufacture. Capitalism, indeed, is of North-Italian origin. It was a Franciscan, Fra Luigi di Pacioli, who invented double-entry bookkeeping. Calvinism gave a new impetus to capitalism but did not invent it. (Aristocratic entrepreneurs in Italy? Count Marzotto with his highly diversified business empire of textile plants, paper mills, hotel chains, and fisheries is a typical example. His labor relations are of a patriarchal nature involving substantial fringe benefits which also characterize Japanese business practice.)

The real animosity against free enterprise did *not* originate with the laborers. Bear in mind that in the early nineteenth century the working class was miserably paid, and this for two reasons: (1) the income from manufacturing was quite limited (true mass production came later) and (2) the lion's share of the profits went into reinvestments while the typical manufacturers lived rather modestly. It is this ascetic policy of early European capitalism which made possible the phenomenal rise of working class standards. Seeing that the manufacturers did not live a life of splendor (as did the big landowners) the workers at first viewed their lot with surprising equanimity. The Socialist impetus came from middle class intellectuals, eccentric industrialists (like Robert Owen and Engels) and impoverished noblemen with a feeling of resentment against the existing order.

As one can imagine, the artificially created ire then was turned first against the manufacturer who, after all, is nothing but some sort of *broker* between the worker and the public. He enables the worker to transform his work into goods. In this process he incurs various expenses, such as for tools, and a part of the costs of marketing. He hopes to make a profit from these transactions in order to render his efforts worthwhile. Curiously enough, his responsibility toward the enterprise is of far greater scope than that of many workers. No wonder that the interest, once centered on accidents in the factories, is shifting more and more to the manager diseases. The entrepreneur sacrifices not only his "nerves" but also his peace of mind. If he fails, he fails not himself alone; the bread of dozens, of hundreds, of thousands of families hangs in the balance. The situation is not very different in a stock company. There, the stockholders sometimes make profits in the form of dividends—and sometimes they do not. The worker *always* expects to be paid. The bigger risks are thus at the top, not at the bottom.

Yet, how well the worker is paid depends on several factors, the first of which is the readiness of consumers to pay for the finished goods a price high enough to warrant high wages. Here we come to the brokerage side of the capitalist. Secondly, there is the decision of the entrepreneur (sometimes the stockholders) how much of the gross profits will be distributed (as dividends, bonuses, and the like) and how much should be reinvested or laid aside. It is evident that the enterprise, being competitive, has to "look ahead" in a far more concrete way than does the often improvident worker. The business usually must be planned years ahead. It not only has to adopt the best means of production (which means the purchase of new expensive machinery), but also needs financial assets as reserves. Finally, the wages have to be in a sound relationship to the marketing possibilities, and also to the quality of the work done, the sense of duty of the workers and employees. Virtue enters the picture. Even the net profits paid out are not necessarily a "loss" to the workers, because a profitable enterprise attracts investors; what is good for the enterprise obviously is good for its workers.

There is a commonality of interests which can be gravely upset by either side. Needless to say, the most common way to upset the applecart is through excessive wage demands which, if yielded to, tend to eliminate the profits and to make the merchandise unmarketable. Politically organized workers also may pressure governments into inflationary policies. Strikes cancel production for a given period and mean economic loss. The inability to sell due to excessive wages and prices or to protracted strikes can bankrupt the economy.

This mutual relationship between costs of production and purchasing power is frequently overlooked—especially in the so-called "developing nations." The insistence on "a living wage," often by well-meaning Christian critics, in many cases cannot be met without pricing the products out of the market. Such critics forget that workers might prefer to work at a low wage rather than not to work at all.

Saving Begins at Home

One thing is certain: *nascent industrial economies have to start on an ascetic, a Spartan level.* This is true of all economies, free or socialistic. The apologists of the USSR can well use this argument in the defense of Soviet economies in their initial stage, but *only up to a point:* the introduction of socialism in Russia effected immediately a tremendous decline of working-class, peasant-class, and middle-class living standards which, compared with 1916 levels, have *improved only in spots.* Large sectors still are worse off than before the Revolution. A microscopic minority, however, lives very well indeed.[1] In the meantime, free economies have made such enormous strides that the gap between Russia and the West is greater than in 1916. There are two reasons for this state of affairs. First, the Eastern Bloc with the exception of Soviet-occupied Germany, Latvia, and Estonia, completely lacks the famous "Protestant Work Ethic." Secondly, free enterprise is basically more productive than state capitalism because of: (a) the snowballing of millions of individual ambitions into a huge avalanche, (b) the element of competition based on free consumer choice which improves quality and efficiency, (c) the strictly nonpolitical management based on efficiency and responsibility.

So, whence comes the wave of hatred directed against

free enterprise? Dissatisfied intellectuals designing utopias and decadent noblemen do not account entirely for the phenomenon. Though nascent capitalism has not yet "delivered the goods" (children can only show promise, no more) mature capitalism has proved that it can provide. Empirically speaking, capitalism has justified itself in comparison with socialism (for the existence of which we have to be grateful in this one respect).

The assaults against free enterprise are launched with the help of theories and of sentiments, sometimes working hand in hand. Frequently these attacks are made *indirectly*, for instance, by criticizing technology. This critique might be genuine, but often serves as a detour. Much of the current antipollution campaign is subconsciously directed at capitalism via technology. (This particular problem is less acute in the Socialist World only because it is less industrialized; it is nevertheless amusing to see the Left embracing all the idle dreams of the old conservative agrarian romanticism.) However, if we examine closely the attack against free enterprise, we find the following elements:

•1. The charge that business cycles are the consequence of freedom rather than political intervention, though proof to the contrary is well established.

•2. The attack against the man-consuming, soul-killing, slave-driving forms of modern production. In this domain, however, the main culprit is the machine rather than the human factor. Technology *per se* is strictly disciplinarian. In this respect, socialism or communism would not bring the slightest alleviation. On the contrary! Let us remember the ideal of the Stakhanovite, the absence in socialist countries of genuine labor unions, the limitless means the totalitarian state has for coercion, regulations, and controls. We must bear in mind that the free world also has a competitive labor market. Man can *choose* the place and conditions of his work.

•3. The critique of "monopoly capitalism," shared in a milder way by the "Neo-Liberal" school, is opposed to all forms of bigness. Still, in the free world we find that most countries have legislation against monopolies *in order to keep competition alive,* to give the consumer a real choice. Any criticism of monopolies by a socialist is hypocritical, because socialism means total monopoly, the state being the only entrepreneur.

Deeper Resentments

Yet these attacks are frequently only rationalizations of much deeper resentments. At the very roots of anticapitalism we have the theological problem of man's rebellion against Original Sin or, to put it in secular terms, his vain protest against the human condition. By this we mean the curse to which we are subject, the necessity to work by the sweat of our brow. The worker is in harness, but so is the manager and so is everybody else. For this uninspiring, sometimes unpleasant state of affairs, the average man will stick the guilt on somebody; capitalism serves as the convenient scapegoat. Of course, work could be greatly reduced if one were willing to accept a much lower living standard—which few people want to do. Without the opportunities free enterprise provides for highly profitable work, the living standards would go down to early medieval levels. Still, the resentment against this order is directed not so much against an abstraction—such is human nature—as against *persons.* Thus, the culprit is taken to be the "Establishment"—of the "capitalists."

This gives us a hint as to the nature of the anticapitalism which has more and more surfaced since the French Revolution and the decline of Christianity: *envy.* Ever since 1789, the secret of political success has been the mobilization of majorities against unpopular minorities endowed with certain "privileges"—particularly financial privileges. Thus, in the nineteenth century, the "capitalist" appeared to be the man who enjoyed considerable wealth though he apparently "did not work" and derived a vast income from the toil of the workers "who have to slave for him." Apart from the incontrovertible fact that they mostly "slave for themselves," there is *some* truth to this.

The Entrepreneurial Role

Almost every worker will usually contribute in a minor way to the income of the entrepreneur or of the stockholders. This is perfectly natural because a broker must always be paid; and an entrepreneur, as we have said before, is actually a broker between the worker and the consumer by providing the former with the necessary tools and guidance in production. (The merchant is a subbroker between the manufacturer and the public.) It is also natural to pay for borrowed tools for the simple reason that their value is diminished by use. (Thus the traveling salesman will have to pay for a rented car, the commercial photographer for a rented camera, and so forth.) Beyond this, the entrepreneur (who is, as we have seen, a broker as well as a lender) takes the risk of failure and bankruptcy. This situation also may be encountered in the USSR where anyone can get an "unearned income" for money he puts into a savings bank or where he can buy a lottery ticket. The purchase of such a ticket is based on an expectation (i.e., to make a profit) but also entails a risk (i.e., not to win anything).

Risk characterizes all of human existence: to make an effort without exactly foreseeing its success. Thus, a writer starting a novel or a painter putting the first lines on his canvas is not sure whether he can transform his vision into reality. He might fail. Often he does. The farmer with his crop is in the same boat. But the typical worker entering the factory can be certain that he will be paid at week's end. It should be noted here that in Austria and Germany, for instance, the industrial laborer works an average of 43 hours a week (the 40-hour week is in the offing), while the self-employed put in an average of 62.5 hours a week. In other words, the rule within our mature economy is this: the "higher up," the greater the work effort—and the higher, too, the work ethics; the slack employee cheats the employer but the slack employer only cheats himself.

Facts and Fiction

The trouble, as Goetz Briefs once pointed out, is that the current notions about the profits of the capitalists are totally out of touch with reality.[2] The reason for these wrong ideas is partly mathematical! Let us look at some statistics. Too many people think that a radical redistribution of profits would truly benefit "the little man." But what do the figures tell us? According to the *Economic Almanac*, 1962, published by the National Industrial Conference Board (page 115), of the national income in the United States, the compensation of employees amounted to 71 percent; the self-employed earned 11.9 percent, the farmers 3.1 percent. Corporation profits before taxes were 9.7 percent of the total national income (after taxes only 4.9

percent) and dividends paid out were 3.4 percent. Interest paid to creditors amounted to 4.7 percent of the national income. Yet, were the recipients of these dividends and interest payments all "capitalists"? How many workers, retired farmers, widows, benevolent associations, and educational institutions were among them? Would this sum, evenly divided among all Americans, materially improve their lot? Of course not.

In other parts of the world the situation is not much different. According to earlier statistics (1958), if all German incomes were to be reduced to a maximum of 1,000 Marks (then $250.00) a month and every citizen given an even share of the surplus, this share would have amounted to 4 cents a day. A similar calculation, expropriating all Austrian monthly incomes of 1000 dollars or more, would in 1960 have given each Austrian citizen an additional 1¼ cents a day!

But, let us return to corporate profits. The 13 largest Italian companies composed in 1965 a full-page advertisement which they tried to place in the leading dailies of the Peninsula. This statement told at a glance what the dividends had been in 1963, what they were over a 10-year period, what salaries and wages were paid, how much industry contributed to social security and old-age pensions. The relationship between the dividends and labor cost was roughly 1 to 12. The companies added that the estimated number of shareholders (obviously from many walks of life) was over half a million—double the number of the employees. Interestingly and significantly enough, two of the dailies refused to carry the paid advertisement: one was the Communist *Unità*, the other the Papal *Osservatore Romano* whose excuse was that it was published in Vatican City, which means outside of the Italian State.

Rooted in Envy

To the advocate of equality, the fact that certain individuals live much better than others seems to be "unbearable." The internal revenue policies which try to "soak the rich" often have their roots in man's envy. It seems useless to demonstrate that a redistribution of wealth would be of no advantage to the many or that an oppressive tax policy directed against the well-to-do is self-defeating for a country's economy. One usually will get the reply that in a democracy a fiscal policy which might be economically sound could be politically unacceptable—and vice versa. Pointing out that the spending of wealthy persons is good for the nation as a whole may bring the snap reaction that *"nobody* should have that much money." Yet, people who earn huge sums usually have taken extraordinary risks or are performing extraordinary services. Some of them are inventors. Let us assume that somebody invents an effective drug against cancer and thereby earns a hundred million dollars. (Certainly, those who suffer from cancer would not begrudge him his wealth.) Unless he buries this sum in his garden, he would help by lending to others (through banks, for instance) and by purchasing liberally from others. The only reason to object to his wealth would be sheer envy. (I would add here that had it not been for the liberality of monarchs, popes, bishops, aristocrats, and patricians it would not be worthwhile for an American to pay a nickel to see Europe. The landscape is more grandiose in the New World.)

Still, it is significant that one of the few outstanding Christian sociologists in Europe, Father Oswald von Nell-Breuning, SJ, not noted for conservative leanings, has recently *(Zur Debatte,* Munich, February 1972) taken a firm stand against the myths of the beneficent effects of the redistribution of wealth. As one of the architects of the Encyclical *Quadragesimo Anno* he emphasized that Pius XI was thoroughly cognizant with this incontrovertible fact but that, in the meantime, this knowledge has been nearly lost and that therefore demagogical ideas have largely invaded Catholic sociological and economic thinking. Especially in the domain of "Third World" economic problems, the learned Jesuit hinted, the hue and cry for "distributive justice" has done a great deal of mischief.

It has become fashionable to attack free enterprise on moral grounds. There are people among us, many of them well-meaning, idealistic Christians, who freely admit that "capitalism delivers the goods," that it is far more efficient than socialism, but that it is *ethically* on a lower plane. It is denounced as egotistic and materialistic. Of course, life on earth is a vale of tears and no system, political, social, or economic, can claim perfection. Yet, the means of production can only be owned privately, *or* by the state. State ownership of all means of production certainly is not conducive to liberty. It is totalitarianism. It involves state control of all media of expression. (In Nazi Germany private ownership existed *de jure,* but certainly not *de facto.*) The remark of Roepke is only too true, that in a free enterprise system the supreme sanction comes from the bailiff, but in a totalitarian tyranny from the hangman.

The Christian insistence on freedom—the monastic vows are voluntary sacrifices of a select few—derives from the Christian concept that man must be free in order to act morally. (A sleeping, a chained and clubbed, a drugged person can neither be sinful nor virtuous.) Yet, the free world, which is practically synonymous with the world of free enterprise, alone provides a climate, a way of life compatible with the dignity of man who makes free decisions, enjoys privileges, assumes responsibilities, and develops his talents as he sees fit. He is truly the steward of his family. He can buy, sell, save, invest, gamble, plan the future, build, retrench, acquire capital, make donations, take risks. In other words, he can be the master of his economic fate and act as a man instead of a sheep in a herd under a shepherd and his dogs. No doubt, free enterprise is a harsh system; it demands real men. But socialism, which appeals to envious people craving for security and afraid to decide for themselves, impairs human dignity and crushes man utterly.

---

1. See "Free Enterprise and the Russians," *The Freeman*, August 1972, pp. 461–470.

2. *Das Gewerkschaftsproblem gestern und heute* (Frankfurt am Main: Knapp, 1955), p. 98.

Higher Education: The Solution or Part of the Problem?

Calvin D. Linton

My title may strike you as odd, whimsical, even wrong-headed. Surely education is a "good thing." It is by its very nature beneficial, not harmful; Promethean, not Mephistophelean; our savior, not our destroyer. The more of it the better.

But every one of these popular beliefs is doubtful. It all depends on what kind of education we are talking about, and what kind of people receive the education.

Let me say at once, therefore, that I am speaking of that kind of education which is secular, largely technological, and chiefly aimed at teaching people how to do things. This is, I believe, the public image. Every member of a liberal arts college has at one time or another confronted bewildered or irate parents who demand to know what, after an expensive liberal arts education, their newly furnished offspring are trained to do—what kind of a job can they get? It is difficult to convince them that the purpose of a liberal education is to develop mental powers, to sensitize one's response to beauty and goodness, to expand and lengthen one's outlook, to teach civilized emotions, and the rest. (It is

Calvin D. Linton is Professor Emeritus of English Literature and Dean Emeritus of the College of Arts and Sciences of George Washington University, Washington, D.C. This article appeared in the June 1968 issue of *The Freeman*.

particularly difficult because, in all conscience, these jobs have often not been done by the liberal arts college. But that is another story.)

The menace of modern education is quite easy to define: Never have so many people, groups, and nations been able, because of education, to do so many things—and we are all afraid that they will now start doing them! To narrow it a bit: The menace is that of incalculable power (the product of knowledge) in the hands of bad or foolish men. The agonizing question now is not whether we can possibly learn how to do this or that, but which of the things we have the tools to do we should, by an act of will, choose to do. The question, in short, is one of conduct, not of knowledge. With this, education, to its own peril, has little to do.

And yet it is the most anciently recognized of problems. Adam faced it, and chose wrong. His problem, like ours, was not knowing *how* but knowing *what*. And the corrective was early stated: "Thou shalt do that which is right and good in the sight of the Lord: that it may be well with thee . . . (*Deut.* 6:18). With the spirit of this commandment, modern education has even less to do. Education's answer to man's problems is more education—as if Hitler would have been made a better man if he had taken a degree or two from some good university.

I submit that modern education presents increasingly the fearful aspects of Frankenstein's monster because of the prevalence of five fallacies or myths.

1. The Myth of Automatic Human Progress

The general tendency of ancient thought was that man had fallen from high estate, whether from some Golden Age or from the bliss of Eden. Not until the eighteenth century and the rise of that strangely irrational epoch called the Age of Reason were doctrines of inevitable human progress widely disseminated. Partly, this was the result of a sort of provincial complacency, and partly ignorance of history. How easily in eighteenth-century writing flow the condescending remarks about the barbarism of the ancient world, the primitive grotesqueness of gothic cathedrals, the ignorance and ineptitude of Shakespeare!

But it remained for the nineteenth century and the rise of theories of evolution for the views to become the dogma that all environments tend inevitably toward perfection. Why this is so was never clearly stated. There simply is faith that the universe is so constituted. "Chance" will see to it. But chance is simply a nonterm, identifying the *absence* of reason, purpose, intention, and will; it is odd that reason should put its faith in that which is, by definition, nonreason.

Reasonably or not, however, the cult of inevitable progress has, in education, placed improper emphasis on novelty, change for its own sake, the gimmick. True, in the world of technology the view that the latest is the best is usually sound—we properly prefer the up-to-date typewriter, automobile, washing machine. But technology advances automatically, so long as we do not forget the practical lessons of past experimenters. Every engineer begins at the point where the last one left off. Advancement is due not to any improvement in the human brain, but to the mere accumulation of experience. The ancient brains that measured the diameter of the earth, that worked out the basic principles of force, leverage, hydraulics, and construction, were almost undoubtedly greater brains than our age possesses. But the modern technologist stands at the topmost height of achievement of all previous craftsmen.

He may himself be a dwarf, but he can see farther than they, for he sits on their shoulders.

Not so in the area of human conduct. Here it is not technology but wisdom that governs. No man becomes virtuous because of the virtue of another. He may be inspired by the wisdom and virtue of others, but he must make that wisdom his own possession. He cannot start out as wise as they simply because they have recorded their wisdom. Every human being, as a moral creature, begins from scratch. Not the *novel* but the *true* controls here.

Julian Huxley once observed that evolution seemingly has not worked in recorded history. Even within the view of evolutionary progress, therefore, there is no ground for believing that the wisdom residing in the most ancient minds was not as great as that held by the latest recipient of a Ph.D. Indeed, in all honesty, most of us would agree that there probably is not alive this day any human being whose wisdom can match that of a Moses, a Job, a Paul, a Marcus Aurelius, an Aristotle, a John—make the list as long as you wish.

And it is precisely this storehouse of ancient wisdom that the Cult of the New denies to the student. How they flock to the latest course presenting results of "an unstructured learning experience bearing upon upward mobility desires in terms of motivational elements in adjustment to a work situation"—but how few choose a course in the ethical teachings of Jesus.

And yet, as we have seen, it is precisely in the matter of choosing wisely what we should do, not in mastering more tools of power, that our future security—if any—consists. Bertrand Russell has written: "If human life is to continue in spite of science, mankind will have to learn a discipline of the passions which, in the past, has not been necessary. . . ." In other words, the upward curve of virtue must parallel that of knowledge.

Professor Ginsberg of the University of London in his book *The Idea of Progress*, correctly states that progress cannot be defined in terms independent of ethics. One can scarcely call it progress if a murderous maniac is progressively handed a stick, a club, a sword, a pistol, a cannon, and finally an H-bomb.

Education must deal with that which has *never* changed: the human heart, its passions, and ideals. *There* are the wellsprings of human well-being or human catastrophe. In an address to the Royal Society, Laurence Oliphant, Australia's top atomic scientist, declared: "I can find no evidence whatever that the morality of mankind has improved over the 5,000 years or so of recorded history."

II. The Myth of the Natural Goodness of Man

This is a delicate subject. One sometimes feels that this dogma is simply a corrective to the reverse obnoxious doctrines of extreme puritanism (the sort seen in medieval asceticism and seventeenth-century extremism) that every impulse of man is totally and inherently evil. (In passing, some even conceive this to be the Presbyterian doctrine of total depravity. Actually, of course, the view declares that the *total* man was touched by sin, that no part of his being remained unaffected. It does not attribute total evil to every impulse.)

But the cult of sensibility, as the eighteenth century termed it, is not a corrective; it is an extreme, untenable, and unreasonable dogma that shows up in modern education all the way from first grade to graduate school.

Simply, it may be called the philosophy of "doing what

comes naturally." At the intellectual level, for example, it is held that there is some magic value in the uninhibited and uninformed opinion if freely expressed. And so discussion groups are held in the grade schools and the high schools on such subjects as "What do *you* think about the atom bomb?" or "teenage morality" or "banning *Lady Chatterley's Lover*" or "implementing freedom among underprivileged nations" or what not. The poor little dears have scarcely a fact to use as ballast. But no matter. The cult of sensibility believes that continuing, free, uninhibited discussion will ultimately release the inherent goodness of natural instincts and impulses. The fad for "brainstorming" has passed, but not the philosophy behind it.

Now, of course, we must encourage discussion. The young need to be encouraged to think and to speak—the former, anyway. But the deadly assumption underlying this sort of thing is that goodness is not a difficult matter of study, discipline, learning, mastery of tough masses of fact, but just a kind of game. It's fun to do what comes naturally. (On reading about the uninhibited conduct of certain grade school classes, with free discussion, finger painting, group games, or whatever the youngsters want to do, an older man said: "That's not a new feature of education. They had that when I was a boy. They called it 'recess.'")

Ultimately, this view of ethics believes that there is no objective standard of morality or ethics. If there were, then what one wanted to do would be either right or wrong according to whether it reflected or violated the absolute standard. Rather, it is the view of the cult that society *determines* morality. The vote of the majority determines the ethical value. To refer to Bertrand Russell again, one remembers his assertion that there is no rational basis for determining ethics. Man, as the random product of an eternal flux of atoms, *feels* certain things—chiefly, that he exists; or rather, he experiences an experience he arbitrarily names "existence." Thus, what are "ethical standards" to one may be unacceptable to another. There is no objective basis for deciding between them. One can only hope, therefore, that he lives in a society in which the majority of the people *happen* to like the same ethical standards one does oneself.

The idea that man is basically good and infinitely capable of self-improvement has ramifications in every area of modern life. It is ardently preached by Freudian psychologists, to whom restraint of any natural desire is bad; by dreamy-eyed social and political theorists who believe that "freedom" is the sovereign remedy for the ills of every primitive tribe and nation; by aesthetic theorists who teach that art is an unplanned eruption occurring when the "artist's biography makes contact with the medium of the art"; and by educationists who teach that what Johnny wants to do is what he must be permitted to do. No concept is more widespread, more taken for granted by millions who have never troubled really to think about it.

It is important to realize that members of the cult of natural goodness believe primarily in the goodness of the *non-rational* faculties—instinct, emotion, impulse, subrational urges. They are not so strong on the natural goodness of the intellect. (The high priest of the cult is D. H. Lawrence.)

There is, consequently, a prevalence of anti-intellectualism in educational circles that manifests itself in a marvelous jargon largely incomprehensible to the rational intelligence. Jacques Barzun gives a fine analysis of this malady in *The House of Intellect.*

III. The Myth of Egalitarianism

This is an even more delicate subject. To seem to question the equality of men is to raise questions about one's attitude toward home and mother and the American way of life. Actually, of course, the situation is not hopelessly complicated. It is simply a matter of identifying those areas in which all men are equal and those in which they are not.

To the Christian, every soul is equal *before God*. All have sinned and come short of the glory of God; all need grace; none is good before God. None can claim social status, investments, political office, or ecclesiastical affiliation to separate him from his absolute equality with all other human souls.

To the believer in the Western tradition of rule by law, every man is also equal *before the law*. The protection of the law, the responsibility for obeying the law, and the duty of understanding the law are equal in distribution and force, without regard to any circumstances save legal age.

But to declare that all men are equally gifted, equal in force of character, equal in abilities and talents, equally deserving of a share of the world's goods, equally deserving of esteem, respect, and admiration, equally deserving of rewards, equal in cultural heritage and contribution—this is irrational nonsense.

No concept has had a deadlier effect upon modern education than this. It has hindered the identification and encouragement of the exceptionally gifted; it has lowered educational standards to a point where no one, no matter how dull, can fail to hurdle them; it has confused the right of every man *to seek* an education with the fallacious belief that every man has a right *to receive* a degree. It has stifled initiative by refusing to grant exceptional reward to exceptional effort. It has encouraged mediocrity by withholding the penalty of mediocrity.

An illustration: A university with which I am very familiar undertook a program to encourage better English in the high schools of the city. The basic idea was competition—the best writers, the most skilled in grammar, the clearest thinkers would be singled out through public contests for reward.

The professional secondary school counselors were horrified. This clearly amounted to "discrimination"—it discriminated between the able and the unable student! In the modern doctrine this is the deadly sin. In sum, the university was permitted to put into effect only a watered-down plan that carefully provided rewards for everyone. Needless to say the program was of only modest effectiveness. Needless to say, too, that high school graduates come to us scarcely sure whether writing is the white or the black part of a page.

I was recently told by a professional educator colleague that the terrible alternative to belief in complete equality in all dimensions is the inculcation of an inferiority complex. From that, he told me, come resentment, insecurity, antagonism, maladjustment, psychoses of various kinds, rebellion—in short, a wrecked society.

This, too, is nonsense. The thing works both ways. Almost everyone has some talent or ability that could be developed beyond the average level. If he properly receives acknowledgment for this superiority, he will be willing to grant superiority in other fields to other people. Is this not inherent in life itself? Do we feel resentful or guilty because we have not the mental equipment of a Pascal or an Einstein? Physically inferior because we cannot bat home runs like Mickey Mantle? Artistically inferior because we cannot play the piano like Rubinstein or Richter? On the contrary, one of the keenest pleasures of life is to be in the presence of a superior person—and to be very still.

That sort of pride which cannot, without infinite anguish, acknowledge the superiority of any other living being is quite literally Satanic. From it flowed all our woes.

IV. The Cult of Scientism

Again, careful qualification is needed. No one can, in the first place, be other than grateful for the marvelous strides science has made in increasing human comfort, controlling disease, providing relief from soul-killing labor. Nor, in the second place, can anyone doubt the validity and effectiveness of the scientific method—in its proper place. What I refer to is the religion of scientism, complete with dogma, faith, ethical system, and ritual.

"Science" is a wonderful word. It means "knowledge." Thus the old term for what we today call "science" was "natural philosophy." The study of nature—physical; perceived by the senses; capable of instrumentation. Indeed, modern science may be called the application of instruments to matter for the purpose of gaining understanding of material forces and thus of gaining control over them for our own purposes.

The cultic aspect arises when (1) science is viewed not as *one* way man has of knowing things (and a sharply limited one) but as the way that embraces everything man can, at least respectably, come to know; and (2) when the teachings of its priests are accepted without question by a faithful congregation.

These cultic aspects are perhaps most perceptible in the development of "mysteries" of the faith, open only to the initiated, not to be comprehended by nonscientists. Writes the great Norbert Wiener: "The present age of specialization has gone an unbelievable distance. Not only are we developing physicists who know no chemistry, physiologists who know no biology, but we are beginning to get the physicist who does not know physics." As a consequence, the mysteries known only to the specialists are accepted without question by those without the necessary knowledge to judge for themselves.

Anthony Standen, distinguished British chemist who is editor of a huge encyclopedia of chemistry, writes: "What with scientists who are so deep in science that they cannot see it, and nonscientists who are too overawed to express an opinion, hardly anyone is able to recognize science for what it is, the great Sacred Cow of our time" (*Science Is a Sacred Cow*, Dutton, 1950).

"Is the universe," he continues, "to be thought of in terms of electrons and protons? Or . . . in terms of Good and Evil? Merely to ask the question is to realize at least one very important limitation of [science]."

The biologists, he says, try to define "life," with ludicrous results. "They define stimulus and response in terms of one another. No biologist can define a species. And as for a genus—all attempts come to this: 'A genus is a grouping of species that some recognized taxonomic specialist has called a genus. . . .'"

The scientist, says Standen, has substituted *is* for *ought*. "That is why," he concludes, "we must never allow ourselves to be ruled by scientists. They must be our servants, not our masters."

The cult has many imitators, all of them injurious to true education. The ritual words of the worship services have been adopted by areas of knowledge where no physical instrumentation is possible: psychology, sociology, aesthetics, morality. When the modern psychologist asks, "What motivational elements predominated in this behavioral manifestation?" he is still simply asking, "Why did he do it?" And the real answer lies far beyond the reach of the cleverest electronic computer or microscope.

In general, the attitude fostered in modern education toward science is unthinking worship. As a consequence, as Martin Gardner states in his recent book *Fads and Fallacies in the Name of Science,* "The national level of credulity is almost unbelievably high."

The menace of this scientific gullibility obviously goes far beyond the classroom. It is the malady of our age, and one of which we may perish. But my immediate point is simply that an environment of anti-intellectual materialism has seriously hampered the development of students' awareness of the moral and spiritual stature of man, by which alone he stands erect.

Most paradoxical is the cult's dogma that there is no room for faith in any true search for truth. The notion is palpably false. Let me quote Warren Weaver, vice-president for the natural and medical sciences of the Rockefeller Foundation: "I believe that faith plays an essential role in science just as it clearly does in religion." He goes on to list six basic faiths of the scientist, including the faith that nature is orderly, that the order of nature is discoverable to man, that logic is to be trusted as a mental tool, that quantitative probability statements reflect something true about nature, and so on ("A Scientist Ponders Faith," *Saturday Review,* January 3, 1959). In sum, he says: "Where the scientist has faith that nature is orderly, the religionist has faith that God is good. Where the scientist believes that the order of nature is discoverable to man, the religionist believes that the moral nature of the universe is discoverable to man."

Dr. Weaver rejects the well-known aphorism of Sir Richard Gregory:

My grandfather preached the Gospel of Christ,
My father preached the Gospel of Socialism,
I preach the Gospel of Science.

But many others accept it with fervor. "God has ceased to be a useful hypothesis," writes Julian Huxley. The problem of the nineteenth century, says another, was the death of God; that of the twentieth, the death of man.

Any humanist who speaks in these terms must be extremely careful, lest he fall into mere carping, deeply tinged by envy of the prominence and prosperity of science. Nothing could be more foolish—or more ungrateful. The lament over the low estate of the humanities in the public mind would be more touching if those responsible for the preservation and dissemination of humanistic studies had something of positive value to say, if they had a Path, a Way of Truth to declare.

V. The Cult of Biologism

I admit that this is a poor term, and perhaps the topic itself were better considered a subheading of the previous one. Essentially, this cult is an outgrowth of materialism, the faith that man is only biology, that he not only *has* glands but *is* glands.

As a consequence, whole segments of educational theory consider man precisely as a physicist considers an atom—one purely objective item among others of its kind, clothed with identity only as it is part of a group, the properties and motions of which are to be determined statistically, in terms of average behavior. (Years ago, Irving Langmuir, speaking of the "burden of irrationality" in science, pointed out that the laws, say, of the expansion of gases tell us how a mass of molecules behave under certain conditions of heat and pressure, but that no one can predict how a single one of the molecules will behave.)

To treat man merely as a capacity for response to stimuli, as totally the product of the forces that impinge upon him, without will or conscience, is to divest him of personality, individuality, and dignity. But the whole science of human engineering is based, more or less, on this concept. The only variation is the difference of opinion among the practitioners as to whether there remains in man some slight indeterminate center of being, inviolate to stimulus or statistical confinement, or whether he is totally susceptible to manipulation.

Among the many ramifications of this cult let me mention only two. First, the dogma that all human actions are social in their implications, to be judged purely by their effect on society. And, second, the dogma that emotions, feelings, are not essentially moral in their nature, nor the product of individual, unique, and sovereign personality, but are merely the conditioned reflexes of quivering biology.

The first, the social dogma, conceives of the individual as the physician thinks of the cells of the body—part of an organic whole, subject totally to the welfare of the organic unit (the state, in the social and political parallel), and to be excised through surgery if a cell rebels.

It is within this belief that a nationally prominent psychologist has defined education as "the engraving of desirable behavior patterns." Through conditioning, teaching machines, Pavlovian devices of various kinds, the individual is created in the desired image. Undesirable behavior patterns are to be eradicated by a form of brainwashing and a new engraving superimposed. Dismissed as utterly outmoded is the view of each human being as a living soul, created in the image of God, with primary responsibilities as an individual to the God of his creation.

And who is to determine what kind of behavior pattern is "desirable"? That's the hitch. The persons who most ardently would like to impose their own behavior patterns on me are the very ones whose patterns I would least like to have engraved.

At worst, this view of human existence is both irrational and evil. It is irrational because it must believe that those who impose the patterns of desirable behavior must be as totally the product of external influence, as completely a consciousness-produced-by-environment, as those who are to be manipulated. It is evil because it denies human dignity and reduces the individual to a cipher.

The second menacing product of the cult of biologism is the belief that emotions and feelings are as purely biological as the purely physiological activities of man. In other words this view denies that the quality of a person's feelings is a measure of his moral stature, of his culture, of his civilization. It denies that the teaching of right feelings is a vital part of true education.

The "natural" emotions of a child are pretty fearful, until they have been civilized, associated with moral values, enriched with culture. Most notably, the child—and the savage—is instinctively delighted by cruelty. A child will pull the wings off a fly. A recent account of life among certain savage South American Indians describes the pleasure of the community at the antics of chickens plucked alive, with perhaps a leg or wing pulled off for good measure.

This may be the "natural" feeling of sin, and it may be an instinctive expression of the savage as biology. But it is the work of civilization, of culture, and above all of religion, to eradicate it. "Natural" man must learn the right emotions—what to laugh at, what to smile at, what to frown at.

Show me what makes a man laugh, what makes him weep, and I know the man. It is ultimately a matter of morality, not biology. Education divorced from moral values cannot teach right feeling.

The deepest and most significant emotion of all, the one this world most desperately needs to be taught, is compassion—the emotion most readily associated with the love of God for sinful man. "The tender mercies of the heathen are cruel," says the Bible. Commandments that we deal gently, forgivingly, tenderly with each other are "unnatural" in biology. They are natural only to the regenerated spirit.

Now, this is a broad indictment. I do not pretend that I have said anything new, or that these problems are peculiar to education. They are maladies of our age. They break into dozens of major subheadings, scores of topics, hundreds of subject headings, thousands of instances.

True Education

But the correction is magnificently simple: True education, as Milton said three centuries ago, is to relearn to know God aright. Education divorced from God is capable of infinite and endless complexities and confusions. He alone is the motionless Center that gives meaning to all motion. What *he is*, not what man is, determines what should be and shall be.

Let me end with a quotation from that rough-mannered philosopher, Carlyle *(Sartor Resartus,* Chapter IX):

> "Cease, my much respected Herr von Voltaire," thus apostrophizes the Professor: "shut thy sweet voice; for the task appointed thee seems finished. Sufficiently hast thou demonstrated this proposition, considerable or otherwise: That the Mythus of the Christian Religion looks not in the eighteenth century as it did in the eighth. Alas, were thy six-and-thirty quartos, and the six-and-thirty thousand other quartos and folios, all flying sheets or reams, printed before and since on the same subject, all needed to convince us of so little! But what next? Wilt thou help us to embody the divine Spirit of that Religion in a new Mythus, in a new vehicle and vesture, that our Souls, otherwise too like perishing, may live? What! thou hast no faculty in that kind? Only a torch for burning, no hammer for building? Take our thanks, then, and—thyself away."

Somewhat modified, these words might be addressed to the kind of dangerous education I have been describing.

Index

Suggestions for Further Study

The following books from FEE are recommended to readers who wish to explore in greater depth the moral case for a free society:

Frederic Bastiat
The Law
A powerful summary of Bastiat's critique of socialism.
76 pages

Ezra Taft Benson
The Proper Role of Government
What government should and should not do.
32 pages

Robert James Bidinotto, ed.
Criminal Justice? The Legal System vs. Individual Responsibility
A thorough review of the crime epidemic in the United States.
320 pages

Clarence B. Carson
A Basic History of the United States
A fresh, comprehensive narrative in five volumes of 200 to 350 pages each.

Burton W. Folsom, Jr., ed.
The Spirit of Freedom: Essays in American History
An anthology of essays and articles on the freedom movement throughout American history.
212 pages

Henry Hazlitt
The Conquest of Poverty
Capitalist production, not government programs, has been the real conqueror of poverty.
240 pages

The Foundations of Morality
The author presents a consistent moral philosophy based on the principles required for voluntary social interaction.
388 pages

Mark W. Hendrickson, ed.
The Morality of Capitalism
A superb collection of essays on the moral foundation of the private property order.
212 pages

Tibor R. Machan
The Virtue of Liberty
A powerful analysis of the connection between liberty and virtue.
176 pages

John Stuart Mill
On Liberty
Mill's observations made in 1859 are relevant to every age.
129 pages

Ludwig von Mises
The Anti-Capitalistic Mentality
A discussion of popular psychological arguments against capitalism.
114 pages

Human Action
Mises' magnum opus: a broadly philosophical work which is indispensable for scholars and students.
907 pages

J. Wilson Mixon, Jr., ed.
Private Means, Public Ends: Voluntarism vs. Coercion
A thought-provoking study of the virtues of private initiative and the failure of public administration.
151 pages

Edmund A. Opitz
Religion and Capitalism: Allies, Not Enemies
A profound discussion of the relationship of biblical religion to free-market economics.
328 pages

Religion: Foundation of the Free Society
An anthology of Reverend Opitz's eloquent essays and articles.
272 pages

Leonard E. Read
Anything That's Peaceful
A philosophical discussion of individual freedom and social cooperation.
243 pages

Government: An Ideal Concept
To Read, government was neither a manager of economic activity nor an almoner of gifts to the people, but a necessary instrument of social order.
149 pages

Hans F. Sennholz
Debts and Deficits
A devastating critique of our propensity to live beyond our means.
179 pages

Robert A. Sirico
A Moral Basis for Liberty
A brilliant essay on first principles.
68 pages

For current price information, or to request FEE's latest catalogue of more than 400 books on economics and social thought, write or phone:

The Foundation for Economic Education, Inc.
30 South Broadway
Irvington-on-Hudson, NY 10533
(914) 591-7230; fax (914) 591-8910;
E-mail:freeman@westnet.com

About the Publisher

The Foundation for Economic Education, Inc., was established in 1946 by Leonard E. Read to study and advance the moral and intellectual rationale for a free society.

The Foundation publishes *The Freeman,* an award-winning monthly journal of ideas in the fields of economics, history, and moral philosophy. FEE also publishes books, conducts seminars, and sponsors a network of discussion clubs to improve understanding of the principles of a free and prosperous society.

FEE is a non-political, non-profit 501(c)(3) tax-exempt organization, supported solely by private contributions and sales of its literature.

For further information, please contact: The Foundation for Economic Education, Inc., 30 South Broadway, Irvington-on-Hudson, New York 10533. Telephone: (914) 591-7230; fax: (914) 591-8910; E-mail: freeman@westnet.com.

If You Liked This Book, You'll Like *The Freeman*

The Freeman is the source of most of the chapters in this book. Since 1956, it has been published monthly by The Foundation for Economic Education (FEE).

The Freeman offers serious readers a unique source of free-market information. No other magazine, newspaper, or scholarly journal introduces readers to so many implications of what the free society is all about: its moral legitimacy, its tremendous efficiency, and its liberating effects in every area of life.

When FEE began publishing *The Freeman*, there was literally no other source of such popularly written information on the free society. Today, dozens of institutions produce thousands of pages of material every year on the topic.

Despite all the competition (and imitation!), *The Freeman* remains the most effective introduction to the fundamentals of the free society. For newcomers and old-timers, for high school students and Ph.D.'s, *The Freeman* offers new insights of significant value each month.

Why should you read *The Freeman*? Because the world is still in the midst of a monumental battle of ideas. The collapse of European Communism in 1989 has only changed the terms of the debate. It has not changed the fundamental issues.

What are these issues? Government compulsion vs. private choice, collective responsibility vs. personal responsibility, the wisdom of central planners vs. the managerial skills of profit-seeking entrepreneurs, compulsory wealth redistribution vs. voluntary charity, Social Security vs. personal thrift.

All over the world, the debate rages. Yet most people don't know where to begin to sort out fact from fiction.

Do you agree? Then you ought to be reading *The Freeman* every month. Find out for yourself. For a free trial subscription, call (914) 591-7230. Or write to FEE, Irvington-on-Hudson, NY 10533.